Post-Revolutionary Peru

Also of Interest

Peru, Victor Alba

*The End and the Beginning: The Nicaraguan Revolution, John A. Booth

*Nicaragua: The Land of Sandino, Thomas W. Walker

*The Dominican Republic: A Caribbean Crucible, Howard J. Wiarda and Michael J. Kryzanek

Arms and Politics in the Dominican Republic, G. Pope Atkins

*Revolution in El Salvador, Tommie Sue Montgomery

*Latin American Foreign Policies: Global and Regional Dimensions, edited by Elizabeth G. Ferris and Jennie K. Lincoln

*Authoritarian Capitalism: The Contemporary Economic and Political Development of Brazil, edited by Thomas C. Bruneau and Phillippe Faucher

Corporatism and National Development in Latin America, Howard J. Wiarda

*Brazil: A Political Analysis, Peter Flynn

*The Continuing Struggle for Democracy in Latin America, edited by Howard J. Wiarda

Insurgency in the Modern World, edited by Bard E. O'Neill, William R. Heaton, and Donald J. Alberts

Development Strategies in Latin America, edited by Claes Brundenius and Mats Lundal

*From Dependency to Development: Strategies to Overcome Underdevelopment and Inequality, edited by Heraldo Muñoz

*Available in hardcover and paperback.

Westview Special Studies on Latin America and the Caribbean

Post-Revolutionary Peru: The Politics of Transformation
edited by Stephen M. Gorman

Whether the nearly twelve years of military rule in Peru--between October 1968 and July 1980--are labeled a "revolution," a "so-called revolution," or simply a "military dictatorship," one fact remains inescapable: the reforms and programs of the armed forces during that period profoundly altered Peruvian society. This book examines the social, political, and economic legacies of the military government and identifies major areas of tension that are likely to pose problems for the new civilian government.

Following a review of the ideology, socio-economic goals, and political performance of the Institutional Revolution of the Armed Forces, the authors analyze the contemporary political economy of Peru and catalog the political and economic policy alternatives available to the Belaúnde regime in the next few years. They discuss the return to partisan politics in Peru, urban and rural conditions, and the way in which real political power has remained with the military forces, despite their surrender of formal authority. Subsequent chapters outline the IMF-imposed stabilization program, revealing its devastating effects on Lima's urban poor, and summarize recent Peruvian foreign policy. A final chapter draws on the prior discussion to present a critical analysis of the transitionary process from military to civilian rule in Peru.

Stephen M. Gorman is an assistant professor in the Department of Political Science at North Texas State University. He has previously served as a translator for Latin American Perspectives and has written extensively on Nicaragua and Peru, his areas of special interest.

Post-Revolutionary Peru
The Politics of Transformation

edited by Stephen M. Gorman

Westview Press / Boulder, Colorado

This is a Westview reprint edition, manufactured on our own
premises using equipment and methods that allow us to keep
even specialized books in stock. It is printed on acid-free paper
and bound in softcovers that carry the highest rating of NASTA
in consultation with the AAP and the BMI.

Westview Special Studies on Latin America and the Caribbean

Copyright © 1982 by Westview Press, Inc.

Published in 1982 in the United States of America by
     Westview Press, Inc.
     5500 Central Avenue
     Boulder, Colorado 80301
     Frederick A. Praeger, President and Publisher

Library of Congress Catalog Card Number: 82-70377
ISBN: 0-86531-265-6

Composition for this book was provided by the author
Printed and bound in the United States of America

10 9 8 7 6 5 4 3 2

For Carol-Ann and Alexandra

Contents

Tables and Figures

Figures

Preface

In 1980 Peru emerged from its longest period of continuous military domination in this century. Fernando Belaúnde Terry, a somewhat charismatic yet enigmatic politician, was returned to the office of president from which he had been ousted twelve years earlier. While there had been scant popular support for Belaúnde when he was overthrown in 1968, in 1980 he regained power with perhaps the most impressive electoral mandate in Peruvian history. Of course this was not only an affirmation of Belaúnde's political appeal, but also a repudiation of the military and its approach to governance. The transition from military rule--which had been styled a revolution--to civilian democracy was actually a protracted and difficult process. As early as 1976 the military's revolutionary program was a manifest failure, and the following year it was announced that government would be returned to civilian hands after the drafting of a new constitution by a popularly elected constituent assembly. The process did not proceed smoothly as labor unrest escalated and the military attempted to emasculate many of the reforms of the early 1970s.

But even if the military's revolutionary experiment is considered a failure from the standpoint of its original objectives, Peru has nevertheless experienced far-reaching social, political, and economic changes. This work attempts to assess the scope and nature of those changes, and what they will likely mean for the present and future leaders of the country. Some of the contributors to this volume suggest that, on balance, the effects of the military's experiment have been positive, even if incomplete. Others are more critical. Similarly, some of the authors are optimistic about the survivability of Peru's new civilian democracy, while others are more pessimistic. Despite these and other divergencies, there is generally more agreement than disagreement among the chapter authors on such questions as the increased complexity of socioeconomic relationships, the importance of new political actors (evolving out of the revolutionary experience) in the electoral arena, and the significance of growing lower-class mobilization and organization. Just as importantly, there is a general consensus that the military-led revolution was a long-overdue attempt to address some of the more tenacious obstacles to Peruvian development, and that many of these obstacles continue to confront the new civilian government to varying degrees. As such, the Peruvian Revolution appears to have been an incomplete revolution, and the present civilian democracy is faced with both new opportunities and some old challenges as a result.

This volume grew out of a panel at the Latin American Studies Association meeting in 1980 dealing with the social, political, and economic legacies of the Peruvian revolution. The chapters by Woy-Hazleton, McClintock, Villanueva, and Scurrah and Esteves were based partly on papers presented on that panel. The chapter by Palmer, who also participated on the LASA panel, is based on a paper presented at a seminar of the Council of the Americas Fund for Multinational Management and Education in New York in December 1980. The chapter on foreign policy by Gorman and St John is an updated and expanded version of a piece by Gorman that appeared in Elizabeth G. Ferris and Jennie K. Lincoln (eds.) Latin American Foreign Policies (Westview, 1981).

Stephen M. Gorman

Acknowledgments

I would like to thank the Faculty Research Committee and the Department of Political Science at North Texas State University for financial and institutional support in putting this volume together. I am also grateful to Rebecca Swartz for typing the manuscript, Mauricio Fernandez for assistance in going over the final product, and Randy Newton for providing the necessary R and R to see me through this undertaking. Finally, I want to thank the contributors for their participation and my wife for her patience.

S.M.G.

Contributors

SANDRA L. WOY-HAZLETON received her A.B. in political science from the University of California at Riverside, and her M.A. and Ph.D. from the University of Virginia. She has taught at California State College, Bakersfield, The University of North Dakota, and is presently at the University of Dayton. Her research efforts focus on political mobilization and popular participation and her published works include "SINAMOS: Infrastructure of Participation" in <u>Citizen and State Participation in Latin America</u>, Seligson and Mitchell, eds. (New York: Holmes and Meier, 1978).

HENRY DIETZ received his Ph.D. in political science from Stanford University in 1972 following service as a Peace Corp volunteer in Peru. He has been a member of the Department of Government at the University of Texas since 1972. He has published a variety of articles, chapters, and monographs on urban poverty and its political consequences in Latin America, including <u>Poverty and Problem-Solving Under Military Rule: The Urban Poor in Lima, Peru</u> (Austin, University of Texas Press, 1980). He has held grants from the Social Science Research Council, the Ford-Rockefeller Foundation Program on Population Policy, and the American Philosophical Society. In January 1982 he will begin research in Peru on a Tinker Foundation Post-Doctoral Fellowship.

MARTIN J. SCURRAH is Professor of Organizational Behavior at the Escuela de Administración de Negocios para Graduados, Lima, Peru, and has worked as consultant for such organizations as UNICEF, the Ford Foundation, OXFAM, and the Inter-American Foundation. He is co-author, with Peter S. Cleaves, of <u>Agriculture, Bureaucracy, and Military Government in Peru</u>, and author and co-author of several articles published in a number of professional journals both in the United States and Peru. A graduate of the University of Tasmania, he received his M.B.A.

degree from the University of Washington, Seattle, and his Ph.D. from Cornell University.

GUADALUPE ESTEVES is a sociology graduate of the Catholic University of Peru and has a B. Phil. in Latin American Studies from the University of Liverpool. A staff member of Peru's National Planning Institute, she has carried out research on the urban labor force and self-managed enterprises in both urban and rural areas of Peru.

CYNTHIA MCCLINTOCK is Assistant Professor of Political Science at The George Washington University. She earned her A.B. from Radcliffe College in 1967 and her doctorate from Massachusetts Institute of Technology in 1976. She is the author of Peasant Cooperatives and Political Changes in Peru (Princeton University Press, 1981), and co-editor of The Peruvian Experiment Reconsidered (Princeton University Press, forthcoming).

VICTOR VILLANUEVA is a former major in the Peruvian Army, and a well-known writer on the political evolution of the Peruvian armed forces and the contemporary political environment in his country. His books include Cien años del ejército Peruano: Frustraciones y cambios (1972), El CAEM y la revolución de la fuerza armado (1973), El APRA en busca del poder (1975), and many others. He presently writes a weekly column for the leftist magazine Marka.

RONALD BRUCE ST JOHN received his Ph.D. from the Graduate School of International Studies at the University of Denver in 1970. He has published articles in Orbis, Journal of Latin American Studies, Inter-American Economic Affairs, and Asian Survey as well as several other journals. St John is on the faculty of the Institute of International Studies, Bradley University.

DAVID SCOTT PALMER is Chairman of Latin American Studies and Coordinator of World Language Advanced Area Studies at the Foreign Service Institute in Arlington, Virginia. He also lectures at the School of Advanced International Studies, The Johns Hopkins University. He received his B.A. from Dartmouth (1959), M.A. from Stanford (1962), and Ph.D. in Government from Cornell (1973). He is the author of numerous articles and chapters concerning Peru. His book, Peru: The Authoritarian Tradition, was published by Praeger in 1980. Professor Palmer has also taught at Bowdoin College, Princeton University, and universities in Peru.

STEPHEN M. GORMAN received his Ph.D. in political science from the University of California at Riverside in 1977. He is presently on the faculty of the Department of Political Science at North Texas State University. His publications include articles in <u>Government and Opposition</u>, <u>Journal of Inter-American Studies and World Affairs</u>, <u>Journal of Latin American Studies</u>, <u>Inter-American Economic Affairs</u> and a number of other journals and chapters in edited works. His field of research over the past six years has concentrated on Peru and Nicaragua.

1
The Peruvian Revolution in Historical Perspective

Stephen M. Gorman

Whether the nearly twelve years of military rule in Peru between October 1968 and July 1980 are labeled a "revolution," a "so-called revolution," or a simple "military dictatorship," one fact remains inescapable: the reforms and programs of the armed forces during that period profoundly altered Peruvian society. The military that overthrew President Fernando Belaúnde Terry in 1968 set out to completely restructure social, political, and economic relations in the country. The objective was to promote urban industrial expansion, head off growing political activism among the lower classes, and strengthen the role of the state as an agent of national development and social reconciliation. Peru's military leaders endeavored to create a corporate social order that would be characterized by moral solidarity, social discipline, centralized authority, and hierarchically integrated self-managing socioeconomic units. The fact that the military failed in many of these objectives, and progressively turned away from reformist policies after 1975, does not alter the fact that the military regime nevertheless intentionally changed the nature of Peruvian political life.

The military's intervention into politics in 1968 is somewhat unique within both Latin American politics generally and Peruvian history in particular. In the first instance, although different military factions had been involved in at least eleven coup d'etats since the election of Peru's first civilian president in 1872,[1] only once before, in 1962, had the armed forces acted as an <u>institution</u> to seize control of the state. On that occasion the military limited its role to convening and supervising "honest" elections, and little more. But in 1968 the armed forces took power with the objective of instituting far ranging reforms with no intention of returning government to civilian hands in the foreseeable future. Secondly, although the military adopted a political program that had been articulated by

1

progressive sectors of the emerging middle class for more
than three decades, the armed forces did not govern as
the representatives of any specific social class (Bamat,
1979: 2-4). This is not to suggest that certain groups
did not benefit more than others from the military's
policies, but this was largely incidental to the broader
goals of national development and political stability
pursued by the armed forces. Finally, the Peruvian
military acted out of extreme nationalism and vigorously
attacked the nefarious forms of political, economic, and
even cultural neo-imperialism that were considered
largely responsible for the country's underdevelopment
and international dependency. Certainly, other Latin
American military regimes have adopted similar
anti-dependency objectives, most notably in Brazil since
the early 1970s, but most of these regimes originally
came to power in response to perceived internal communist
threats. But for the Peruvian military, the breaking of
the linkage between North American imperialism and Peru's
ruling oligarchy was an important motivating
consideration in the overthrow of the civilian
government.

While Peru found itself in worse economic condition
in 1980 than in 1968, with growing class conflict and a
deepening dependency on international financial
institutions controlled by North America, important and
potentially beneficial transformations were brought about
(not always intentionally) by the military government.
Other chapters in this work will examine the consequences
of military rule in specific areas of Peruvian politics
and attempt to outline some of the difficulties that will
be faced by the new civilian government headed by
Fernando Belaúnde Terry. The purpose of the present
chapter is to provide a general review of the military
revolution, both as a background to the following
chapters and in an attempt to identify the primary
factors that combined to frustrate the military's program
of government and eventually force it from power.

The twelve years of military rule (the docenio) are
normally divided into the First Phase, corresponding to
the presidency of Juan Velasco Alvarado (1968-1975), and
the Second Phase, corresponding to the presidency of
Francisco Morales Bermudez (1975-1980). In point of
fact, however, there was a brief period between the
overthrow of Velasco in August 1975 and the Lima riots of
July 1976 which stands apart from both phases. The First
Phase was a period of reformism while the Second Phase is
considered rather reactionary, since President Morales
Bermúdez presided over the emasculation of many earlier
reforms. Morales Bermúdez himself originally
characterized the Second Phase as a period of
"consolidation" intended to rationalize the reforms that
had been effected under Velasco. Throughout the first

year of his regime the emphasis actually appears to have
been on consolidating earlier revolutionary gains during
a period of economic difficulties. Only after the Lima
riots and an attempted right-wing coup within the armed
forces in July 1976 were liberal officers purged from the
government and a systematic assault initiated against
many of the progressive reforms of the earlier period.
This shift in governmental policy apparently resulted
from the failure of many reforms to produce the results
intended by the military.

In the remainder of this chapter we will outline the
ideology and political objectives of the military, the
specific reforms enacted to promote those objectives, and
the actual impact of reforms and programs on Peruvian
society over the course of the docenio. The actual
causes for the failure of the military-led revolution
will be found to be complex. But two contributing
factors that stand out in particular were: inadequate
conceptualization and poor execution of reforms. What I
choose to term the "bad luck" explanation mentioned by
some analysts (see for example Werlich, 1981; and Herbol
1979), which cites the failure to discover exportable
resources in anticipated amounts and the international
recession that began in 1974 as important factors
contributing to the collapse of the military's economic
programs, will be largely discounted here. As the
following section will attempt to illustrate, the
military assumed power with an ideology that claimed to
understand the past errors of civilian governments that
had produced Peru's underdevelopment and international
dependency, including the nature of the country's
subordinate integration into the global capitalist
system. Yet, the military rulers proceeded to predicate
the success of revolutionary reforms on the expansion of
the country's integration into the international market
(albeit with some diversification of products, trading
partners, and marketing techniques). The result
economically was that the generals' approach to
development failed in much the same fashion as civilian
regimes before them, but on a grander scale.

IDEOLOGY AND GOALS

One of the important characteristics of the Peruvian
military is that its officer corp has not been drawn from
the upper classes. In fact, officers after the turn of
the century were drawn increasingly from the middle and
lower-middle classes, especially in the case of the army.
Thus, the armed forces, dominated by the army, were not
strictly speaking an extension of the ruling classes
athough they frequently acted in defense of upper-class
interests prior to 1968. The essentially middle-class
composition of the army officer corp rendered it

especially susceptible to the reformist currents that gained steadily after the early 1930s. Because of early hostilities between the army and the main carrier of progressive middle-class reformism, the Peruvian Aprista Party (or APRA), however, the army was inhibited from embracing the dominant reformist ideology for some time. But with the establishment of the Center of High Military Studies (CAEM) an indirect process of officer indoctrination in middle-class progressivism was initiated under the aegis of military professionalization (Villanueva, 1973b; and Stepan, 1978: 144-147).[2]

Among the courses offered at CAEM were many dealing with the political history and socioeconomic conditions of Peru. A significant number of the civilian instructors brought in to offer such courses were, at least indirectly, influenced by the writings of Peru's early socialist José Carlos Mariátegui (1895-1930) and the political platform advanced by APRA. New officers became ever more sensitive to the political and economic corruption of the national oligarchy, the domination of the country by foreign economic interests, and the superficiality and decadence of Peru's purely formal democracy and personalistic political parties. All of this promoted a rejection within the army of the sterility of politics and a decrease in respect for the legitimacy of civilian rulers. The final step in the gradual politicization of CAEM officers was the conceptualization of national development as an integral dimension of national defense. If development was indeed essential to a strong national defense, and if civilian politicians were, as the army came steadily to believe, incapable of promoting development, then the army would be compelled to assume the direction of the state in order to fulfill its own mission of national defense.

Without implying that the following goals were universally held within the armed forces, or clearly and consciously understood by the entire circle of military rulers at the outset of the revolution, we can nevertheless identify four major concerns that oriented the military after 1968: 1) Social Justice, 2) Popular Participation, 3) National Independence, and 4) Development.

Social Justice was a primary and all inclusive goal of the military revolutionaries, but it was defined in only the vaguest manner. Generally, Social Justice combined a concern for the material well being of individuals with the teachings of Catholicism. As such, it was analogous to Christian Humanism. But its main emphasis was on the collectivity over the individual, and social responsibility over personal interest. Velasco (1973: 134) explained early in the revolution that the military leaders were "humanist revolutionaries" who were intent on moralizing Peruvian society with a set of values completely different from "those that sustain capitalism or communism." The goal of the revolution was to create a society that would "reprieve" man as part of a broader collectivity.

The concept of Social Justice precluded social conflict, which was considered to be a by-product of social stratification based on the special privileges and monopoly over wealth enjoyed by an egotistical minority. Accordingly, Social Justice required that all people share equitably (although not necessarily equally) in both the wealth and "destiny" of the country. This would be possible only when there arose "free citizens" occupying their "just place in society" (La Prensa, June 25, 1969). It should be stressed that this was not a call for strict egalitarianism since it did not propose a leveling of society, but only a more "just" distribution of social wealth.

Finally, Social Justice imposed certain limitations on formal or legal rights, including property ownership. Stated Velasco (1973: 41), "The Revolution recognizes the legitimacy of all those rights whose observance does not signify perpetuating injustice. . . ." Conversely, the military government refused to respect certain formal rights whose observance "would signify, necessarily, condemning the majority to eternal poverty. . . ." This clearly encompassed property rights. The notion of Social Justice assumed that property might be held in private ownership, but that this would not relieve it of its social obligations. In other words, the right of private property in the productive sectors was conditioned on the use of that property to promote socially beneficial ends (Gorman, 1978c: 28).

Participation of the masses in the revolution was another important component of the military's ideology. But participation was redefined and placed within a moral and economic context instead of an essentially political one. That is, participation was not understood in electoral terms. Elections were considered the window dressing of the purely formal democracy which had worked only to the advantage of elites in Peru prior to 1968. In a speech to the nation on the 148th Anniversary of Peruvian Independence, Velasco (1973: 55) made it clear that the military had no intention of respecting the institutional norms of the civilian political system, including elections, since these had merely permitted the privileged few to deceive and manipulate the vast majority. Not only did participation as defined by the military reject the need for national elections, it also excluded the need for intermediaries such as political parties. Intermediaries were considered unnecessary, in the first instance, because the national leaders were "interpreters" of popular aspirations, not mere representatives of it. The government and people were

one and the same (Velasco, in El Comercio, July 29,
1969), and thus the functions of interest articulation,
aggregation and communication which political parties
purportedly perform to link government and people were
superfluous in the case of revolutionary Peru.

What the military meant by participation was the
right and duty of all citizens to share in the burdens
and benefits of Peruvian development. Also, individuals
were to be allowed a wider and more meaningful
participation in the operation of social and economic
institutions that directly touched upon their own
immediate lives, such as neighborhood councils, workers'
councils in factories, or other localized units. Yet,
such grass roots participation was not intended to serve
as a process of reconciliation between opposing
interests. The military argued that true participation
could only take place within a context of moral
solidarity, which meant that it could not occur in the
presence of competing interests or values. Consequently,
the revolutionary goal of promoting participation had

> . . . as its end the construction in [Peru] of
> a social democracy of full participation, that
> is to say, a system based on a moral order of
> solidarity, not individualism; on an economy
> fundamentally self-managing, in which the means
> of production are predominantly social property
> . . .; and on a political order where the
> decisionmaking power, far from being
> monopolized by the political and economic
> oligarchies . . . [is grounded in] social,
> economic, and political institutions directed,
> without intermediation or with a minimum of it,
> by the men and women that form them (Velasco,
> 1973: 205).

The organic and solidary definition of true
participation, thus, entailed a progressive
depoliticization of Peruvian society and a somewhat
Burkean integration of citizens into disaggregated social
units.

National Independence was another important
objective of the Peruvian revolution, which was dedicated
to breaking the country's political, economic and
military dependency on North America. Dependency was
defined as the subordination of national will to
"imperialist" interests. For the military, subordination
occurred whenever national decisionmakers yielded to
foreign pressures or influence. The oligarchy prior to
the revolution was considered to have been the active
agent of imperialism, and therefore bore primary
responsibility for the dependency of Peruvian society.
The military promised to resist any and all forms of

foreign political influence in the formulation of Peru's domestic and foreign policies.

Nationalism meant, pre-eminently, national liberation. It required that the government conduct its foreign affairs in strict relation to the national interest, and not in accordance with such outmoded international configurations as the East-West split. Nationalism also meant cultural and intellectual emancipation. A nationalist ideology, for instance, could only be based on, and understood in reference to, the unique heritage of a particular people. Appropriately, Velasco (1973: 38) insisted that the Peruvian revolution was neither capitalist nor communist, but predicated on strictly indigenous values and ideas.

Most significantly, nationalism and the struggle against dependency was taken to mean that Peru should join with the vanguard of underdeveloped nations in pressing for a restructuring of the international political and economic order. To assert the country's new independence, Peru's military leaders broadened diplomatic and commercial ties to include many communist bloc nations, and turned away from the United States as the country's chief arms supplier. Lastly, National Independence presupposed national development oriented toward the satisfaction of domestic needs and greater international economic equality with trading partners.

National Development, which was the fourth major revolutionary objective, was intended both as a justification of the revolutionary process (the end that would justify the means), and as a condition that would facilitate the realization of the other revolutionary goals (Social Justice, National Independence, etc.). First and foremost, development required the construction of a modern industrial society, supported by a modern and efficient agrarian sector. Production had to be oriented both toward increasing internal consumption and improving Peru's competitiveness in the international finished goods market. The military realized that foreign capital would be necessary for development, but would have to be closely controlled to insure that it benefited Peru as much or more than it benefited foreign investors (Gorman, 1978c: 32). It would also require a greater mobilization of Peru's own domestic resources which would be channeled to the industrial sector. Consistent with these two principle requirements, the revolutionary leaders redefined the rules for investment and altered the incentives to encourage greater private investment in specific areas of production, while reserving certain "key" industrial sectors to the state.

Underlying the military's approach to development was a strong belief that the state should play a larger role in industrialization and exercise tighter supervision of foreign capital to direct it into those economic activities most beneficial to Peru. But even while the state was to expand its economic role, the military still intended to rely heavily on private domestic investment, for which reason it was predisposed to permit increasing profits in modern industries to stimulate the accumulation of capital for further investment. Agrarian reform to stimulate greater production for domestic consumption, coupled with price controls to hold down the cost of living for urban workers (and hence the cost of labor for industrialists) were integral elements of the military's approach to national develpment (Bamat, 1979: 3-4). And in a more general context, the military assumed that complete development would ultimately require national integration in the broadest possible sense. Only through a simultaneous process of economic, cultural, political, and linguistic integration would it be possible to fully mobilize human and material resources and build a modern industrial society.

It should be reemphasized that the four principle objectives of the revolution outlined above evolved gradually over the first year or so of the military regime. In other words, the military did not take power with a clear conceptualization of purpose, but rather came slowly to define its political program through the actual exercise of power. Toward the end of the Velasco period, one of the president's close advisors argued that the military had been pursuing a detailed secret plan of government almost from the outset (Zimmermann Zavala, 1974). But the actual conduct of the military government between 1968-1975 strongly suggests that many reforms were ad hoc responses to unanticipated developments, while others (like the agrarian reform and creation of so-called Industrial Communities) may actually have been part of a "grand strategy." In the following section we will examine the major reforms of the First Phase of the Peruvian revolution.

THE FIRST PHASE OF THE REVOLUTION

Under Velasco, the military government committed itself to creating a "pluralistic" economy and a "Social Democracy of Full Participation." These duel objectives required some far-reaching economic reforms and a comprehensive reordering of the national political environment. On the economic side, a variety of different forms of economic organization were promoted in industry and agriculture, the state assumed a greater role in planning the economy and stimulating industrial expansion, and workers were provided with varying degrees of participation in profits and management. On the political side, the government endeavored to reduce (and eventually eliminate) the role of unions and political parties in the society, depoliticize higher education and increase technological training, and deprive the upper class of its traditional monopoly over political resources (such as control of information). Naturally, economic and political reforms overlapped and were highly interdependent. Nevertheless, it is possible to differentiate between primarily economic and political reform measures in the following discussion for purposes of clarity. While all of the important reforms cannot be reviewed here for reasons of space, we can identify the major programs initiated by the military during the revolution's First Phase.

Economic Reforms

The goal of promoting national development within a context of economic pluralism took the form of recognizing different ownership patterns and organizational forms throughout the economy. The four chief economic sectors that emerged were: State Property (involving a government monopoly over certain business, financial, and commercial activities of special importance to Peruvian development), Reformed Private Property (involving worker participation in the profits and management of private industrial firms), Unreformed Private Property (in which companies with less than six employees or $250,000 in annual sales remained essentially unaltered), and Social Property (modeled after Yugoslav worker ownership of industries). Aside from promoting a variety of organizational forms throughout the economy, the military government attempted to restructure the overall economy itself by channeling a greater share of national resources to the modern industrial sector, providing increased opportunities for private capital accumulation, and expanding agricultural production for both export and internal consumption. One of the first and most important moves the Velasco government undertook to stimulate development was agrarian reform.

Agrarian Reform. On June 24, 1969 the Velasco regime decreed a comprehensive agrarian reform intended, among other things, to increase production in order to generate surplus capital for investment in the urban-industrial sector (Velasco, 1973: 9-13). The reform applied to most coastal properties above 150 hectares and sierra holdings above 35 to 55 hectares (with regional variations). While expropriated holdings were compensated for with bonds payable over twenty to thirty years (Caballero, 1977: 147), the actual value of compensation was "sharply reduced by inflation and lax law enforcement" (McClintock, 1977: 11). Although some observers perceived the reform as an attempt by the

military to head off peasant unrest in the highlands, the
pattern of application suggested that increasing
productivity was the primary motivation for the law. The
large export-oriented coastal estates were expropriated
almost immediately while the provisions of the reform
were applied only gradually to the highlands on a
regional basis (Harding, 1975: 236; and Philip, 1978:
119-120).

The reform originally called for transferring
roughly 11 million hectares (out of a national total of
perhaps 21 to 23 million hectares of agricultural land)
to some 340,000 rural families (out of perhaps 700,000
rural families).[3] Through subsequent decrees,
expropriated properties were organized along four primary
lines, depending on the size, productivity, and previous
organization of the holdings. Large, profitable coastal
estates were constituted as Agricultural Production
Cooperatives (CAPs) while the best sierra holdings were
organized as Social Interest Agrarian Societies (SAISs).
Fully seventy-six percent of expropriated properties were
eventually organized into CAPs or SAISs, while the
remainder was distributed as individual plots in either
Campesino Cooperatives or Campesino Communities (both of
which suffered from a scarcity of government assistance
and credit) (Caballera, 1977: 148-149). While the
peasants in CAPs and SAISs were guaranteed a dominant
voice in the management of their cooperatives
(McClintock, 1977: 13-14), conflicts between cooperative
members and state appointed technocrats were frequent
over such questions as the allocations of surpluses
toward reinvestment or increased pay (Philip, 1978: 120).
Other conflicts concerned the demands of large numbers of
peasants who failed to qualify as beneficiaries of the
reform because they had been non-tenant laborers on
highland haciendas or only temporary or part-time
employees on coastal estates before the reform. Finally,
a considerable amount of land escaped expropriation in
the highlands because government delays allowed owners to
carry out their own parcelation of holdings among family
members and/or others.

As George Philip (1978: 119) has suggested, the
agrarian reform suffered from a certain ambiguity of
purpose from the outset. The "developmentalist" officers
viewed the reform as a measure to increase agricultural
productivity, while so-called "radical" officers favored
the reform as a means of income redistribution (that
would mobilize popular support behind the military
regime). The revolutionary rhetoric that accompanied the
declaration of the reform aroused the expectations of
landless sierra peasants, but in practice the government
concentrated on increasing productivity on the already
highly efficient coastal estates rather than meeting the
demands of highland peasants for the swift and complete

expropriation of haciendas. The percentage of Agrarian
Bank loans allocated to the agro-export sector increased
during the First Phase, and the bulk of public investment
in agriculture went toward large-scale irrigation to
benefit coastal estates (McClintock, 1980b: 7). The fact
that most part-time agricultural laborers and non-tenant
peasants failed to benefit from the agrarian reform led
to serious labor tensions along the coast and land
invasion in the highlands (Harding, 1975: 242-248).

Partly in response to tensions in the countryside,
the military government created the National Agrarian
Confederation (CNA) as "the one legitimate organ of
expression of farm interests" (Bourque and Palmer, 1975:
191). Established in 1972 by Decree Law 19400, the CNA
did not hold its first national convention until late
1974. The CNA was intended to join together all
individuals who worked in the agricultural sector to both
communicate their interests to government and coordinate
regional and national agricultural policies. However,
the CNA was "basically a mechanism to enhance the labors
of the government" since peasant interests were to be
defended by the CNA only to the extent that they were
"compatible with the national interest as determined by
the Military Government" (Bourque and Palmer, 1975:
191-192). Although problems continued to disrupt
government policies in the countryside even after the
formation of the CNA, as the expectations unleashed by
the agrarian reform contributed to growing political
instability, the situation remained within manageable
limits throughout the Velasco period. And although the
agrarian reform did not measure up to all of the rhetoric
that surrounded its initiation, it nevertheless qualified
as one of the most important changes effected by the
military (Quijano, 1971: 15).

Reformed Private Property. The First Phase
government attempted to stimulate industrial expansion
and harmonize worker-owner relations through the
introduction of a series of reforms in 1970. The General
Law of Industries (D.L. 18350) required private companies
with more than six employees or $250,000 in gross income
to re-invest 15 percent of their profits in the name of
the workers as a group until workers acquired 50 percent
ownership, provide participation in management
proportionate to worker ownership in the company, and
distribute another 10 percent of net profits directly to
individual workers (Jaquette, 1975: 428). This was
followed by Decree Law 18384 which established the
organizational form of the Industrial Communities in each
firm through which workers were to share in profits
(Knight, 1975: 367). Finally, Decree Law 18471 in
November 1970 significantly tightened the conditions
under which industrial workers could be fired or laid

off.

According to David Scott Palmer (1980: 110), "the Industrial Law permitted important advances in worker participation in management and profits of those relatively few fortunate enough to be already employed in this privileged sector." But the reform of private industrial property did not significantly expand production nor did it reduce labor problems as the military had anticipated. As Anibal Quijano (1971: 93-94) observed after the introduction of Industrial Communities (CIs), in spite of the apparent benefits offered to workers,

> . . . the [CI] is a cleverly designed instrument for fulfilling the purposes for which it was intended: to ally the proletariat with the interests of capitalist enterprise in order to introduce into this class even greater differences and sources of friction and thus prevent a growing class solidarity, to try to subordinate class consciousness to the individual interests of its members, and to try to eliminate class struggles between workers and capitalists, in accordance with the doctrine which the regime upholds, i.e., that conflicts between 'capital and labor' are only 'apparently irreducible.'

Regardless of the intentions of the reform to reconcile the interests of labor and management, worker unrest increased. During the two years preceeding the reform of industrial property (1968-1969) there had been 735 strikes involving over 200,000 workers (about 10 percent of the labor force), while during the two years following the measure (1971-1972) there were 786 strikes involving 292,000 workers (about 15.4 percent of the labor force). More important, the severity of strikes increased. During the period 1968-1969 a total of 7.3 million man hours were lost through strikes. This increased to 17.2 million man hours during 1971-1972 (Palmer, 1980: 14; and Sulmont, 1977). What also changed was the cause of strikes. Whereas in 1968-1969, 23.1 percent of all strikes involved layoffs and firings, 17.7 percent involved pay demands, and 15.9 percent involved contract disputes; in 1971 fully 35 percent of all strikes involved pay demands, while the other two issues declined in importance (see Pease García and Verme Insúa, 1974: 48, 128, 126, 348, and 462). Certainly not all of these strikes affected the Reformed Private Property Sector, but they do reflect the intensification of labor conflicts in the better organized sectors of the economy which industrial reforms failed to stem.

Even together with a modified form of Industrial

Communities for State Enterprises (in which workers received bonds instead of stock), industrial reform measures benefitted only a minority of Peru's modern work force, In 1972, there were roughly 53,100 workers in mining, 485,200 workers in manufacturing and 171,700 workers in construction, which together represented 16.2 percent of Peru's labor force (ILO, 1976: 86-87). Yet, by the end of the reform period in 1975 only approximately 200,000 workers belonged to CIs, representing less than 4.3 percent of Peru's economically active population (Palmer, 1980: 110; Knight, 1975: 367). These workers, who were organized into more than 3,500 CIs by the close of the Velasco period, came to pose something of a political challenge to the military government after 1973 when the Ministry of Industry and Tourism sponsored the First National Congress of Industrial Communities. Although the government had not intended to form a permanent national body to aggregate and communicate the interests of CIs (as is had done in the agricultural sector with the formation of the CNA), the workers themselves formed the autonomous National Confederation of Industrial Communities (CONACI) in October 1973 which called upon the government to 1) convert all reformed property to Social Property, 2) increase worker participation in management, and 3) cancel the agrarian debt owed to former land owners (Pease García and Verme Insúa, 1974: 482). By mid-1974 CONACI had become a serious embarassment to the regime because of its efforts to push the revolution further left than the generals desired to go. The military responded with an effort to divide CONACI and bring it back within the ideological parameters of the revolution.

The State Sector. The expansion of the Peruvian government's direct involvement in the economy under Velasco has been characterized by many observers as a form of "state capitalism" (Fitzgerald, 1976; Quijano, 1971; and Bollinger, 1977). Aside from its other economic reforms, the military created a heterogeneous state sector composed of a collection of industrial, financial, and commercial enterprises. The First Phase government did not intend to either replace or discourage private domestic and foreign investment. Rather, state investment in certain "strategic" areas of the economy was intended to guarantee a rapid development of the industrial infrastructure (e.g., steel production) and promote the expansion of the domestic market. Major export activities were also nationalized to insure that export earnings were maximized to finance the military's ambitious industrial investment program. Finally, the creation of a state sector was intended to breakup certain monopolies held by domestic and foreign capitalists in Peru which acted as obstacles to what the

military perceived as the inherent dynamism of the
economy (Thorp and Bertram, 1978: 304). Thus, while
foreign investment was still encouraged, it was no longer
allowed to freely choose the area and scope of its
activities. It was expected to be consistent with, and
contribute to, the government's developmental strategies.

Two primary characteristics of the state sector were
that it was formed primarily on the basis of existing
(mostly foreign) industries, and grew largely out of the
pursuit of other objectives, such as the rationalization
of a particular area of production or the reduction of
external dependency (Fitzgerald, 1979: 192). While the
military became intent on centralizing what it perceived
as strategic economic activities, it nevertheless
remained committed to a notion of "economic pluralism"
and had no intention of moving toward a completely
state-managed economy. E.V.K. Fitzgerald (1976: 32-34)
has classified the state sector firms that emerged during
the First Phase of the revolution into three major
categories. In the first group were state enterprises
formed from expropriated foreign holdings (including
PETROPERU, ENTROMIN, HIERROPERU, ENTELPERU, and ENAFER).
These state enterprises gave the government dominant
control over the important extractive industries (oil,
copper, iron) and public services (electricity and rail
transportation). In the second group were formerly
domestically owned industries taken over after economic
collapses. The fishmeal industry is the chief example,
which was converted into the state enterprise PESCAPERU
in 1973 at a time when the sector was in severe decline.
The third group was made up of already existing and newly
created state enterprises, like the steel firm SIDERPERU.

Apart from these primarily extractive and
manufacturing firms, the government assumed a dominant
position in marketing and credit. Through the purchase
of stock, the government came to control most of the
banking industry. State monopolies were also created in
the foreign marketing of minerals and other products, the
domestic wholesale of basic foodstuffs, and industries
oriented to processing primary exports to increase the
value added.

The military had intended to have the state augment
private investment, not replace it. But the rhetoric of
the revolution created a climate of uncertainty in the
business community that discouraged both domestic and
foreign private investments in the economy. Thus, the
state's share of fixed investment rose from 29.8 percent
in 1968 to 44 percent in 1973 (Pease Garcia and Verme
Insua, 1974: xxix). Over the long run the military
rulers expected primary exports (especially oil and
copper) to finance state investments in heavy industry.
But over the short run the government turned to private
international credit which, as it happened, was readily

available at reasonable terms during the early 1970s
(Thorp and Bertram, 1978: 309-315). Indeed, it was the
abundance of private credit during this period that
allowed the Peruvian government to escape almost
completely the effects of the cutoff of official
bilateral credits and aid from the United States. The
cutoff was in retaliation for the uncompensated
expropriation of the International Petroleum Company in
1968, and was not ended until the 1974 Greene Agreement
between Peru and the United States resolved all
outstanding claims against the revolutionary government.

Even with heavy foreign borrowing, however, the rate
of fixed capital formation by the close of the Velasco
period remained virtually the same as during the early
1960s (United Nations, 1977: 649-660). And the growth of
industrial output generally, and manufacturing in
particular, remained virtually unchanged between the
periods 1961-1970 and 1971-1975 (United Nations, 1977:
680-682). What did change was the economy's dependence
on state investment and the country's external public
debt (which began to increase almost exponentially). The
expansion of the state sector also brought the government
into an employer-employee relationship with a sizable
proportion of the Peruvian work force. This eventually
posed serious political difficulties for the government
after 1974 when the military began to react to the first
signs of economic crisis by "rationalizing" state
controlled industries (i.e., reducing labor costs).

Social Property. As early as July 1971, President
Velasco let it be known that the Revolutionary
Government's reorganization of property ownership would
not stop with the formation of agrarian cooperatives,
Industrial Communities, and the expansion of the state
sector. He announced that an entirely new form of
property--Social Property--would be created as the
foundation for Peruvian socialism (Pease García and Verme
Insúa, 1974: 290). It was not until August 1973,
however, that the government finally issued a draft law
of Social Property for public comment. After eight
months of sometimes intense public debate, resulting in
the deportation of certain leading critics (see Lecaros,
1975; and DESCO 1975), the Law of Social Property (D.L.
20598) was decreed on April 30, 1974. This law provided
for the formation of a Social Property Sector composed of
Social Property Enterprises (EPSs) which, it was planned,
would come to constitute the dominant form of production
in the country over the course of twenty or thirty years
(Fitzgerald, 1979: 125-126).

The Social Property Sector was to be presided over
by the National Commission of Social Property (CONAPS)
which would be responsible for approving the creation of
individual EPSs, supervising their early operations, and

coordinating policy for the sector as a whole. While EPSs could be formed in any economic field either from scratch or through the conversion of an existing company upon the request of its workers, preference was initially given to the establishement of entirely new firms. To provide state capital for the formation of EPSs, the government set up the National Fund of Social Property (FONAPS) to finance the growth of the new sector. Finally, the law provided for a national Social Property Sector Assembly to consist of EPS representatives elected through regional associations. This national assembly was to meet biannually: in November to plan programs for the sector for the coming year, and in April to evaluate the performance of the sector during the previous year.

The government devoted considerable time and effort to detailing the structure and function of the sector since it was supposed to become the priority area for future public investment. Within the individual EPSs all employees (including part-time workers who were normally excluded from reform benefits in the other property sectors) were to be members entitled to share in the management and profits of the company. Elaborate provisions were outlined for the self-management and democratic governance of the EPSs. However, a limit on the amount of profits which could be distributed to EPS members was established (with the surplus to be transferred to FONAPS to finance the creation of additional EPSs.) And CONAPS retained the right to intervene in the management of companies until the state had recovered its investment to insure that the EPSs were administered efficiently. Also, some of the earnings of the EPSs were to be allocated to providing certain social services to members which, under normal circumstances, should have been provided by the state (Decree Law 20598, Article 101). (Even so, such profits were still subject to taxation even though they were used to provide services that would normally be paid for by taxes.) Finally, although Social Property Enterprises were to become entirely self-managing after a supposedly brief period of state-supervised gestation, the fixed assets of each company could not be freely disposed of by workers since they were legally considered the property of society as a whole (Gorman, 1977: 316-318).

The introduction of Social Property received an enthusiastic response from most workers and leftist intellectuals, but was bitterly opposed by business leaders who feared that it threatened the concept of economic pluralism and was intended to subvert private property. The success of Social Property, however, was jeopardized from the outset by two major difficulties. First, by 1974-1975 the military government's investment resources were already severely strained which in turn limited the expansion of the new sector. Second, as

Fitzgerald (1979: 126-127) has noted, the high
concentration of production in the various branches of
modern industry in Peru where EPSs were to be formed
threatened the economic viability of the new firms.
Their competitiveness within such monopolistic conditions
could not be guaranteed even with state imposed
restrictions on the expansion of existing private
manufacturers. As a result, demands increased toward the
end of the First Phase for the conversion of existing
companies into EPSs, rather than the formation of new
enterprises. These and other problems delayed the
expansion of the sector, and by the close of the Velaso
period only a handful of EPSs were in operation (with
perhaps another one hundred in various stages of planning
or formations). The actual growth of the Social Property
Sector failed to satisfy the expectations that the reform
aroused among workers and intellectuals, and the
government's commitment to the social property concept
waned quickly after 1975.

Political Reforms

While the military's basic approach to development
reflected a high degree of confidence in technocratic
solutions to economic problems, its approach to the
representative duties of government was influenced by a
deep distrust of politics and politicians. Labor unions,
to the extent that they were taditionally either the
creatures of political parties in Peru or, at a minimum,
politically oriented, were also highly suspect in the
military's eyes. The traditional political system in
Peru had operated on the basis of the marginalization of
the highland rural population and the segmentary
incorporation of different urban and coastal groups by
political parties that became their patrons (see Cotler,
1968; Delgado, 1974; and Bourque, 1970).

The client-patron relationships that developed
between the various political parties and their
constituencies led to a situation in which the national
interest was neglected in favor of particularistic
interests. When, as often happened, competing narrow
interests could not be reconciled and a concensus for
action arrived at, the situation gave rise to the
stagnation of the national govermental process. Politics
was overwhelmingly a forum for sectarian competition
between essentially personalistic political parties.
Thus, the military committed itself to the complete
depoliticization of Peruvian society and the imposition
of what Julio Cotler (1975) termed a "new mode of
domination." The following measures, although in no way
comprehensive, stand out as some of the more important
political reforms enacted by the First Phase government
to restructure the political environment and foster the

growth of a corporatist society in Peru.

   Mobilization and Participation. The military, or at
least a certain faction within the military, was
interested in mobilizing support for revolutionary reform
and increasing lower-class participation in restructuring
Peruvian society. As Henry Dietz (1980: 178) observes,
three options were open to the government: it could
create its own revolutionary political party, work
through one of the existing political parties (such as
the pro-government Communist Party), or attempt to
completely redefine the nature and process of
mobilization and participation. The military opted for
the third alternative and estalished what Alfred Stepan
(1978: 314-315) has termed a "bureaucratic sponsored
organization": the National System for Support of Social
Mobilization (SINAMOS). The law establishing SINAMOS
(D.L. 18896) in June 1971 and the subsequent statute (D.
L. 19352) outlining its organization and procedures in
April 1972 assigned the agency a number of
responsibilities. The most important duties of SINAMOS
were to 1) train and organize the popular classes at the
local level to promote the implementation of national
policies, 2) elaborate a corporatist definition of
participation in which individuals would cooperate in
localized activities directed from above by the
government, 3) coordinate self-help activities among the
poor, and 4) undercut the traditional role of political
parties as integrative agents for "marginalized" groups
(see Palmer, 1973: 89-99; and Gorman, 1977: 325-326).
   SINAMOS was given a wide field of operations,
including the cooperatives formed by the agrarian reform,
the Industrial Communities formed by the Industrial Law
and, most importantly, the squatter settlements (pueblos
jóvenes) surrounding Lima. To facilitate its manifold
responsibilities, SINAMOS was given a duel organizational
structure. Along side a variety of functional
departments (dealing with rural organization, labor
organization, community development, etc.) the
government created a pyramidal national structure with a
central office at the top, ten regional offices
(presiding over two to five departments) and numerous
zonal offices (ideally presiding over about two provinces
each). Finally, at the lowest level, were the actual
field operatives--or "contact points"--of SINAMOS who
initiated or coordinated community activities. As David
Scott Palmer (1973: 93) noted in one of the earliest
studies of SINAMOS, while citizens were not to be
permitted actual participation in the making of national
policies themselves, they were allowed a role in deciding
how these policies would be carried out in their
immediate areas.
   SINAMOS was beset with difficulties almost from the

outset. In the first instance, the formation of the agency was a response to the autonomous formation of Commmittees for the Defense of the Revolution that sprang up around Lima and throughout the country in 1970 (Palmer, 1973: 85-87). At least one observer (Philip, 1978: 128) has speculated that the appearance of these committees precipitated something of a crisis within the armed forces. Some military hardliners wanted these committees disbanded, while other officers viewed them as an opportunity to expand the revolution's base of support. Whether this is true or not, SINAMOS was also an attempt to overcome the military's lack of grassroots structures within the society by which the popular classes could be linked to the government, and give substance to the military's rhetoric of "participation." As Henry Dietz (1980a: 172) has written:

> the absence of meaningful mechanisms for participation among the lower levels of society explained in large part why formal democracy had always maintained an elitist and discriminatory character in Peru, and why it had always had something of a foreign character about it: it failed to relate to the experiences and lives of the lower sectors (the majority) of society.

At least in the thinking of the more radical officer corp and many of the civilian intellectuals supporting the government (like Carlos Delgado), SINAMOS presented an opportunity for promoting a uniquely Peruvian participatory system.

But Alfred Stepan (1978: 314) and others have argued that SINAMOS could not escape from the consequences of its own inherent contradictions. While it could not adjust to fluid political conditions with the flexibility or independence of a poltical party (since it lacked autonomy from the military), neither was it in a position to radicalize government policies to meet the expectations that its own activities unleashed among the populace (see Philip, 1978: 127-130). SINAMOS programs throughout most of the society were visible failures by late 1973; with some notable exceptions, such as in the pueblos jóvenes of the Lima/Callao areas (Collier, 1975: 155; and Dietz, 1980a). Stepan (1978: 315) has observed that SINAMOS encountered opposition from virtually every political sector: government technocrats resented its efforts to interject politics into economic planning, the target communities feared its manipulative potential, and the political parties and unions opposed the efforts of SINAMOS to deprive them of popular leadership. Most significantly, SINAMOS was unable to control many of the mass-based groups it helped bring into existence.

Paradoxically, although the military originally created SINAMOS to undercut the appeal of unions, by 1974-1975 the government virtually abandoned SINAMOS and in turn attempted to compete with unions directly by forming state-sponsored syndicates in a variety of economic sectors.

Education. The military considered the rationalization and modernization of Peruvian higher education essential to national development, and therefore moved quickly to impose major university reforms. In a highly controversial move, the government issued Decree Law 17437 in February 1969 in a sudden and unexpected manner. The law reduced student participation in university governance from one-third to one-fourth, reorganized faculties into disciplines, and attempted to depoliticize student politics by setting academic standards for election to student organizations and barring re-elections. Most threateningly, the law effectively abolished the traditional autonomy of Peruvian universities by placing them under the supervision of a National Council of the Peruvian University (CONUP) that was placed under the authority of the Ministry of Education (see Pease García and Verme Insúa, 1974: 62). Because of intense reaction from practically all university groups, especially students and professors, the Velasco regime made progressive modifications in the law throughout the remainder of the year (Drysdale and Myers, 1975: 257-261). Finally, in November 1969 the government attempted to modify the university community by appointing an Educational Reform Commission under the supervision of the Ministry of Education to write a new comprehensive educational reform proposal with public input.

It took the Reform Commission until September 1970 to publish its first report for public comment which sparked considerable public debate. As far as possible, the commission--sometimes under direct pressure from President Velasco himself--endeavored to incorporate the demands of important groups into a new reform proposal (Lowenthal, 1975: 37). By early 1971 the commission had produced a draft law, but this was not released for public comment until December. After still further modifications in the law in response to pressures and demands from both within and without the universties, the Velasco government finally issued its General Law of Education (D.L. 19326) in March 1972 (more than 34 months after the military's first educational reform initiative).

The law recognized "humanism, nationalism, and democracy" as the three "ideological pillars" of the educational system in Peru and formalized three distinct levels of instruction: preliminary education for children

up through age 5, basic education for ages 6-15, and
vocational and academic higher education (Drysdale and
Myers, 1975: 261-265). Although CONUP remained in
existence, its authority was reduced somewhat and the
principle of university autonomy, and student and
professor participation in university governance, were
upheld (Pease García and Verme Insúa, 1974: 381-382).
However, the law also required both public and private
universities to serve as free and open resource centers
to their surrounding communities and delayed the
promulgation of a General Statute of the Peruvian
University which would outline the precise administrative
structure of each universty. In effect, despite the
military's efforts to involve the public in the
formulation of the General Law of Education, the process
failed to produce public support for the reform package
and stopped short of definitively resolving some of the
most sensitive issues (such as the exact authority of
CONUP over universities).

Conflict between the government and the educational
community continued at all levels after 1972. In higher
education, two major issues of conflict concerned pay for
teaching and non-teaching personnel (which failed to keep
pace with inflation) and the alleged interference of
CONUP in university self-governance. Both the
pro-government Revolutionary Students of Peru (formed
with the assistance of SINAMOS) and the more radical
Student Federation of Peru (FEP) criticized or opposed
the reformist measures of CONUP. And the National
Federation of Teachers of the Peruvian University
(FENDUP) vigorously attacked the government's
"rationalization" program in education (Pease García and
Filomeno, 1977a: 1252, 1329, and 1363). Within lower
education popular opposition to the government on a wide
range of issues became increasingly radical. In 1970 the
strongest teachers' union had been the National
Federation of Educators of Peru (FENEP), whose membership
was split between followers of the pro-government General
Confederation of Peruvian Workers (CGTP) and left-wing
Apristas. The Apristas withdrew and formed the Sole
Syndicate of Workers of Peruvian Education (SUTEP) which
adopted an extremely militant opposition to the military
regime (Gorman, 1978b: 299; and Philip, 1978: 143n).

When the government sponsored elections in the
educational establishment in 1973, SUTEP emerged as the
dominant teachers' union. The Velasco regime reacted by
withdrawing recognition from SUTEP and forming a
government sponsored Syndicate of Educators of the
Peruvian Revolution (SERP) (Cotler, 1975: 74). The
continued dominance of SUTEP among educators, however,
led the government to seek a dialogue with the union in
July 1974 (Pease García et al., 1975: 881-882). The
"dialogue" came to an end, however, shortly after SUTEP's

Secretary General, Horacio Zevallos, labelled the
military's education reform as an attempt to promote the
interests of the country's "dependent bourgeoisie" at a
national congress in November (Pease García et al., 1975:
1001-1002, and 1068). By early 1975 SUTEP had formulated
a political program calling for the overthrow of the
existing "bourgeoise government" and its replacement by a
proletarian regime, total opposition to the General Law
of Education because of its bias in favor of "power
groups," and the formation of a united front to resist
the manipulative agencies of the military government
(such as SINAMOS and the Ministry of Education) (Pease
Garcia and Filomeo, 1977a: 1218).

In reality, the military's approach to education
became ever more equivocal after 1973 as opposition
mounted to reforms. At times the government adopted a
hard line policy, as with the promulgation of Decree Law
20201 in October 1973 that authorized the Minister of
Education to dismiss any instructor suspected of
"subversion" without appeal over the course of a year.
At other times, the government (acting through CONUP)
struggled to appease student and teacher demands,
especially during the first half of 1975. In spite of
its obvious disappointment with the response to its
reforms, the Velasco government continued to attempt to
effect major changes in education right up to the end of
the First Phase. For example, in May 1975 Decree Law
21156 established the Indian language of Quechua as one
of the official languages of the country, mandated
obligatory instruction in the language by the 1976 school
year, and gave the judicial system until January 1977 to
acquire the capacity to conduct proceedings in the
language when requested by defendants.

Information and the Press. The Velasco government
enjoyed generally good relations with the Peruvian press
during its first year in power, but the increasing tempo
of reforms invariably caused tension between the military
and the wealthy owners of the leading national dailies
(see Gilbert, 1979). The government's first effort to
exercise control over the press came in December 1969
with Decree Law 18075. This law imposed stiff penalties
for libel against government officials and state
entities, and prohibitied either foreigners or Peruvian
nationals living abroad from owning newspapers. As the
government's treatment in the press worsened, more direct
measures were taken. In March 1970 two important dailies
(Expreso and Extra) were expropriated and turned over to
their workers (who were under the influence of the
pro-government Communist Party). The papers, which
belonged to Manuel Ulloa who had served as a minister in
the Belaunde government, were accused of defending the
interests of foreign capitalists and the Peruvian

oligarchy. In 1971 a third important daily came under indirect military influence when the goverment purchased the stock of the Banco Popular after the collapse of the financial empire of one of the nation's leading oligarchic families. The bank had served as the holding company for the diverse investments of the Prado familiy, including the Lima daily La Crónica. The paper was renamed La Nueva Crónica and placed under the management of an editorial council sympathetic to the revolution. Finally, in January 1972, the government issued Decree Law 19270 that gave the workers in each paper the first option to puchase their dailies should the owners be forced to sell under the provisions of Decree Law 18075 of 1969.

The crux of the growing conflict between the government and the independent press was that practically all of the leading dailies were owned by extremely wealthy individuals who were deeply involved in the political and economic issues on which their papers editorialized (Gilbert, 1979: 370-374). Indeed, with the exception of El Comercio (which was the primary investment of the Miro Quesada family) the leading papers had been purchased by members of the oligarchy precisely in order to protect their investments in other areas of the economy (Gilbert, 1979: 373). In other words, left-wing accusations that the national dailies were little more than political organs for the upper class had a great deal of substance. Nevertheless, the rights of the private owners of the press were defended by the more moderate members of the revolutionary government (especially the representatives of the navy), and the efforts by radical officers to take more decisive actions against the press precipitated a political crisis within the Velasco regime between late 1973 and early 1974 (Philip, 1978: 137-140). Only after these moderates were purged from the inner council of the Velasco regime did the revolutionary government proceed with its plan for guaranteeing "popular control" of information.

In a preliminary move, the government created the National Information System (SINADI) in March 1974 to monitor all mediums of communication to 1) guarantee "truth" in reporting on government programs, 2) "harmonize" reporting with the objectives of the national development plan, and 3) modify the content of news to insure that it "serve culture" (See Pease Garcia et al, 1975: 803-804). The system was placed under the administration of a Central Office of Information (OCI) whose director was given ministerial rank. The major offensive was contained in Decree Law 20680 isssued secretely on July 23, 1974 and put into effect dramatically a few days later. Under its provisions, all national dailies (papers with a circulation of more than 20,000 or distribution in more than half of the departmental capitals) were expropriated. Each of the expropriated papers was assigned to a different sector of the population whose government-recognized participatory organizations were to elect the civil associations that would oversee the editorial policies of each daily. La Nueva Crónica, in turn, was placed directly under the authority of the OCI as the official government press.

The law brought about the expropriation of the five remaining major dailies (La Prensa, El Comercio, Correo, Ultima Hora and Ojo) which, together with Extra and Expreso, were designated as the representatives of different socioeconomic groups such as urban labor, campesinos, the service sector, and professional organizatins. Although the law was justified as a measure to increase popular participation in the mediums of information, as Dennis Gilbert (1979: 382) observed, "the manner in which sectors to be served by individual dailies were defined had, from the outset, the effect of withholding media representation from much of the population." For example, only campesino interests organized in the government-sponsored CNA were allowed input into the editorial policy of El Comercio, while the large following of the non-government sponsored Campesino Confederation of Peru was denied representation. And while the law originally proposed only a brief period of transition before the papers were to be placed entirely under the control of organized sectors of the population, in practice the government resisted surrendering ultimate authority over the dailies.

While the papers remained generally supportive of the revolutionary government up through mid-1975, they nevertheless exhibited considerable editorial independence. As the government encountered increasing financial difficulties and important reforms failed to meet the growing expectation of the population, this editorial independence became increasingly intolerable to the First Phase regime. Finally, during the last month of the Velasco government, the military reacted to what it perceived as a radicalization of the press with the first of many purges of "subversive" journalists (Gilbert, 1979: 388; and Gorman, 1978b: 302-303). The Second Phase government subsequently tightened press controls and, finally, completely abandoned the idea of a socialized press in Peru.

THE SECOND PHASE AND THE END OF REVOLUTIONARY CHANGE

Although many of the reforms of the First Phase were either incomplete or poorly executed, a considerable redistribution of national resources was accomplished benefiting the lower classes. The new or increased responsibilities of the central government in industrialization, public welfare and other areas, however, placed severe strains on the treasury. With the onset of the international recession induced by increasing energy prices in early 1974, Peru began to encounter serious balance of payments problems. Many of the Velasco-era development projects had been financed with private foreign credit, which was to be repaid with the earnings from expanding primary exports. The international recession that set in early in 1974 placed the Velasco regime in a difficult posture: on the one hand the revolutionary government had become committed to extensive public expenditures, while on the other hand it needed to come to terms with international creditors who began to press for austerity measures to stabilize the Peruvian economy. The political situation was further complicated by President Velasco's deteriorating health and increasingly personalistic style of rule.

By mid-1975 a coalition of conservative officers within the army had formed around Velasco's Prime Minister, General Francisco Morales Bermúdez. Morales Bermúdez, who was next in line for the presidency on the basis of military seniority, favored conservative fiscal policies to improve the country's national accounts, but otherwise professed support for the objectives of the revolution. In a well coordinated putsch on August 29, 1975, Velasco was overthrown without bloodshed when the country's five regional army commanders issued an Institutional Manifesto naming Morales Bermúdez president. The action was quickly endorsed by the air force and navy, and encountered virtually no opposition from the popular organizations created by the revolution.

Morales Bermúdez announced that the coup merely signaled a change in personnel, and not a rejection of the goals of the revolution. The government would continue to pursue the objectives of the First Phase, only without "personalismo" or "desviaciones" (personalism or deviations). Nevertheless, the so-called Second Phase reordered government priorities, reduced the influence of reformist officers in decisionmaking, and began to stress the themes of labor discipline and sacrifice. The Second Phase government attempted to "rationalize" First Phase programs, which usually entailed increasing the profitability of public enterprises by adopting wage or employment policies injurious to the working class. Also, a succession of austerity measures (that actually began under Velasco) were imposed that reduced public welfare expenditures and generally raised the cost of living. During its first year, the Morales Bermúdez government kept most of the working class organizations in line by stressing that Peru's economic difficulties were the result of the collapse of the international capitalist system. The seemingly antipopular policies of the government, it was explained, were only temporary expedients to deal with a transitory crisis. The political space of the Second Phase regime, however, was narrowing as a disproportionate amount of the burdens of the austerity measures fell on the very groups to which the revolution had originally looked for support. By mid-1976 it was clear that the piecemeal austerity measures adopted over the previous year were insufficient to either satisfy Peru's foreign creditors or stabilize the economy. In order to obtain a refinancing of the foreign debt, attract foreign investment, and stimulate exports, drastic action was required. In late June 1976 the ministerial cabinet finally agreed on a set of policies that the ranking reformist officer in the government was forced to announce on national television on June 30. Although numerous reformist officers had been forced into retirement after the Morales Bermúdez coup, enough remained in the Second Phase government to block some of the more onerous policy demands of the most conservative generals. These holdovers from the First Phase were grouped behind General Jorge Fernández Maldonado Solari, who served as Prime Minister and Commander of the Armed Forces by virtue of seniority. The ability of the conservative generals to maneuver Maldonado into announcing the austerity measures, which he certainly had fought against in the cabinet, was probably designed to blunt the public's reaction and direct resentment away from the president.

The austerity package was draconian. It provided for a 12.4 percent cut in government investment in state enterprises (see Table 1.1), a 12.8 percent reduction in the national budget (Table 1.2), a steep increase in consumer prices (Table 1.3) and a devaluation of the national currency by 44.4 percent. To help offset the effects of these actions, it was also announced that wages would be increased by 10 to 14 percent (Table 1.4). The wage increases, however, did not come close to covering the rise in the cost of living (compare Tabls 1.3 and 1.4). One immediate effect of the policies was a dramatic increase in the cost of gasoline, which was not compensated for by a corresponding increase in public transportation fares. To protest this fact, the Lima/Callao transportation cooperatives went on strike the following day. The transportation strike, in turn, sparked three days of rioting that required a full scale military operation to contain. The violent popular reaction, which was largely directed against government institutions, profoundly altered the military's attitude toward the masses and appeared to confirm the fears of conservative generals that the First Phase had created revolutionary organizations that the government could not be sure of controlling. Many of the organizations created during the First Phase (such as the CNA, CONACI, the Confederation of Workers of the Peruvian Revolution,

TABLE 1.1
Investment Cutbacks in State Enterprises, June 30, 1976

State Enterprise	Investment Reductions (million soles)
SIDERPERU (Steel)	250
EMSAL (Water Supply)	27
ENTURPERU (Tourism)	50
EMPRESA PUBLICA IND. CHICAMAYO	6
INDUPERU (Industrial Services)	375
ENAPU	185
ENTERPERU	165
SIMA (Ship Construction)	580
PETROPERU (Petroleum)	4,000
MINEROPERU (Mining)	3,415
ELECTROPERU (Electricity)	567
TOTAL	9,666

Source: Official Communique, Correo, June 30, 1976

TABLE 1.2
Budget Reductions for Ministries, June 30, 1976

Ministry	Budget Reductions (million soles)
Agriculture	600
Fishing	550
Industry and Tourism	600
Transportation and Commerce	900
Housing and Construction	350
Education	140
Health	140
SINAMOS	50
Food	800
Earthquake Relief for Ancash	100
Other	270
TOTAL	4,500

Source: Official Communique, Correo, June 30, 1976

TABLE 1.3
Consumer Price Increases, July 1, 1976

Product	Former Price	New Price	Percent Increase
Rice	s/.16.50	20.00	21
Pasturized Milk	13.70	17.60	28
Evaporated Milk	13.00	15.60	20
Prime Beef	104.00	129.00	24
Beef	91.00	112.00	23
Prime Lamb	91.00	112.00	23
Lamb	83.00	101.00	22
Chicken	80.00	91.00	11
Noodles	21.00	26.50	26
French Bread	.75	.95	26
Flour	12.00	18.10	50
Loaf of Bread	30.00	33.30	11
Cooking Oil	28.00	44.00	57
Vegetable Oil	16.80	25.00	48
Margerine	45.30	54.00	19

Source: La Cronica, July 2, 1976

TABLE 1.4
Authorized Wage Increases, July 1, 1976

Income Group (in soles)	Percent Authorized Wage Increase
Up to 5,000 per month	s/.720 per month or s/. 24 per day
5,001 - 7,000	14
7,001 - 9,000	13
9,001 - 11,000	12
11,001 - 13,000	11
13,001 - 15,000	10
15,001 - and above	s/.1,500 per month or s/.60 per day

Source: Correo, June 30, 1976

etc.) joined together in the Front for the Defense of
the Revolution that functioned simultaneously as a source
of political support for the government and a powerful
pressure group designed to push reforms through to
completion. As late as June 24, 1976 the Front had
remained committed to the military government, but
bitterly resisted the conservative orientation of certain
officers. In a public communique, the Front declared:

> We believe that the world economic crisis and
> its consequences in Peru, together with the
> imperialist's and reactionary right's offensive
> . . . have disrupted the rhythm of the advance
> of the Revolution in the past ten months. But
> we are sure that the earlier transforming
> orientation will be regained shortly, without
> deviations or foreign influences of any kind.
> Therefore, we are in the same trench of battle
> as the Armed Forces, supporting the President
> of the Republic, General Francisco Morales
> Bermudez, and remain confident that he will
> keep the Revolution on the same road that the
> People and Armed Foces have been following
> heretofore (El Comercio, June 24, 1976).

Three days later, reacting to rumors that a major
austerity package was under consideration in the cabinet,
the coordinating committee of the Front issued another
communique stating that:

> Whoever has proposed such measures to the
> government has not considered the suffering of
> our people, the future of the Revolution and of
> the country, and therefore we are not in
> agreement with such policies. (Pease García
> and Filomeno, 1977b: 2020-2023).

As an alternative, a number of counter measures were
proposed that would attack what the Front termed the
capitalist infrastructure of the country, and place the
major burdens for contending with the economic crisis on
the upper classes. The austerity program unveiled on
June 30, therefore, represented a major political defeat
for both the remaining reformist officers in the
government and the mass-based organizations created under
Velasco. Popular support for the military government
after the rioting virtually evaporated and the armed
forces found themselves politically isolated.
The final blow to the Peruvian revolution came later
in the month of July when a power struggle ended in a
complete purge of reformist officers from the government.
During the rioting in Lima between July first and third,
the conservative commander of the Center for Military

Instruction (CIMP) ignored standing orders and deployed his troops to protect upper-class suburbs instead of seizing communications centers. General Bobbio Centurión, a strong supporter of austerity measures, incorrectly assumed that mobs were about to attack Lima's upper-class residential districts and took defensive actions without authorization from General Maldonado. Afterward, on July 9, Maldonado used the incident to demand Bobbio Centurión's early retirement. The commander of Lima's second most important military garrison then declared himself in rebellion (expecting support from the arch-conservative navy). After a brief battle, Bobbio Centurión was placed under arrest and sent into exile after the five regional army commanders and the Joint Chiefs of Staff issued a pronouncement in support of the existing government (LAPR, July 2, 1976; July 16, 1976; and July 23, 1976; and personal observations).

Although the power struggle appeared to have been won by Maldonado, the declaration of the armed forces against Bobbio Centurión was not so much an endorsement of the reformists in the government as an attempt to maintain the outward appearance of military unity and discipline. In reality, Maldonado's actions against Bobbio Centurion solidified the right-wing officers within the armed forces who then forced Maldonado and the other remaining reformists officers into early retirement later the same month. By August 1976 the revolutionary process was over in Peru, and a wide range of First Phase programs were either terminated or, at best, ignored. As Henry Pease García and Alfredo Filomeno (1977b: iii) observed: "1976 is thus a year of redefinition of the military political project. At times, the government appeared to be a new regime, distinct from the one that ran the state during the previous eight years." The attack on revolutionary programs was swift. Just five days after Maldonado's forced retirement on July 16, the government announced that the conditions for transferring the socialized press to complete citizen control did not yet exist, and the papers would therefore have to remain under the administration of government representatives. (Gradually, the military came full circle on the notion of a socialized press and favored the return of the Lima dailies to their former owners.) The following month in a major address, President Morales Bermúdez declared that the term "socialism" would be dropped from the government's vocabulary because it was a vague and confusing word that merely discouraged private investment in the country. By mid-1977 the government began negotiations with the International Monetary Fund in an effort to appease foreign creditors and investors which the First Phase government had pledged would never again influence Peruvian decisionmaking. Finally, the government adopted a policy of "labor discipline" to replace the earlier policy of "labor stability," meaning that employers were given a freer hand to dismiss workers for reasons of either profitability or discipline.

The slackening and eventual termination of revolutionary change after the overthrow of Velasco prevented some programs (like Social Property) from ever getting off the ground, and others (like agrarian reform) from expanding their beneficiaries. The case of the agrarian reform is particularly interesting since it is generally considered to have been the single most important consequence of the revolution. The 1969 agrarian reform had originally aimed at transferring up to eleven million hectares of land (well below the total arable land in Peru) to some 340,000 rural families. Yet in June 1976 the Morales Bermúdez government declared the agrarian reform at an end (with one year permitted for resolution of all pending cases) with only 6.7 million hectares having been distributed among 269,437 families: 4.9 million of it as CAPs and SAISs (El Comercio, June 23, 1976; and La Prensa, June 24, 1976). All told, a total of seven million hectares were distributed by the close of the revolution, leaving as much as twelve million hectares unaffected. And even if the original target of 340,000 families had received land (which they did not), those benefited would still have represented only a fraction of an agricultural work force that was calculated in excess of 1.5 million in 1972 (ILO, 1976: 86-87). In essence, the armed forces simply lacked the resources and resolve to carry through to completion the reforms begun in the First Phase.

In July 1977, President Morales Bermúdez declared that the military would sponsor elections to return government to civilians. The armed forces had exhausted their political capital and seriously damaged their institutional prestige and solidarity. But the military's withdrawal from power proved to be slow and painful. Elections were held for a Constituent Assembly in 1978 that drafted a new constitution which was promulgated the following year. In May 1980, general elections were held for the national legislature and the presidency. During the three years between the announcement of elections and the actual surrender of power by Morales Bermúdez in July 1980, the military found it necessary to rely on openly repressive measures to contend with growing labor militancy. The armed forces ended up devoting their last three years of rule to brutalizing the popular classes in whose name they assumed power in 1968.

Notes

1. The following is a list of military coups in Peru since 1872.

   1883 General Miguel Iglesias
   1886 General Andrés A. Cáceres
   1914 Coronel Oscar R. Benavides
   1930 General Maria Ponce
   1930 Comandante Luís M. Sanchez Cerro
   1931 Comandente Gustavo Jimenez
   1948 General Manuel A. Odría
   1962 General Ricardo Perez Godoy
   1968 General Juan Velasco Alvarado
   1975 General Francisco Morales Bermúdez

   In addition, there were three notable civilian coups.

   1879 Nicolás de Piérola
   1895 Nicolás de Piérola (called a revolution)
   1919 Augusto B. Leguia

2. The historical rivalry between the military and APRA dates from the 1931 presidential election and an Aprista uprising that followed. Aprista supporters in Trujillo attacked a military garrison and killed a number of soldiers. The military responded with mass executions (see Stein, 1980, Ch. 7).

3. The exact amount of arrable land in Peru is not known (see McClintock, 1976: Appendix 2). The amount of land distributed by the reform by the close of the Velasco government is discussed by McClintock (1977: 11-13), while the final amount distributed at the close of adjudication in July 1977 is reported in Latin American Political Report (July 1, 1977: 197-198). The estimate of the total land unaffected by the reform is based on Ernest Feder (1971: 104), who placed the agricultural land in Peru in 1960 at 18.6 million hectares. Subsequent irrigation projects added at least a half million hectares. McClintock (1977: 12) suggests that by 1976 the reform had distributed only 26 percent of the agricultural land in benefit of only 20 percent of Peru's rural families.

2
The Return of Partisan Politics in Peru

Sandra L. Woy-Hazleton

On May 18, 1980, the citizens of Peru participated in presidential and parliamentary elections for the first time in seventeen years. Representative democracy had been suspended on October 3, 1968 when the armed forces overthrew President Fernando Belaúnde Terry. For seven years General Juan Velasco Alvarado led a self-declared revolutionary experiment that sought to structurally alter the political, social, and economic bases of Peruvian society. This period, designated the First Phase, was characterized by the initiation of some ambitious reform programs and the ambiguous promise to return power to "the organized sectors of the population" when the structural changes had become "irreversible." The Second Phase, the last five years under General Francisco Morales Bermúdez, amounted to the systematic repeal of most reform legislation, the dismantling of the popular organizations and, finally, the return to power of civilian political parties. Thus, on July 28, 1980, Fernando Belaúnde Terry was inaugurated president of Peru.

Had nothing changed in twelve years? Was the second election of Belaúnde a desire to turn the clock back to 1968? Had the political system moved in a full circle so that revolution ended with restoration? Of course, it is hardly that simple. While there are numerous relationships to be explored, one of the most basic is the political party system. An important factor contributing to the fall of Belaúnde in 1968 was the narrow base of popular support for the party system. Major groups in the population were deprived of participation in the political process that was monopolized by elite sectors. Such deprivation stemmed from psychological, social, economic and legal factors and resulted in little popular resistence to the military's intrusion into political life. Although the revolutionary junta attempted to institutionalize alternative means of popular participation, this failed and partisan politics returned to Peru.

The purpose of this chapter is to identify the bases of the new partisan alignment and the balance of power between major civilian political forces. Specifically, it will address the question: Is there any reason to believe that the contemporary system will prove more viable than the former one? In an effort to answer this question and to better understand the political party system in Peru in the 1980s, we will focus on the most salient events in the construction of the new party system: the opening of democratic participation through the Constituent Assembly, the establishment of a national leadership with the 1980 presidential and parliamentary elections, and the consolidation of mass participation at the grassroots in the municipal elections.

THE OPENING OF DEMOCRATIC PARTICIPATION

The bases of the new partisan alignment certainly have their roots in the prerevolutionary era, but a simple comparison of the 1963 and 1980 elections would be more misleading than instructive if the 1978 Constituent Assembly election and the legacy of the revolutionary experiment were ignored. Although it can be argued that the 1978 election is not comparable to the others in purpose, districts, laws, or electorate involved, and that the writing of the Constitution essentially endorsed the old system, the experience was a crucial one in the military's transfer of power to civilians. First, the Constituent Assembly was the vehicle for the rise and fall of the Peruvian Aprista Party. Second, it initiated the popular left into the game of electoral democracy. Finally, it served firm warning to the political center and right that the ideological bases of partisan competition had taken a substantial step toward the left, with greater representation of the more populous urban areas and the emergence of the popular sectors as a politically relevant force.

In July 1977 when the junta decided to hold elections for the formation of a constituent assembly, they faced mounting social unrest, a growing economic crisis, and persistent demands for political participation. To a certain extent their decision represented a tactical maneuver to occupy the politicians and defuse the brewing social explosion, as well as to buy more time in which to reach an agreement on refinancing the national debt and obtaining foreign loans. None of these reasons alone would have been sufficient for beginning a transfer of power, and given the changing situation, none alone would have precluded the military from cancelling or postponing the entire project. The military was most interested in initiating a long, carefully controlled transition to stable civilian government. As Henry Pease García (1979) noted, the means of choosing a constituent assembly had little juridical meaning coming as it did during the "counter-reformation" period. Instead it provided: 1) an opportunity for the military to assess the distribution of political opinion in the nation; 2) the optimal forum in which to "reactivate political organizations and electoral activity with no offering of power to the winners;" 3) the means for those groups preferable to the military to lay the groundwork for increasing their stability and insuring their victory in the subsequent general elections; and 4) a way for the military government to exit with honor, turning power over to a popularly elected civilian government (Pease García, 1979: 325). This plan was by no means endorsed by all sectors of the armed forces, and the election results increased doubts about returning to civilian rule as shown in Table 2.1.

At first glance the composition of electoral choices indicated that not much had changed in ten years inasmuch as power was being restored to traditional political parties, rather than to the popular organizations such as the National Agrarian Confederation (CNA). To be sure, the revolutionary experiment to provide an alternative system of participation through the National System for support of Social Mobilization (SINAMOS) had failed, but a great deal had changed. During the military docenio political parties were not, generally speaking, vigorously repressed; rather, they were denied their representative functions. In the nonelectoral system the groups that were best able to survive were those with stable cadre organizations, those with a significant popular base that rested on nonelectoral activities (such as unions, adult education, sports activities, study groups, etc.), those which appealed to relevant group value orientations and/or those which had consistent and high-quality leadership. Ten years of ostensibly nonpartisan politics did little damage to most prerevolutionary politicl parties. In fact, the atmosphere of the revolutionary process actually stimulated political activism whether in support of or in opposition to the military's initiatives. Far from replacing political parties or unions, the base units established by the promotores of SINAMOS expanded the participatory opportunities of these groups. From 1968 to 1978 union membership grew, as did union activities, with strikes increasing in quantity and intensity. This was due to greater competition for membership by three new union confederations that had been created since 1968 (Pease García and Verme Insúa, 1974; and Bollinger, 1980: 26). The increased number of political parties in 1978 is yet another indicator of greater politicization under the revolutionary government.

TABLE 2.1
Registration and Results for the 1978 Constituent Assembly Election
by Party and Leader of Party Lists

RIGHT	Registration	%	Final Vote	%	Seats
Movimiento Democrático Peruano (MDP) (Javier Ortiz de Zevallos)	57,104	6.0	68,619	1.95	2
Unión Nacional Odriísta (UNO) (Victor Freundt Rosell)	68,001	7.2	74,134	2.11	2
Partido Democrática Reformista Peruano (Carmen Leguía)(FDRP)	50,876	5.4	19,594	.55	0
Partido Popular Cristiano (PPC) (Luis Bedoya Reyes)	154,850	16.3	835,294	23.78	25
	330,746	34.9	997,644	28.39	29
CENTER					
Acción Popular (AP) (Fernando Belaunde Terry)	137,000	14.5			
Partido Aprista Peruano (APRA) (Victor Raul Haya de la Torre)	77,777	8.2	1,241,174	35.34	37
	214,777	22.7			
LEFT					
Frente Nacional de Trabajadores , y Campesinos (FNTC) (Roger Cáceres Velasquez)	86,000	9.1	135,552	3.86	4
Partido Democrata cristiano (PDC) (Hector Corejo Chavez)	70,000	7.4	83,075	2.37	2
Partido Socialista Revolucionario (PSR) (Leonidas Rodríguez Figueroa)	54,479	5.8	232,520	6.62	6
Acción Revolucionaria Socialista (ARS) (Mario Villaran)	41,130	4.3	20,164	.57	0
Partido Comunista Peruano (PCP) (Jorge del Prado)	50,000	5.5	207,612	5.91	6
Frente Obrero Campesino Estudiantil y Popular (FOCEP) (Genaro Ledesma)	47,194	4.9	433,413	12.34	12
Unión Democratica Popular (UDP) (Víctor Cuadros)	53,004	5.6	160,741	4.58	4
	401,807	42.6	1,273,077	36.25	34
TOTAL	947,330	99.2	3,511,895	99.98	100

Source: Oiga, No. 4 (February 6-13, 1978), p. 6 and Enrique Bernales, Crisis
politica: solucion electoral? (1979), pp. 44-45.

The supporters of the revolutionary experiment and the civilian theorists who worked to establish an alternative to traditional partisan participation attribute their failure largely to the no-party thesis of SINAMOS's civilian director, Carlos Delgado. This rejection deprived the revolutionary supporters of an integrative multisectoral and interdepartmental political organization or "party" through which to mobilize their supporters. The civilian theorists underestimated both the resilience and benefits of political parties. Their experiences had predisposed them to see parties as the protectors of the status quo and as instruments of political elites. Their communitarian beliefs led them to overestimate the potential of societal unity. They viewed parties as the cause of divisiveness rather than as a reflection of actual differences in interests. Finally, as "militants," they were never able to see their ideals as one position among many on the Peruvian political spectrum (Woy-Hazleton, 1978a: 9-14).

However, the results of this experiment in "social democracy with full participation" produced important changes in behavior and attitude. First, nonelectoral participation in social and economic activities at the local and regional level meant those individuals who had been marginal in previous electoral systems (e.g., peasants and illiterates) were provided greater and more varied participatory experiences through workplace and neighborhood democracy. Second, related to their broader experience with participation, there was an increase in politicization and a concomitant growth in the political demands of the Peruvian population. Third, the center of the poltical party system gravitated to the left on the ideological spectrum. And fourth, there was an expansion of the electorate in regard to age, and pressure increased to include illiterates in natonal suffrage.

Thus, the results of the election for the Constituent Assembly revealed a politicized and polarized electorate as shown in Table 3.1. The center-right won a majority with the Partido Aprista Peruano (APRA) receiving 35 percent and the Partido Popular Cristiano (PPC) 24 percent of the vote. But of perhaps greater import was the impressive strength of the left, especially when it is taken into account that illiterates were not able to vote; the popular organizations were not allowed to participate with a quota as they had demanded; the electoral requirements were arranged with the assistance of APRA; there was extensive harassment and repression against the leftist parties and their leaders (fourteen of them were exiled); and funding for the center and rightist parties was far greater than that available to the left. This shift to the left was matched, however, by the reappearance of a stable, if small, right wing. Consequently, the elements of a variegated, pluralistic, multiparty system were present in the Constituent Assembly with three distinct divisions--left, center, and right (for details on the framework of analysis employed, see Sartori, 1976: 132-139).

It is often difficult to locate parties along a left-right continuum, but self-identification, media identification, and other party designations are generally consistent on the Peruvian spectrum. The major exceptions are found when a party is internally divided and no ideological resolution has been achieved (e.g., APRA). Perhaps the most relevant dimension on which to compare the active political parties is their relationship to the economic, political, and social changes of the military government. The far left is represented by minuscule, but vocal and violent, factions that argued that the Velasco reforms were bourgeois and detrimental to true revolution. They refuse to participate in the new electoral system. The more orthodox marxist and nonmarxist left, the so-called "responsible" left, generally supported the Velasco initiatives though not the corporatist framework. Their goals in 1978-1981 were to maintain popular gains and further structural changes of the system. They continued to favor state intervention and/or communitarian control and sought stricter scrutiny of foreign enterprises, along with broader international ties to lessen dependence on the United States. The democratic center and the right represented the largest share of politically active groups in Peru. Those parties that were reformist in orgin--APRA and Accion Popular--maintained intransigent opposition to the First Phase military regime because it violated democratic norms. While Velasco's reforms reflected much of APRA's early program, the party had moved to support more middle class objectives, free enterprise, and a pro-western foreign policy. As one moves toward the right, there is less and less support for state intervention in the economy for social reasons and more interest in promoting a capitalist economy with strong ties to the United States. The groups on the far right are relatively small, most had once been personal campaign vehicles for presidential candidates in the pre-1968 system. By 1978 they had dwindled to narrow circles composed of those who had suffered most in the reforms--landowners, manufacturers, and commercial and financial elites--with no mass base.

The three most salient features of the assembly were the absence of Acción Popular, the prominence of APRA, and the size of the left--divided among representatives of the popular organizations, the intellectual left, and the revolutionary far-left. With a certain degree of hindsight, Belaúnde's decision not to have AP participate in the Constituent Assembly appears to have been a master stroke. By keeping aloof from the military's show, AP retained the status of deomcratic opposition to the revolution, a role APRA had now relinquished. By denying the legitimacy of the assembly, AP felt less restrained by the parameters of the Constitution. With the party's strong revival in the 1980 elections, it is tempting to dismiss the assembly results as an aberration. But the decision not to participate in the Constituent Assembly election was a calculated risk on the part of AP, and it was not arrived at easily. From the time the elections were announced, AP leaders began returning from exile to reestablish partisan activity. Although they consistently called for immediate general elections, discussions to form a democratic coalition with the PPC, and even APRA, were undertaken. More importantly, the party did register as required. But AP's disappointing percentage of the total registered voters who signed party petitions (14 percent) convinced its leaders that a loss in an election they considered unnecessary on principle was not worth the risk. While AP's nonparticipation certainly undermined the assembly's claim to broadbased representation, AP's interests were well represented by others. Indeed, it seems likely that the PPC's vote total was considerably inflated by AP loyalists, as party secretary Javier Arias Stella had suggested AP followers vote for the center-right party (DESCO, Resumen Semanal, 1st semana, May, 1978: 1).

It is hard to exaggerate the impact that APRA has had on the Peruvian scene. Hugo Neira (1973: 399-400) has called it the "common denominator" of Peruvian political life.[1] The Apristas' protracted struggle with the traditional oligarchy from 1931 to 1956 set the stage for many contemporary political issues. Party doctrine was reformist, innovative, nationalist, and antioligarchic. For this the party was proscribed periodically from participating in the political system. As Peru modernized in the postwar era, and the circle of politically active individuals widened with middle-class bureaucrats, white-collar workers, and professionals, popular support became an important political resource and elite omnipotence began to crumble.

In 1956 some elites recognized the desirability of a popular base and they turned to APRA--the largest mass party in the nation. For their part, the Aprista leadership had long sought incorporation into the political system as legitimate participants, and they were willing to ally with their former enemies to do so. By this time the political elites could no longer count on the middle-class military as their auxiliary arm in governing, and the agreement with APRA reinforced the patron-praetorian split.

APRA-military relations had a long, bitter history

of unflagging opposition. During the initial years of
the Velasco period, APRA remained a major component of
the intransigent opposition despite the congruence
between the early Aprista program and the military's Plan
Inca in terms of antiimperialism, economic organization,
decentralization, and Peruvianization. By 1974, however,
the military's policy of undermining traditional
political party support was taking a toll on APRA.
Membership in its labor confederation was declining,
student involvement was diminishing, and there was a
continued migration of talented Apristas into the ranks
of the revolutionaries. Party leadership was divided,
but the faction calling for conciliation after five years
of progressive, reformist military government was
becoming stronger. APRA's interest in peaceful
coexistence with the military coincided with the
beginning of the Second Phase. The party offered the new
leadership support from the only noncommunist political
entity with mass organizations acceptable to the patrón
sector. After 1956, APRA had become a potent force on
behalf of liberal capitalism, middle-class entrepreneurs
and a pro-Western foreign policy (Monteforte, 1973: 128).
Thus, the historic accommodation of military and Arpista
interests was the background against which the transition
to civilian rule unfolded.

The Aprista party approached the Constituent
Assembly with a great deal of enthusiasm and
anticipation. As they were in the controlling position
to establish the new framework of government, they
confronted three major problems: 1) establishing a
relationship between the military and assembly, 2)
establishing an alliance in drafting the constitution,
and 3) establishing the bases of electoral compatititon
for the general election.

With regard to the assembly's relationship to the
military government and its capability to intervene in
national politics, APRA had to walk a tightrope between
maintaining the military's favor and gaining popular
respect. The Aprista president of the assembly, Víctor
Raúl Haya de la Torre, described the body as "the main
power of the state," thus proclaiming its autonomous
existence, separate and equal to the military regime.
But he was not prepared to accept the proposal of leftist
leader Hugo Blanco that recognition of the Morales
Bermúdez government be withdrawn and the assembly declare
itself sovereign (LAPR, July 28, 1978: 230; and August 4,
1978: 238). In fact, APRA leaders were willing to
forcefully constrain the assembly to insure the general
election would be held--their major goal. The leftist
delegates wanted to discuss the regime's economic
policies, worker strikes, and military repression, but
this conflicted with the military's wishes that such
sensitive topics not be subject to debate. Therefore,

soon after the opening session Haya announced that the assembly's duties were to be construed narrowly and confined to writing the constitution (Pease García, 1979: 339-340, 350).

As the confrontation politics of the leftist delegates clashed with the collaborationist politics of APRA, the latter moved closer toward an alliance with the Partido Popular Cristiano (PPC) whose liberal democratic policies found their greatest support in the wealthy suburbs of Lima. The APRA-PPC assembly majority agreed upon a working relationship with the military--peaceful coexistence--for two reasons. First, the economic crisis was so grave they preferred not to be involved, and second, their silence was rewarded by the free rein given to APRA in efforts to recapture control of various unions and student organizations and to set up new unions (LAPR, October 20, 1978: 41).

To formulate the constitution APRA needed support for their initiatives, and they had to turn either to the right or the left to obtain agreement on each of the major parts: organization of economic life and the nature of the state, constitutional rights, and the organization of popular participation. The creation of a National Economic Congress had long been a stated goal of the Aprista party, but for the party out of power never a real option. Now that the opportunity presented itself, however, the party was divided over this goal. Party leader Armando Villanueva del Campo attempted to establish an agreement between APRA's social democratic faction and the left. But his efforts were not supported by the old-guard Apristas in the assembly who were satisfied with a PPC compromise on a plural economy rather than an economic congress. Not only was no change made in the form of the legislature, but alteration of the nation's economic structure was also denied. Any illusions that reforms from the First Phase would be enshrined in the constitution were squelched by the refusal to name the social property sector as part of the plural economy. The APRA-PPC majority accepted three bases for the Peruvian economy: 1) freedom of industry and commerce, 2) a market economy, and 3) a plural business system with the emphasis on the private sector. The final document thus ratified the foundations of a liberal capitalist system (DESCO, Resumen Semanal, May 5-11, 1979: 8).

The left had greater influence on portions of the document dealing with constitutional rights and guarantees as the Apristas could not entirely ignore popular concerns. The old-guard group coalescing around Andrés Townsend in the assembly was under great pressure to prove their ability to keep the rank-and-file, coalescing around Villanueva, happy by demonstrating some differences from the PPC. The constitutional rights

which were guaranteed in the final draft reflect
traditional and contemporary rights (the right to life,
freedom from torture, a healthy environment, etc.), but
definitional interpretations, legal "exceptions," and the
ability to suspend such guarantees provoked skepticism as
to how much improvement this made over the 1933 document.
In the area of labor rights, for example, the right to
strike was recognized but subject to limitations of the
law, that is, to parliamentary authority. The same was
true for guarantees of collective bargaining and labor
stability. In addition, there was recognized a right to
a minimum wage necessary to live and the right to work,
even though the guarantee could not insure its
fulfillment (DESCO, Resumen Semanal, June 2-5, 1979: 2;
and June 16-22, 1979: 3).

The philosophical or theoretical aspects of the
constitution did not have as great an importance to many
Aprista leaders as did the political framework which
would set the stage for the upcoming elections. They
were willing to accede on idealistic goals to insure
their pragmatic objectives. This is best demonstrated in
the bitter struggle over the presidential formula. The
Aprista position was to include in the constitution a
minimum percentage required to be elected president with
the provision that the parliament select among the two
highest vote getters if no one candidate achieved the
minimum, which would be established at 33 percent. The
PPC, with some leftist support, proposed that a majority
be required with a run-off election between the top two
candidates if no one attained fifty plus percent, a
situation that was extremely likely (DESCO,
Resumen Semanal, May 19-25, 1979: 5). The compromise
eventually reached was perhaps the most disingenuous deal
worked out by a party that had long-specialized in such
political maneuvers. It was decided that the two-stage
election would be written into the constitutoion, but the
1980 election would be decided by a plurality with a
minimum of 36 percent, or by the parliament if no
candidate received the minimum.

The Constitution of 1979, signed by Victor Raúl Haya
de la Torre on his sickbed, was a classical liberal
document that differed little from the 1933 formulation
in doctrine. Although generally in accordance with the
views of the majority coalition, criticism from that
arena included charges that the new constitution had "too
many regulations," was "too rhetorical," "repeated the
obvious," made "concessions to puerile demagoguery," and
was too long with 307 articles and 18 transitory
dispositions (Oiga, July 16-23, 1979: 9).

The military immediately made known its objections
to four of the transitory dispositions: proposals for
agrarian debt relief, the free trade of bonds, the
ratification of the international Treaty on Civil and

Political Rights and of the International Labor Oranization Convention protecting the right to unionize by public administration workers. The military also wanted specific authority to suspend guarantees and opposed the immediate enforcement of the articles which abolished the death penalty, allowed consitutional norms precedence over legal norms, and prohibited the application of the military code to civilians (DESCO, Resumen Semanal, July 7-13, 1979: 1).

Overall the military had been fairly successful with the Constituent Assembly. It had not become a forum for debating regime policies and work had been limited to drafting a constitution. But the military could not completely control the outcome which resulted from a political process, that is, from accommodation and compromise, not decree. They could, however, set the whole project aside. Thus, after the assembly unanimously rejected the government's requested modifications and dissolved itself, President Morales Bermúdez announced that the military government would continue to rule under the Revolutionary Statute and the Constitution of 1933, thus ignoring the transitory dispositions and undermining the legitimacy of the new document. Earlier, general election had been delayed. This meant the new Constitution would not come into effect until July 28, 1980. The reason for the delay, according to Morales Bermúdez, was that the Jurado Nacional de Elecciones (JNE) had to prepare new regulations and the Registro Electoral had to register the illiterates who would become part of the electorate under the terms of the new constitution (DESCO, Resumen Semanal, May 19-25, 1979: 1).

This lengthy postponement was unpopular with most party leaders because of the loss of a forum in which they could attract enough attention to keep the military firmly on the road to transfer. There was a great deal of speculation as to the military's reasons for the delay. Promulgating electoral regulations did not seem sufficient and the mere desire to stay in power, as charged by Equis X and El Tiempo, did not seem to explain it as well as the desire of some military factions to give their favorites time to get ready for the election (Equis X, May 30 - June 5, 1979: 4; and DESCO, Resumen Semanal, July 29 - August 3, 1979: 2). The Apristas, for example, needed time to adjust to a new era and to select a successor to Haya, who was obviously terminally ill. Interestingly enough, the pro-Aprista forces in the military seemed to be more protective of the party than did its leaders, who were so embroiled in a power struggle that they thought only in personal terms.[2] Those in the high command who supported Acción Popular also perceived that a delay between the Constituent Assembly and elections would bolster their presidential candidate by allowing the attention and fanfare paid to APRA throughout the assembly to die down. Moreover, the major institutional concern was a stable civilian government. The military leadership believed that economic conditions would improve enough by 1980 to deflate major left-wing agitation, but the center-right had to be sufficiently strong to benefit. The size of the leftist vote in the assembly election continued to play upon the minds of many in the armed forces, despite the fact that the leftist bloc never realized its political potential.

NATIONAL ELECTIONS: 1980

Even before the assembly ended, the nation's political parties turned their attention to the elections announced for May 19, 1980. the Apristas had the initial advantage with their leading role in the assembly, and they sustained their cooperation with the military by containing union struggles and concentrating on electoral programs rather than criticizing the military (see the chapter by Villanueva). The left had every incentive to cooperate. While the assembly itself may have been an exercise in futility, the size of their contingent did indicate the depth of the popular movement. Given the standard of living of the average Peruvian family, the level of discontent, the prolonged teacher's strike, and the inclusion of the illiterate population in the electorate, the left was expected to retain its one-third share of the vote. The mystery factor was Belaúnde Terry's Acción Popular. The prevailing assumptions by the Apristas and the left were that Bedoya's PPC vote was inflated by AP loyalists and that those "centrists" who sat out the 1978 elections would be offset by the presumably "leftist" illiterates entering the electorate. In addition, there was the feeling, perhaps more wishful than reasoned, that the military would not return the government to the very man they ousted in 1968. Thus at the outset, it was believed that the election was APRA's opportunity to win and the left's opportunity to be spoiler; not to win but to keep the percentage of victory low. The closer it came to election day, however, the more obvious it became that APRA was mortally wounded, that the left had committed fratricide, and that AP would win.

The Performance of APRA

APRA's perceived advantage rested upon a vision of a strong party, supported by the military, which could utilize favorable electoral law. Only the latter condition was even slightly close to reality. When Decree Law 22652 was issued on August 27, 1979 by the

TABLE 2.2
Active Peruvian Political Parties and Their Presidential Tickets in
the 1980 Presidential and Parliamentary Elections

RIGHT

Unión Nacional (UN), formerly the Union Nacional Odriísta
    Carlos Carrillo Smith   Maria Delgado de Odría   Raúl Beraun
Movimiento Democratico Peruano (MDP)
    Alejandro Tudela Garland   Javier Ortíz de Zevallos Alfredo Corzo Masias
Movimiento Popular de Acción e Integracion Social (PAIS)
    Waldo Fernandez Durand   Víctor Villavicencio   Juan Marmol

CENTER-RIGHT

Partido Popular Cristiano (PPC)
    Luis Bedoya Reyes   Ernesto Alayza Grundy   Roberto Ramírez
                                                            del Villar
CENTER

Acción Popular (AP)
    Fernando Belaúnde Terry   Fernando Schwalb   Javier Alva O.
Partido Aprista Peruano (APRA)
    Amando Villanueva del Campo   Andrés Townsend Ezcurra   Luis Negreiros

NONMARXIST LEFT

Acción Popular Socialista (APS)
    Gustavo Mohme   Alfonso Benavides Dorrea Enrique de la Cruz
Partido Socialista del Perú (PSP)
    Luciano Castillo   Raul Torres Fernandez   Maria Cabredo
Frente Nacional de Trabajadores y Campesinos (FNTC)
    Roger Caceres   Jorge Zevallos Ortiz   Julio Arce Catacora
Organizacion Política de la Revolución Peruana (OPRP)
    Javier Tantalean Vanini   Daniel Bossio   Ismael Frías

MARXIST LEFT

Partido Revolucionario de los Trabajadores (PRT), joined by the Partido Socialista
    de los Trabajadores (PST), and the Partido Obrero Marxista Revolucionario
    Hugo Blanco   Ricardo Napuri   Enrique Fernandez C.
Unión de Izquierda (UI), formed by the Partido Comunista Peruano, Partido Socialista
    Revolucionario, Partido Vanguardia Revolucionario, Comite Obrero Revolucion-
    ario and the Movimiento de Izquierda Revolucionaria.
    Leonidas Rodriguez F.   Jorge del Prado   Isidoro Gamarra
Frente Obrero Campesino Estudiantil del Perú (FOCEP)
    Genero Ledesma   Manuel Scorza   Laura Caller
Union de Izquierda Revolucionaria (UNIR), formed by Vanguardia Revolucionaria, PC,
    MIR-Peru, FLN, Partido Comunista del Patria Roja and Partido Comunista
    Revolucionario-Clase Obrero
    Horacio Zeballos   Rolando Brena   Angel Castro L.
Unidad Democratico Popular (UDP), formed by a large group of extreme leftists
    Carlos Malpica   Edmundo Murrugarra   Cesar Levano

Jurado Nacional de Elecciones (JNE) it was greeted with cries that it looked like APRA wrote the law (Oiga, September 10-17, 1979: 12). The complaint rested with the distribution of deputies per department when electoral density was considered.[3] Of the twelve departments that received more deputies than they had in 1963, eight had supported APRA with better than 40 percent of their votes in 1978. The three departments which were inflated the most were Cajamarca, Loreto, and Piura. Cajamarca is the second strongest Aprista department and in Loreto and Piura the party showed its largest gains between Haya's vote in 1963 and the party vote in 1978. It seems hard to sustain the notion of deflation of power, however; those departments that lost representatives had also lost population relative to the more urban areas.

The distribution of deputies was not the only complaint of those who saw compromise and partiality in the law. Challenges ranged from the theoretical to the technical, but were all based on whom was perceived to benefit. What the left saw as insuring the freedom to form parties, the center-right parties saw as regulations aimed at impeding the direct election of the president or frustrating the popular will through parliamentary juggling and official pressure (Oiga, September 10-17, 1979: 12-13). In the assembly, the left had managed to keep any strict definition of a political party, written in terms of an acceptable party ideology, out of the constitution. Thus, regulations from the JNE provided for the registration of any group obtaining 40,000 valid signatures on their petition. This meant that in early September 1979 there were already eleven valid parties and 23 other groups with petitions in circulation (DESCO, Resumen Semanal, September 22-28, 1979: 3). The worry was that such splintering of the vote would lead to a weak "boliviano" form of government. The use of proportional representation in the parliament was criticized from this same perspective.

While fragmented in terms of party competition, the Peruvian political system under the new law was to be centralized along another dimension. The senate "district" was the entire nation (election at large) which meant Lima, with its 37 percent of the electoral population, would have a heavy influence on the formulation of the party lists. In addition, with almost one-quarter of the seats in the Chamber of Deputies (Lima and Callao total 47), the urban interests would have a much greater impact than in the past. Acción Popular and Belaúnde complained that this concentration in Lima was detrimental to a "national focus" and, presumably, to AP's areas of strength (DESCO, Resumen Semanal, September 8-14, 1979: 8).

The leftist groups argued that many of the technical

aspects of the law, such as the elimination of the preference vote, the obligatory voting age limit of 70, and accrediting each person on papel sellado, favored the well-financed, well organized, older party; that is, APRA. Perhaps the most disturbing thing about the electoral regulations was the number of modifications, changes, and alterations that occurred along the way.[4] For example, all the deadlines for registration were extended, usually in response to charges that registration was difficult, delayed, or done improperly (DESCO, Resumen Semanal, May 3-9, 1980: 1).

During the Constituent Assembly it appeared as though the Aprista leadership was in firm control with a parliamentary partner (PPC), a patron (the military), and a populace (more than the traditional one-third). But as the campaign began in the summer of 1979 the party's situation deteriorated as rapidly as did its leader's health. Fist, internal divisions that had been held in check only by Haya's commanding presence came to the surface in a protracted and bitter fight for succession. Second, the military's support, which was contingent upon the party's stability, became less assured. And, finally, the other political parties realized that an Aprista victory in the general elections was not a foregone conclusion, and they eagerly entered into the electoral battle.

The major cleavage in APRA appeared between the more conservative old guard represented by Andres Townsend Ezcurra, Luis Alberto Sanchez, and Ramiro Priale, and the more populist oriented group led by Armando Villanueva del Campo. The most serious problem for APRA was its inability to deal with a successor to Haya de la Torre until the founder and leader had actually died. (He was still proclaimed the party's presidential candidate as late as July 31, 1979 and he died on August 2.) Haya was unwilling to designate an heir apparent as both factions reflected important aspects of his life and philosophy--one his idealistic youth (Villanueva), the other his mature pragmatism (Townsend). While these contradictions could be subsumed in the personality of the leader, in the party they became irreconcilable differences. The Andresista faction had prevailed in the Constituent Assembly, but at the Twelth Party Congress in July 1979 and the Party Plenary in August 1979, the Armandistas emerged stronger. The major issues at stake were: party structure and control; party philosophy and direction of electoral alliance or legislative coalition-building; and party presidential candidate and platform for the May elections.

Since 1974, APRA had had a collegial leadership, but Villanueva wanted to return the party to a single secretary providing greater strength and more definitive leadersip. The Townsend-Sanchez group, on the other hand, believed the collegial mechanism was the best in which to contain their ambitious rival. The major difference between the two factions was one of political philosophy. While Villanueva lost his attempt to control the party alone before the election, he did manage to influence points in the program such as support for turning the newspapers over to workers organized in cooperatives; support for the teacher's strike; a change in the union leadership; ratification of the anti-imperialist doctrine; rejection of transnational influence, totalitarian communism, and the reactionary right; and a call for immeidiate municipal elections (DESCO, Resumen Semanal, June 29 - July 6, 1979: 10). As Villanueva explained, "We Apristas are leftists because we believe that the fundamental objective of our policy should be the solution of mankind's problems in an ultimately classless society. . . . The first priority is to improve the living conditions of our masses" (Caretas, July 30, 1979: 28-31). Thus he managed to distinguish himself from his competitors by his theme of creating a dialogue with the "responsible left." Townsend's response to this was that "the only responsible left is APRA, we are, were known, and will be the party of the left" (DESCO, Resumen Semanal, October 13-19, 1979: 1). Villanueva's plan was to clearly emphasize the party's origins, going from the popular base to challenge the marxist left. The Townsend faction, however, felt that while a populist stretegy might win a few votes, it would cost them more in the middle sectors.[5]

The national nominating convention was held in Lima in Ocotober 1979. After a violent and acrimonious debate, Armando Villanueva's position prevailed and he received the nomination as presidential candidate. In a conciliatory effort, Townsend was offered the first vice-presidency; he refused it, but was then elected by acclamation. It took four days of negotiating for him to agree to take the position. At this point the party factions were being held together only by their mutual interest in the election. Yet, with Villanueva controlling the secretariat and Sanchez the policy committee, it was uncertin whether the electoral campaign could be carried out in harmony. This in turn affected APRA's relationship with the military leadership.

The Armed Forces desired 1) a broad-based government, 2) a stable governing party or coalition, and 3) an "acceptable" president. A broad-based government, they felt, was necessary to govern in the face of rising inflation, continued social unrest, and endemic economic crises. At the same time, the electoral law made it almost impossible to expect one party to be able to establish such a government. Therefore, in September 1979, conversations were initiated by Prime Minister Pedro Richter Prada with the various parties about establishing an electoral accord. Solutions proposed ranged from a "democratic national front," to an interparty program as in Venezuela's Pacto de Punto Fijo, to a gentlemen's agreement to accept the highest vote getter as president (DESCO, Resumen Semanal, September 8-14, 1979: 3; and 22-28 September 1979: 2). In the final analysis, the junta wanted a strong, popular, centrist candidate who would respect the military institution. APRA with Villanueva seemed less and less capable of fulfilling these objectives.[6] But the military's attempts to forge an electoral front, propose a consensus candidate, and secure the autonomy of the armed forces proved unsuccessful.[7] By this time the parties were willing to gamble that the military was committed to the elections. The junta's populartity was at its lowest ebb with IMF-imposed austerity measures exacerbating the steadily rising cost of living, and any alteration in plans to hold elections could have sparked violent protests. Thus, the parties were not easily dissuaded from launching their first electoral battles since 1963, and the incentives to form a front before the elections were negligible. They all believed that "responsible democrats" would be able to cooperate afterward. The only possibility to force a union would have been a significant threat from the left, but that never materialized as disunity sapped the strength of the reformist and revolutionary groups.

The question still remains: To what extent did APRA "lose" the election? As indicated earlier, the stage had supposedly been set for an Aprista victory. The Aprista share of the vote turned out to be 27 percent at the presidential, senatorial, and deputy levels. This represented an 8 percent decline from the party's share in the 1978 election. The loss was "great" for two reasons: expectations were so high after APRA's assembly role, and more importantly, APRA's regional bases showed significant signs of erosion. At the presidential level, Villanueva and Townsend claimed only the departments of Cajamarca, La Libertad, and Lambayeque; and in the parliamentary races the party added Amazonas into the fold. This slippage in the party's traditional territory must be blamed in large part on the organization's festering internal problems. Taking over after fifty years of Haya's domination was not easy. No one could replace the founder and any successor was bound to have trouble. But Villanueva's attempts to consolidate control were considered so brutal by those on the inside that they became public knowledge. These wounds did not heal before the election (Caretas, May 5, 1980: 25). As the north (APRA's traditional stronghold) proved none too solid, the party's hopes to expand its base of support were also dashed.

Many reasons have been advanced for the inability of

the Apristas to widen their base, not the least of which
is the continuing strength of emotional anti-Aprismo.
But, the party was also compromised for having worked
with the military government during the Constituent
Assembly and it was widely perceived that the elections
had been tailored to APRA's needs. At the same time,
however, APRA's special relationship with the military
had deteriorated to the point that the official media
adopted an anti-Aprista tone and behavior that contrasted
greatly with their earlier treatment of the party.[8] In
addition, during the campaign Villanueva's personality
and behavior served only to reinforce the image of APRA
as an aggressive, intolerant organization (Werlich, 1981:
1). APRA was also perceived as one of the greatest
perpetrators of violence during the campaign, using it
for internal discipline as well as against other parties
to break up rallies, sack headquarters, and generally
agitate. Even the Aprista media campaign was cited as
counterproductive. The compulsive propaganda, which
saturated the air waves, showed a well-regimented party
ready to take over power and induced more fear than
support (DESCO, Resumen Semanal, May 10-16, 1980:1).
Internal struggling damaged the party from within, its
friendly relationship with the military cooled, and its
campaign image checked any significant growth beyond its
traditional loyalists. Thus the once proud Peruvian
Aprista Party entered the 1980s split asunder and
humilitated.

Factionalization of the Left

An important feature of the Constituent Assembly had
been the large number of delegates representing the
political left. Over one-third of the assembly actually
believed in radical change as the only solution to Peru's
severe economic, social, and political problems. But the
delegates' ability to act in coordination was limited and
their potential to influence was largely unrealized in
the assembly. Notable efforts were made, however, to
create a leftist front for the 1980 elections. The major
questions for unification concerned what would be the
program, which groups would be included, and who would be
the candidates.
There existed agreement on at least a minimum
program--unification to defeat the reactionary parties of
APRA, AP, and the PPC. Frente Obrero Campesino
Estudiantil del Perú (FOCEP) leader Genero Ledesma said,
"the unitary front, as taught by Mariategui, should be
formed from all activist parties in the popular sector
which support workers' and peasants' struggles, which are
moving in the direction of socialism, and which are
fighting rightist groups and imperialism" (La Prensa
August 13, 1979: 4). All attempts to form such a broad

front failed because there existed doctrinal differences which time after time shattered each front. The most successful leftist group in 1978 had been FOCEP, formed from radical rural and industrial organizations, Trotskyist parties, and student groups. Hugo Blanco had received the third highest number of votes and FOCEP had obtained 12.34 percent of the vote with twelve delegates to the Constituent Assembly. But the central position of FOCEP proved to be a major problem to unification because its two most prominent and popular leaders, Blanco and Ledesma, represented two very different political tendencies. While Ledesma was willing to accept all who would support him, and the broad based elements of the left were willing to do so, Blanco would not accept particpation with bourgeois, Velasquista, or reformist sectors even though they were willing to support him. He claimed such willingness came only from electoral ambition and he insisted that FOCEP could form an alliance only with workers and campesinos--"ni patrones, ni generals" (DESCO, Resumen Semanal, June 23-28, 1979: 6). Therefore, it was disappointing to the advocates of unity, but not surprising, that the Trotskyist forces decided to go it alone and run Blanco as their presidential candidate (DESCO, Resumen Semanal, January 5-11, 1980: 3).

The split in January 1980 was between the Union de la Izquierda (UI) formed of Ledesma's FOCEP, PSR, and PCP, and the Trotskyist group (Partido Obrero Marxista Revolucionario--POMR, Partido Sociaista de los Trabajadores--PST, and the Partido Revolucionario de los Trabajadores--PRT). The other fronts had to decide on their own strategy. The Unidad Democrático Popular (UDP), a combination of maoist groups and the Fuerzas Revolucionaries Anti-imperialistas por el Socialismo (FRAS), a marxist-leninist union, both continued to feel pressure from popular demand and journalists' urgings to avoid having a third bloc competing in the elections. Alfonso Barrantes Lingan, the UDP's contender for the presidency, proved willing to join with Blanco, creating the Alianza Revolucionaria de la Izquierda (ARI, which means "yes" in Quechua) (DESCO, Resumen Semanal, January 12-18, 1980: 2).

The persistent dilemma was the purpose of unity. Was it to gain electoral strength, unify the program and strengthen the party, or to spread propaganda? The difference, Marka explained, between the ARI and UI blocs, was based on their interpretation of 1) the existence or not of the objective and subjective conditions for revolution, and 2) the role of the bourgeois state vis-á-vis revolution. the UI believed that a transfer from popular democracy to socialism was possible in a non-violent manner and a government contolled by the people could in fact bring about that transfer. The groups in ARI denied the possibility of constructing socialism within the existing system, but the UDP and others supported the positive role of government for a brief period before the revolution. The Trotskyists, however, proposed immediate destruction of the state (Marka, No. 139 in DESCO Resumen Semanal, June 19-25, 1980: 3). Given these philosophies on the utility of elections and the reasons for participation, the strategy chosen by each group is quite clear. At no time did the Trotskyists see the elections as something that should be contended in a goal-oriented manner. To spread propaganda, embarrass officials, challenge government institutions, generally to raise the level of popular consciousness, yes; but to seek electoral victory, no. Ironically, the single most popular leader was Hugo Blanco. Thus, it was clear to those who saw electoral unity as important that Blanco was an essential component in any attempt to gain popular strength.

But electoral unity, or combining forces to contest an election, requires that decisions be made as to program and candidates. Blanco wanted each front to maintain its own program and the lists were to be divided 40 percent to the PRT, POMR, PSR-ML, and 60 percent to the UDP, UNIR and PC-M (DESCO, Resumen Semanal, January 19-25, 1980: 2). But, the pro-Chinese factions from both the UDP and UNIR combined to ask for more places on the parliamentary lists. Their argument was that the Trotskyists were trying to dictate policy even though they were weaker in terms of local strength than were groups like the PCP-Patria Roja which could count on SUTEP (The teacher's union) for support (DESCO, Resumen Semanal, February 23-29, 1980: 2). Thus, the alliance fell apart two days after it was officially formed.

While no one expected one large bloc to emerge, the disintegration of the leftist groups progressed beyond the greatest hopes of the right. Even Ledesma's FOCEP left the UI in late February [9]. The inability of the left to cooperate is an endemic characteristic stemming from ideology and structure. The first major obstacle is doctrinal rigidity. For the left, a program is not something which is worked out as a compromise or an accomodation between members' desires. Rather, a program is induced from principles or deduced from goals. The program becomes revealed truth to remain inviolate—a measure of dedication, adherence and loyalty. This in turn produces what in self-criticism is called "hegemonic tendencies." The inability to compromise means that to cooperate a party must coopt others and enforce its beliefs on its would-be allies. Those who waver even slightly must form "new" parties because heresy cannot exist within the organization. The result is extreme sectarianism.

Unity is not possible unless it performs a function conceived of as furthering the group's goals. For most of the revolutionary left, elections were not viewed as practical or appropriate mechanisms for reaching their goals. Yet, they believed that if an opportunity existed to use this means against a common enemy, then it should be taken. Thus, the second barrier to cooperation was one of defining who was friend and who was foe. An "anti-imperialist" was too broad a designation; it could even have included the Apristas. But, self-declared "revolutionaries" were also deemed to be mere reformists, and therefore suspect as allies. The desire for litmus-test revolutionaries reduced the capacity of the Trotskyists (who represent the far left in Peru) to operate in a wider, broad-based organization.

Ideology has a great deal to do with the structures that exist on the left of the political spectrum, but those structures themselves are obstacles to unity. Individuals form groups, the groups may join others and call themselves a party. These parties are often so small that action can be taken only by joining with other parties in a "front." The fronts then attempt to form into blocs. It is this level of organization that would be necessary to have an impact on the Peruvian political system. Yet, the importance, independence, and integrity of each unit at each level is so essential that unanimity is required for action. More improbable for competition in representative democratic politics, each unit maintains this virtual equality regardless of the volume of its political support. The result for the Peruvian left in the national elections was the isolation of the "leaders" from the masses, the absence of a coherent alternative to the center-right parties, and the lack of a popular opposition bloc of any significant size in the new parliament.

Yet, when the 1980 showing of the left is compared with such representation prior to 1968 as shown in Figure 2.1, it is evident that major changes had occured in Peruvian politics. The center of the political party system had gravitated to the left on the ideological spectrum with the disappearance of the far-right and the emergence of a fairly large group of 20 percent who voted for parties whose programs called for major structural change. The left lacked a party and a leader behind which to unify, but the depth and breadth of the popular, anti-establishment vote was impressive. While the various parties polled only 15.9 percent of the total for their presidential candidates, they managed 20.9 percent in the Senate and 20.8 percent in the Chamber of Deputies races as shown in Table 2.3. Because this was split, they received only 10 percent of the total representatives--fourteen deputies and ten senators. It is important to note that the appeal of the left was

FIGURE 2.1
Percentage of National Vote Along an Ideological Spectrum; 1962, 1963, 1978 and 1980

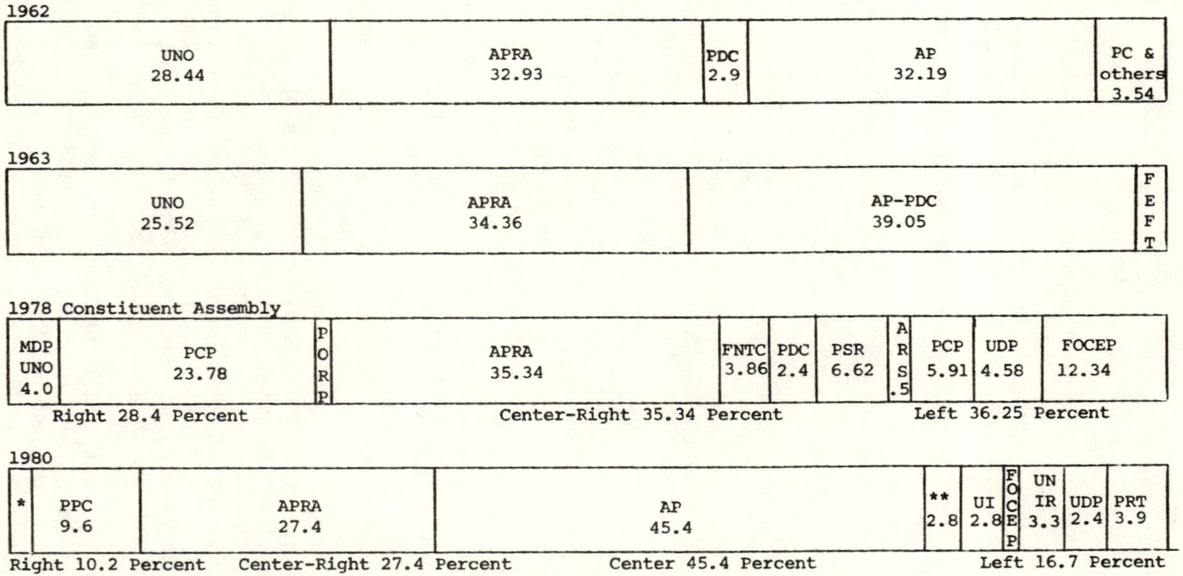

1962

| UNO 28.44 | APRA 32.93 | PDC 2.9 | AP 32.19 | PC & others 3.54 |

1963

| UNO 25.52 | APRA 34.36 | AP-PDC 39.05 | F E F T |

1978 Constituent Assembly

| MDP UNO 4.0 | PCP 23.78 | P O R P | APRA 35.34 | FNTC 3.86 | PDC 2.4 | PSR 6.62 | A R S .5 | PCP 5.91 | UDP 4.58 | FOCEP 12.34 |

Right 28.4 Percent   Center-Right 35.34 Percent   Left 36.25 Percent

1980

| * PPC 9.6 | APRA 27.4 | AP 45.4 | ** 2.8 UI 2.8 | C E P | IR 3.3 | F O C E | UN | UDP 2.4 | PRT 3.9 |

Right 10.2 Percent   Center-Right 27.4 Percent   Center 45.4 Percent   Left 16.7 Percent

* UDP .2 percent, UNO .4 percent.
** ORPR .4 percent, FNTC 1.9 percent, APS .3 percent, PSP .2 percent.

Source: Adapted from Henry Pease García, Los caminos del poder (1979).

TABLE 2.3
Voting by Party and Office , 1978 and 1980

	1978 Constituent Assembly[1]			1980 Presidential		1980 Senatorial[2]			1980 Deputy[3]	
	Vote	%	Seats	Vote	%	Vote	%	Seats	Vote	Seats
AP				1,870,864	45.4	1,701,136	40.9	26	1,620,932	98
APRA	1,241,174	35.39	37	1,129,991	27.4	1,148,357	27.6	18	1,105,679	58
PPC	835,249	23.78	25	394,592	9.6	389,335	9.4	6	376,060	10
UNIR				134,321	3.3	189,292	4.6	2	191,163	2
PRT	329,100	9.37	12[1]	160,713	3.9	165,551	3.9	2	159,800	3
UI(PCP,PSR)	440,132	12.53	12[2]	116,890	2.8	146,534	3.5	2	150,190	2
FNTC	135,552	3.85	4	81,647	1.9	92,984	2.2	1	97,417	2
UDP	160,741	4.57	12[1]	98,452	2.3	145,487	3.5	2	166,582	4
FOCEP	104,313	2.97	2	60,853	1.4	69,814	1.7	1	71,030	3
UNO	74,137	2.11		18,170	.4	25,599	.6	0	33,850	0
OPRP				17,737	.4	23,400	.6	0	24,141	0
APS				11,607	.3	19,167	.5	0	24,023	0
MDP	68,619	1.95	0	9,875	.2	17,803	.4	0	25,499	0
PSP				8,714	.2	11,421	.3	0	10,266	0
PAIS				9,350	.2	12,783	.3	0	18,097	0
PDC	83,075	2.36	0							
ARS	20,164	.57	0							
PDR	19,594	.55	0							
Independents									14,353	0
	3,511,895		100	4,123,776		4,158,663		60	4,098,082	180

Source: 1. DESCO, Resumen Semanal, May 17-23, 1980, No. 71, p. 2.
2. DESCO, Resumen Semanal, June 28-July 4, 1980, No. 77, p. 4.
3. Ibid., p. 5.

nationwide; only in San Martín and Amazonas departments did the vote for deputies fall below 10 percent as shown in Table 2.6. Areas of particular strength included Puno (58.26 percent), Moquegua (48.72 percent), and Tacna (40.56 percent). Puno presented a special case in that the FNTC is a regional party and it is consistently denied entree into coalitions with the radical left. But it must be considered with the leftist opposition in terms of its delegates' stated purposes, relationship to the government, and its votes in parliament. Moquegua and Tacna both had been sites of continuous and intense union strike activity and partisan organizing by the UNIR and the PRT. Those groups which were most successful on the left were those with political party infrastructure and/or ties to significant labor organizations that generated the physical and economic capacity to launch a nationwide campaign. Thus, UNIR received the most votes in nine departments, the UDP placed ahead of the other leftist groups in six departments and the UI won in five (DESCO, Quehacer, No. 5, 1980: 30). UNIR's support was based on its connections with SETUP, the teachers' union, and both the UDP and UI had organizational infrastructures from their participation in the assembly elections. The major losers were Hugo Blanco and his PRT and Genero Ledesma and his FOCEP. The UI also suffered a decline if the totals of its components--the PSR and PCP--from 1978 are compared to the 1980 elections in terms of support for its presidential candidate. Thus, those who ran personalist campaigns, or those who were perceived as "reformers," did poorer than the more radical conglomerate fronts.

Acción Popular

Fernando Belaúnde Terry won a striking victory in May 1980. He polled 45.39 percent of the valid votes to gain 10 percent more than the constitution required, a feat which had seemed impossible considering the fifteen candidates in the field. But the architect ran well ahead of his nearest rivals; Villanueva received 27.40 percent and the third place went to Luis Bedoya Reyes (PPC) with only 9.57 percent. In fact, Belaúnde ran ahead of AP's parliamentary list by a significant margin. After voting for senators and deputies, parties on both the right and the left saw their members migrate toward Belaúnde for their presidential selection. Acción Popular's appeal was not limited to its leaders, however. The size of Belaúnde's mandate strengthened by the party's dominance nationwide. In nineteen of twenty-five districts, from the barriadas to the sierra, Acción Popular's organization proved capable and its philosophy attractive, electing deputies in every department and

being the majority party in all but Amazonas (APRA),
Cajamarca (APRA), Callao (tied three-three with APRA), La
Libertad (APRA), Lambayeque (APRA), and Puno (FNTC). AP
emerged with a clear majority in the Chamber of Deputies
and within five votes of a majority in the Senate.

Perceptions of AP's strength had been
underestimated, initially, for various reasons.[10]
First, there had been no partisan activity for twelve
years, except to gather petitions necessary to register
as a party in 1978. Another problem of AP's was its
reputation for being a "collection of notables," or a
grouping of independents rather than a party with
organizational stability. Its party apparatus was
believed to go no deeper than its ex-leaders. This view
was heightened by the fact that many of the most
prominent AP members had spent the military _docenio_ in
self-imposed exile abroad. In addition, the process of
politicization of the masses during the revolution hardly
promised great gains for Belaúnde's nondoctrinaire,
mildly reformist party. Finally, there was considerable
speculation that the military leaders would be loath to
return power to the very man they felt was too
incompetent to run the country in 1968. Most of these
"weaknesses" related to perceptions of a situation which
was changing more rapidly than the popular frame of
reference. Attention had been so vividly focused on the
success of APRA and the emergence of the left in the
Constituent Assembly that expectations for these two
groups were extraordinarily high. When compared to APRA
and the left as a unit, AP had one major advantage--a
single, charismatic leader who was unchallenged within
the ranks of his party, who was nationally known and
respected, and who had had presidential experience.
Despite the fury of campaign attacks, the reappearance of
"painga once," and the threat of a military veto,
Fernando Belaúnde Terry seemed to personify all that Peru
needed at this point in time--a loving father figure
whose rhetoric spoke to the hearts of the people. As
Caretas took great pleasure in pointing out, Belaúnde was
"antimilitary but not irresponsible" (meaning he would
not destroy the institution literally or figuratively).
He was also "ideologically flexible and nondoctrinaire"
(meaning he appealed to a large group of people with a
vague, comforting program). Pragmatism with charisma
equalled the "resurrection of Belaúnde" (_Caretas_, May 5,
1980: 23). His victory can be seen as a combination of
these sentiments, plus a good dose of anti-Aprista
activity.

Belaúnde's victory was hailed as a triumph of
democracy over dictatorship, or liberal civilian rule
over corporatist or "socialist" military experimentation,
and as a return to normalcy. But the breadth and depth
of the AP win, while statistically impressive, was hard

TABLE 2.4
Distribution of Vote by Political Tendency in Each Department, 1980 Presidential Election

	Left			Center		Right	
	Marxist (PRT, FOCEP, UI UNIR, UDP)	Non-Marxist (APS, OPRP, PSP, FNTC)	Total Left	AP	APRA	PPC	Far-Right (PAIS, MDP, UN)
Amazonas	6.14	.76	6.90	44.34	44.23	4.15	.37
Ancash	15.76	1.25	17.01	39.19	37.76	5.44	.62
Apurimac	11.82	1.32	13.14	64.22	18.57	3.28	.78
Arequipa	14.82	3.22	18.04	59.50	10.93	10.78	.75
Ayacucho	21.31	1.69	23.00	56.83	17.49	1.84	.86
Cajamarca	9.08	.68	9.76	34.36	53.04	2.31	.52
Callao	11.20	1.94	13.14	38.83	30.18	16.99	.87
Cuzco	15.01	1.29	16.30	66.85	14.31	2.16	.37
Huancavelica	21.18	1.76	22.94	52.98	15.97	5.18	2.93
Huanuco	10.27	2.11	12.38	50.47	26.71	9.49	.95
Ica	13.81	1.79	15.60	49.76	27.80	5.91	.92
Junín	17.14	1.43	18.57	57.65	14.24	6.90	2.64
La Libertad	7.09	.64	7.73	18.40	67.88	5.53	.47
Lambayeque	11.61	1.32	12.93	35.26	35.26	5.26	1.37
Lima (Metro)	12.51	1.32	13.83	47.10	22.95	15.39	.74
Lima (Province)	15.23	1.90	17.13	48.07	26.46	7.45	.89
Loreto	7.12	.73	7.85	63.65	24.92	3.09	.48
Madre de Dios	8.30	.72	9.02	60.39	28.09	2.19	.30
Moquegua	35.52	2.25	37.77	43.77	13.07	4.63	.76
Pasco	19.60	1.55	21.15	59.55	14.83	3.82	.65
Piura	20.27	5.64	25.91	37.81	28.12	7.04	1.12
Puno	25.01	31.15	56.16	25.17	14.16	2.75	1.76
San Martin	6.30	.28	6.58	50.74	40.02	2.47	.20
Tacna	28.42	3.17	31.59	47.96	11.13	8.38	.94
Tumbes	13.31	1.88	15.19	52.41	27.58	4.20	.62
TOTAL	13.86	2.90	16.76	45.37	27.40	9.57	.91

Source: DESCO, Lima 1980.

TABLE 2.5

Percentage Distribution of Vote by Political Tendency in Each Department, 1978 Constituent Assembly and 1980 Senatorial Elections

	Marxist Left		Nonmarxist Left		Total Left		Center AP	Center-Right APRA		PPC		Far-Right	
	1978	1980	1978	1980	1978	1980	1980	1978	1980	1978	1980	1978	1980
Amazonas	11.24	6.50	6.21	.79	17.45	7.29	43.83	63.81	47.67	15.21	3.87	.35	.35
Ancash	23.49	17.36	11.02	1.43	34.51	18.79	37.72	50.69	37.71	13.45	5.07	1.35	.73
Apurimac	31.31	12.85	10.63	1.33	41.94	14.18	63.23	43.84	18.33	11.43	3.19	2.80	1.07
Arequipa	33.24	21.76	14.82	4.02	48.06	25.78	51.28	23.44	11.35	24.87	9.57	3.64	2.04
Ayacucho	36.97	23.32	13.71	1.95	50.68	25.27	54.09	34.43	17.69	12.87	1.94	2.02	1.01
Cajamarca	19.65	9.93	3.79	.70	23.44	10.63	33.66	59.60	52.88	14.44	2.25	2.53	.57
Callao	27.82	15.42	5.29	3.24	33.11	18.66	33.45	29.69	29.32	32.98	2.30	4.22	1.57
Cuzco	38.85	17.76	9.98	1.44	48.83	19.20	63.94	38.75	14.03	10.51	17.00	1.90	.61
Huancavelica	39.77	20.91	10.72	1.92	50.49	22.83	54.29	34.60	16.27	11.18	5.20	3.74	1.41
Huanco	17.47	10.41	4.76	2.65	22.23	13.06	50.04	49.01	26.42	20.91	9.05	7.85	1.43
Ica	29.63	16.56	2.63	2.07	32.26	18.63	46.12	41.38	27.87	24.66	5.94	1.69	1.45
Junin	35.15	18.96	6.68	1.82	41.83	20.78	51.96	34.26	17.79	13.41	5.39	10.50	4.09
La Libertad	11.97	9.35	1.94	.76	13.91	10.11	15.99	72.46	67.64	11.89	5.66	1.76	.62
Lambayeque	17.38	13.25	2.59	1.71	19.97	14.96	32.46	56.32	45.22	15.23	5.24	8.49	2.10
Lima (Metro)	32.88	18.19	5.30	2.14	38.18	20.33	39.99	25.58	23.15	32.38	15.27	3.87	1.25
Lima (Province)	27.24	17.12	5.43	2.24	32.67	19.36	45.81	38.73	26.35	25.65	7.35	2.95	1.13
Loreto	18.53	7.76	7.74	.91	26.27	8.67	62.26	49.83	24.61	22.09	3.91	1.83	.56
Madre de Dios	25.42	7.91	7.58	.76	33.00	8.67	59.49	55.96	28.78	7.95	2.00	3.08	1.08
Moquegua	49.25	40.80	7.26	2.66	56.51	43.46	34.37	29.02	17.70	12.12	3.43	2.35	1.03
Pasco	53.33	19.25	2.27	1.70	55.60	20.95	56.22	30.41	18.25	12.15	3.77	1.85	.79
Piura	21.94	21.46	5.67	6.42	27.61	27.88	36.08	36.97	27.71	14.37	7.01	21.05	1.34
Puno	40.72	24.31	29.58	33.51	70.30	57.82	23.31	23.55	13.96	5.43	2.78	.73	1.86
San Martin	19.98	6.69	1.66	.22	21.46	6.91	50.49	58.53	39.85	17.96	2.48	1.87	.26
Tacna	52.58	32.31	9.25	3.67	61.83	35.98	42.32	17.23	12.91	13.62	7.14	7.32	1.26
Tumbes	9.56	13.61	38.36	2.41	47.92	16.02	50.74	41.60	27.97	4.27	4.52	6.23	.74

Source: For 1978 figures, Bernales (1979); for 1980 figures, DESCO.

TABLE 2.6

Distribution of Vote by Political Tendency in Each Department, 1980 Deputy Election Percentages

	Left			Center		Right	
	Marxist (PRT, FOCEP, UNIR, UDP)	Non-Marxist UI (APS, OPRP, PSP, FNTC)	Total Left	AP	APRA	PPC	Far-Right (PAIS, MDP, UN)
Amazonas	5.92	1.00	6.92	43.48	45.16	4.44	1.00
Ancash	17.24	1.28	18.52	37.72	37.62	4.91	.48
Apurimac	12.83	.97	13.80	62.90	19.38	3.91	4.66
Arequipa	23.21	4.54	27.75	48.32	10.59	8.67	.91
Ayacucho	27.15	2.56	29.71	50.31	17.36	1.71	1.24
Cajamarca	10.68	.50	11.23	33.01	52.82	1.71	1.67
Callao	15.15	3.06	18.21	31.92	28.89	15.72	1.22
Cuzco	17.75	1.63	19.38	63.70	13.52	2.10	1.52
Huancavelica	22.45	1.38	22.83	53.38	16.53	4.74	2.24
Huanuco	11.09	2.84	13.93	48.08	25.48	9.57	1.93
Ica	16.39	2.27	18.66	45.44	27.23	6.73	8.52
Junin	20.13	2.51	22.64	49.49	14.32	5.04	.70
La Libertad	9.95	.73	10.68	15.37	68.05	5.21	5.01
Lambayeque	13.30	1.32	14.62	30.16	44.09	5.12	1.35
Lima (Metro)	19.01	2.38	21.39	39.38	22.70	15.17	1.87
Lima (Province)	17.81	2.01	19.82	44.40	25.92	8.00	.30
Loreto	10.07	.83	10.90	58.15	23.49	3.34	.39
Madre de Dios	9.86	.57	10.43	33.72	22.11	1.68	1.43
Moquegua	47.38	2.65	50.03	31.62	13.99	2.94	.47
Pasco	20.43	1.65	22.08	56.32	17.32	3.81	1.67
Piura	22.33	6.75	29.08	34.88	27.42	6.94	.98
Puno	24.40	37.42	61.82	21.03	13.30	2.88	.12
San Martin	7.92	.14	8.06	49.19	39.71	2.92	
Tacna	36.73	3.81	40.54	40.52	12.85	6.08	
Tumbes	19.13	3.32	22.45	43.19	23.88	10.03	.45
TOTAL	18.06	3.81	21.87	39.64	27.04	9.20	1.89

Source: DESCO, Lima 1980.

Independents received .35% of the national vote (with a high of 31.68% in Madre de Dios).

to calculate and critics were not merely fantasizing when they noted that the electoral coalition could prove to be highly volatile and unstable in that many voted for Belaúnde not as their first choice, but as the "mal menor."[11]

GRASSROOTS CONSOLIDATION: THE 1980 MUNICIPAL ELECTIONS

It would be a mistake to conclude from the general election results that Peru had restored the system of the mid-1960s. While the Constituent Assembly election by its nature exaggerated the strength of the middle and popular sectors, the general elections with their emphasis on the presidency also presented a skewed view of popular political opinions. The November 1980 elections for district and provincial councils and mayors provided yet another indicator to be weighed in seeking to understand the character of the Peruvian political system of the 1980s.

As an indicator of popular appeal, the voting totals of the municipal elections are distorted by extremely low turnout. Less than one-half of the registered voters participated, making it the worst turnout in Peruvian electoral history. Low interest was variously attributed to apathy, certainty of outcome, skepticism about the importance of local government, and complicated electoral regulations. Nevertheless, the campaign and its results had important implications for the partisan realignment in Peru because of the consolidation of the government's power, the coordination of the opposition, and the disintegration of the center.

Only four parties contested the elections nationwide--Acción Popular, Izquierda Unida (IU), APRA, and the PPC. As was expected, AP won, but the results were characterized by Caretas as an earthquake. Acción Popular was shaken up, the left caused the movement, and the epicenter where the greatest damage was done was APRA headquarters (Caretas, November 26, 1980: 25).

Acción Popular received important support with wins in sixteen department capitals and ninety provinces. Major magazines emphasized that winning in the majority of the district and provincial councils proved that AP was really a party with nation-wide appeal, and not merely a figment of Belaúnde's charisma. In Lima, Eduardo Orrego won with 36 percent of the vote ahead of IU's Alfonso Barrantes with 27 percent, PPC's Richard Amiel, who polled 21 percent, and APRA candidate Justo Enrique Debereiri, with 17 percent (Caretas, November 26, 1980: 25; unofficial returns).

But the results also served notice that discontent was high, and that AP's opposition, while outnumbered in the parliament, was formidable indeed. Unofficial results showed the distribution of council seats in Lima

to be AP fourteen, IU twelve, PPC nine, and APRA six.
Thus, at the local level, AP's reliance on the PPC grew.
The united left coalition of Izquireda Unida won a
majority in six capitals--Arequipa, Huaraz, Huancayo,
Moquegua, Puno, and Huancaelica--and in many other
economic and population centers throughout the country.
IU's success in Lima was characterized as "astounding,"
and "instructive." As La Prensa put it, "a red belt
surrounds Lima." In addition to winning in six districts
in Lima, the IU came in second in six others, and even
succeeded in placing members on the councils in upper
class San Isidro and Miraflores (La Prensa, November 30,
1980).

The success of the leftist front was "surprising"
for several reasons. As had been true in the other two
post revolutionary elections, the grounds of fair
competition were muddied by registration irregularities,
by the election authorities' (JNE) decision to use party
numbers rather than symbols and to give a different
number to each party in the front. There were delays in
publishing the location of voting places, and not all
parties had equal access to radio and television. In
addition, the campaign against the left was hard-hitting
and sustained by newly "liberated" newspapers.
Differences in spending were considerable and the
government party let out all the stops. In Arequipa, for
example, COFIDE approved 3 billion soles for city
services, the government suspended interest repayments on
agricultural loans, and started housing and irrigation
projects (Caretas, December 2, 1980: 8). Such
expenditures could not help the AP candidate overcome his
problems in the southern city, however. The AP labor
lawyer with corporate ties was soundly defeated by the IU
candidate, Jose Villalobos Ampuero, a forty-nine-year-old
doctor to the poor.

The strength of the left was seriously
underestimated by the major poll, Peruano Opinión Pública
(POP). In fact, the polls were so far off that leftists'
complaints about the poll's partiality--perhaps even a
contract with AP--may have been justified. In the last
poll before the election, the distribution of preferences
in the mayor's race in Lima was projected: Eduardo Orrego
(AP) 42 percent, Richard Amiel (PPC) 13 percent, Alfonso
Barrantes (IU) 10 percent, and Justo Enrique Debereiri
(APRA) 10 percent, with one-quarter of those asked unsure
(Caretas, November 3, 1980: 70). This meant the straw
poll was 7 percent off on every candidate except
Barrantes, who was misjudged by 17 percent.

Finally, the leftist coalition surprised the country
by its ability to coalesce, demonstrating that a lesson
had been learned from their poor showing in the May
election. The core of the organization was established
by the left in parliament, but soon the Trotskyiste PRT

was out and the coalition was broadened. Izquierda Unida was created by UDP, PSR, PCP, UNIR, FOCEP and PCR, with a single candidate, Alfonso Barrantes Lingan, in Lima. Thereafter meetings were organized throughout the nation to coordinate grassroots campaigns and elections. The results indicated that the united left was a credible electoral force.

Nothing succeeds like success. In the aftermath of the municipal eletions, there was a clear realization that unity had brought strength. The question then became how to utilize that strength in the district and provencial councils: to work constructively and expand local services or to be obstructionist and concentrate on the political destabilization of an already beleaguered regime? No longer on the outside, the left had to demonstrate practical and alternative programs of governing. The impatience of the masses with those parties and politicians who were willing to sacrifice small gains for illusions of total change, or sacrifice electoral strength for doctrinal purity, was demonstrated by the decline of Hugo Blanco in May; and the negative impact of Trotskyist divisionism was also apparent in November in Tacna where the POMR and the PST participated separately, giving the victory to AP. It appeared, however, that the "electoral" or "responsible" left recognized that as part of the government its members had to cooperate and deliver tangible benefits to their districts. In fact, in Maynas' provincial council, the IU representative from UNIR joined with AP to form the majority coalition (Caretas, January 5,1981: 16).

On the other hand, the task of unity is an arduous one. Soon after the elections, IU held regional meetings in Lima, Piura, Pucallpa, and Arequipa to bring together all officials elected under the IU banner. Their goals were to pressure for continued reforms that benefit the masses and to preserve the legal status of the marxist left. The consolidation of minifactions began when several of the small groups called for a permanent structure of IU with Barrantes as its leader (DESCO, Resumen Semanal, December 6-12, 1980: 2-4). But the ability of the desparate groups to continue to work together remains to be seen. Factors enhancing cooperation include past success and the left's status as the legitimate opposition. Yet, factors which inhibit cooperation continue to be the lack of coherent programs and the absence of a single organization and set of leaders.

Even more than the renewal of civilian rule after the docenio, the disintegration of APRA heralded the end of an era. The party's decline was vividly shown by the decreasing number of departments in which it received a plurality of votes. In 1963, APRA had won nine departments (using presidential votes), in 1978 the party carried thirteen, but this reflected the absence of AP from the election. In 1980 APRA received a plurality in only four departments, and in the municipal election only three of the department capitals registered a victory for the Apristas--Trujillo, Huanuco, and Chiclayo. The same trend is visible in Lima where the percentage of votes captured by the Apristas, or more specifically their party leaders, declined from 25.58 percent for Haya to 22.95 percent for Villanueva to 17 percent for Debereiri.

APRA entered the eighties split in two. The "official" group, that one occupying the party's headquarters in Alfonso Ugarte in Lima and controlling the party appartus headed by Villanueva, expelled Andrés Townsend Ezcurra on January 9, 1981 for "creating internal dissension, using the party's name without authorization, damaging the faith of followers in leaders, and a lack of ethics and fraternity," among other things (DESCO, Resumen Semanal, January 1-9, 1981: 3). The real reason was that Townsend had called for a total repudiation of the leadership which had steered the party into such a disaster in the May and November elections. He blamed the loses on "incoherent policies and marxist infiltration" (DESCO, Resumen Semanal, January 1-9, 1981: 11).

Despite repeated attempts to negotiate a reconciliation and offers of amnesty to those expelled, by February 1981 the split of APRA into two parts seemed irrevocable.[12] The "Día da la Fraternidad," the party loyalty celebration on Haya de la Torre's birthday, was dubbed "La Noche de Fratricidio" as two rival meetings took place within one kilometer of each other. Turnout was measured as though it were a party referendum and although observers agreed that the official group was larger, Townsend's showing was significant enough to be called a triumph (DESCO, Resumen Semanal, February 21-27, 1981: 2). Thus, APRA was split oganizationally and the cleavage was reinforced by ideological, generational, experimental, and role differences.

The APRA in parliament was, for the most part, older and more conservative. The party appartus controlled by Villanueva is younger and more oriented toward the left. The Aprista organizaton, historical memory, and sense of discipline insures its existence; the question will be, on which side of the spectrum will the main body of the party remain? In the past, all dissidents have moved to the left, but the 1980s may see a division with the smaller contingent going to the center-right. The other political parties are vitally interested in this situation. Since the party represents almost one-third of the electorate, a tilt of the majority toward the government or the opposition is extremely important. The democratic center fears that Villanueva's radicalized portions will ally with the left and they have been quite supportive of Townsend who, with his followers in the senate, represents an important coalition group with the government. Villanueva's acceptance by the left is more problematical, but it was inhanced by the January 1981 work stoppage which marked the first time that the Aprista union (CTP) joined with the three others in a coordinated effort.

CIVILIAN GOVERNMENT AFTER ONE YEAR: AN ASSESSMENT

After one hundred days in office, it was aready obvious that Prime Minister and Finance Minister Manuel Ulloa Elias' economic programs to control inflation and stimulate growth were causing considerable dislocation in the population. They had generated animosity in almost every sector of the economy. The budget was one which placed a higher priority on debt repayment and military expenditures than on social services; the petroleum law renewed fears of increasing foreign influence and raised nationalist complaints; and the agrarian legislation seriously compromised the gains of Velasco's reforms without addressing the major failures such as the clash between the comuneros who had benefitted and the comunidades which had not. The continued rise in the cost of living along with salary freezes provoked such a protest that for the first time in Peruvian history all four labor centrals joined together in a general strike (DESCO, Resumen Semanal, January 24-30, 1981; LAWR, January 9, 1981: 12). In addition, Ulloa's policies led to a division within AP as two distinct factions emerged. The first was headed by Ulloa and consisted of the old guard who, generally, spent the military docenio in exile, who were more concerned with their technical contributions to Peru's recovery than with partisan unity, and who were serving for the most part in the executive branch. The second group, led by Second Vice President Javier Alva Orlandini, represented somewhat younger acción populistas who experienced the military revolution, who were conscious of building a strong party organization, and who, by and large, served in the legislature and were therefore in closer contact with minority views and complaints.

Alva's differences with Ulloa began with the latter's economic policies. In fact, Alva gathered to his base in parliament an economic advisory group to evaluate and introduce alternatives to Ulloa's team (DESCO, Resumen Semanal, March 21-27, 1981: 1). In addition, Alva challenged Ulloa's proposal to increase the power of the Prime Minister vis-á-vis the rest of the Cabinet. This conflict went even deeper in that executive-legislative relations had become a complicated and controversial issue as the Peruvian civilian government completed its first year in office. Under the

constitution, when parliament is in its 90 day recess
work is carried on by a Permanent Commission. Contrary
to the expectations and constitutional interpretions of
most representatives, the commission was kept to a purely
formal role with AP President Oscar Trelles limiting its
functions and responsibilities.[13] It was quite clear
that the executive faction was, at least initially,
successful in keeping the legislature in a weaker,
subordinate role. Extraordinary power granted to the
executive during the recess resulted in the preparation
of several important legislative proposals at the cabinet
level. On the other hand, a significant number of
minority senators and deputies of the Alvista wing of AP
were frustrated by the manner of initiation and the
content of these proposals, and they demanded
modifications and open debate in the second legislative
session. Interestingly enough, Alva Orlandini was to be
the president of the Senate during that session (DESCO,
Resumen Semanal, March 21-27, 1981: 2).

Although the dissension between Ulloa and Alva was
based on substantive policy differences (with Alva
decrying the continued harsh consequences of Ulloa's
economic package with little improvement recorded,
rejecting the expanding role of the executive in relation
to the legislature, and disagreeing with the proposed
centralization of municipalities, among other points),
there was an important element of personal political
ambition involved in their competition. Even in early
1981 manuevering had begun within the party organization
to position favorites for the 1985 presidential
elections.[14]

Belaúnde, unable to succeed himself, was placed
above the fray as a conciliator and moderator between his
hard-line policymakers and the others who attempted to
soften the economic blows. While wholeheartedly
supportive of Ulloa, the president at the same time
encouraged the initiatives of Minister of Labor Alfonso
Grados Bertorini to create a consultative mechanism in
the form of a National Tripartite Commission in which
management, government and labor could negotiate on labor
problems and demands. Precipitated by the January 15,
1981 general strike, the mechanism was criticized by the
left as a means "to distract attention from more central
problems" and that rather than dealing with a
re-evaluation of the entire economic policy, it would
result only in a forum for collective bargaining for the
represented sectors at the national level (DESCO,
Resumen Semanal, March 7-13, 1981: 11). The AP
administration, of course, was hoping that such official
awareness of problems and the willingness to discuss them
would succeed in buying labor peace.

Social peace and order remained a primary objective
for the Belaúnde government. In the last six months of

1980 there were 232 acts of terrorism attributed to a small pro-Maoist organization--Sendero Luminoso.[15] Generally, their activities involved dynamiting the doorways of public buildings and disrupting utilities and communications networks. In the face of persistent violence, AP took a combative position. Prime Minister Ulloa stated that he saw no reason for terrorism "now that there is a democracy" and he felt that the government should "deal with firmness and bring to bear the full weight of the law against those who attempted to create chaos and anarchy" (La Prensa, October 20, 1980: 3). An attempt to pass an anti-terrorism law in the first legislative session failed but under the extraordinary powers granted the executive the controversial Decree Law 46 was promulgated. The parliamentary minority had argued that the criminal code was sufficient to deal with terrorists and that the provisions of this law were so vague they could serve as a justification to repress almost all government opposition.[16] The tone of this law was ominous for democratic participation and it suggested a governing party with an embattled mentality, but there was considerable opposition within the legislature and vociferous demands for modification. More importantly, the party itself was divided as to its application and Belaúnde, Minister of the Interior de la Jara, and the Armed Forces consistently de-emphasized the magnitude of the problem.

Thus, there were some disturbing similarities between the situations faced by Belaúnde in the mid-1960s and the early 1980s. He remained fiscally conservative, favored foreign investment and a capitalist economy, and remained an avowedly progressive liberal democrat. He faced social unrest, high unemployment, serious inflation, rural tension, and guerrilla terrorism. But there were also some important differences. The government party had a working majority coalition, the military continued to be discredited, and the popular forces enjoyed parliamentary access and representation. The result presented the prospect of a polarized, multiparty system, but as long as the opposition continued to be treated as legitimate, Fernando Belaunde Terry's chances of serving out his term seemed better than they were in 1963, most importantly because of the legitimacy adhering to the civilian system of government.

Notes

1. Hugo Neira, "Peru," in Guide to the Political
    Parties of South America, ed. Richard Bott, trans.
    Michael Perl (Middlesex, England: Peguin Books,
    1973), pp. 399-400. For more detail on APRA also
    see: Robert Alexander, Aprismo: The Ideas and
    Doctrines of Victor Raul Haya de la Torre (Kent,
    Ohio: Kent State University Press, 1973); Grant
    Hilliker, The Politics of Reform in Peru: The
    Aprista and Other Mass Parties of Latin America
    (Baltimore: Johns Hopkins Univeristy Press, 1971);
    Harry Kantor, The Ideology and Program of the
    Peruvian Aprista Movement (Berkeley: University of
    California Press, 1953); and Peter F. Klaren,
    Modernization, Dislocation, and Aprismo: Origins of
    the Peruvian Aprista Party (Austin: University of
    Texas Press, 1973).

2. Luis Alberto Sanchez and Andrés Townsend wanted
    elections as soon as possible to forestall
    Villanueva's gathering strength and attention after
    the Constituent Assembly was over and they were out
    of the limelight (DESCO, Resumen Semanal, May 12-18,
    1979: 1). Vilanueva himself was so concerned about
    "hiding" his ambition that he said in an interview
    as late as July 30, 1979 that Haya would be the
    candidate (Caretas, July 30, 1979: 28-31). Haya de
    la Torre died on August 2, 1979. That the party
    could not come to grips with the task of choosing a
    viable candidate caused its military supporters
    great dismay. Morales Bermúdez said in May 1979,
    "APRA is the party that has popular support, that
    has organization, that has a definite ideological
    position and for this it is very important that they
    resolve their internal problems" (DESCO, Resumen
    Semanal, May 12-18, 1979: 1).

3. The distribution of deputies per department was at
    first criticized on the basis that the volume of
    illiterates had not been considered. Those
    departments losing delegates when compared with 1963
    were Ayacucho, Huanuco, Apurimac, Huancavilica, and
    Pasco, all of which had high percentages of
    illiterates. But the criteria in the transitory
    clause was electoral and demographic density and
    these departments had also lost population relative
    to the more urban areas.

4. Examples of changes made during the campaign were:
    Citizens who had enrolled as members of a party in
    the 1978 elections were told in November that they
    could not sign a petition for new parties. This

appeared to be aimed against the attempts of the left to unify. Peruvians overseas were belatedly told they needed their libreta electoral, not just a passport. The use of indeliable ink was supposed to take care of possible fraud at transient polling booths, but finally the JNE revoked this privilege in early May because of the quantity of duplicate librestas electoral for which they had received applications--an estimated 200,000 to 300,000 persons were affected by this change (DESCO, <u>Resumen Semanal</u>, May 3-9, 1980: 1).

5. The theoretical guide for Villanueva was <u>El anti-imperialismo y el APRA</u>, while the andresistas found their inspiration from <u>Trenta años de aprismo</u>, in which Haya evaluates the previous book in light of actual experience. Haya would not allow the first one to be republished until 1970 because he thought it was outdated, that APRA had moved beyond those goals. But many Apristas believed they were still the most important ones (DESCO, <u>Resumen Semanal</u>, October 13-19, 1979: 1).

6. William Bollinger cites Víctor Villanueva as saying that the military sought assurances not only on the capability of the new government to stop the advances of the left, but also to guarantee that there would be no investigations of the military and that the Armed Forces would be autonomous in regard to budgets, promotions, and assignments. Apparently with Haya such an understanding had been reached, but Armando Villanueva's succession as the party's candidate brought this arrangement into doubt. See William Bollinger, "Peru Today: The Roots of Labor Militancy," (<u>NACLA: Report on the Americas</u> XIV:6 November-December, 1980: 31).

7. Not only did there appear to have been some pressure to form an alliance, there may also have been pressure from the armed forces to select an alternative coalition candidate. The re-election of Belaunde was as distasteful to some officers as the nationality of Villanueva's wife (Chilean) was to others. The name most frequently connected to various proposals for candidacy was Carlos Garcia Bedoya, after he resigned as foreign minister (DESCO, <u>Resument Semanal</u>, November 3-9, 1979: 1; and <u>LAPR</u>, November 6, 1979: 27).

8. During the last weeks of the election, Villanueva was talking of voluntad de fraud, citing as evidence that the government refused to run a program by Carlos Lorel de Mola on the IPC matter on a

television program (DESCO, Resumen Semanal, August 10-16, 1980: 1).

9. It appeared that between the time UI was created in August 1979 and February 1980, Ledesma's FOCEP bases were gradually being undermined. Only a conglomerate of parties and groups, when the Trotskyists decided to withdraw, the FOCEP union was considerably weakened. Originally the presidential candidate with first place in the line for senators, and control over one-third of the deputy candidates, Ledesma was asked to accept second place on the senate list and cut back on the number of FOCEP deputies. He resigned, considering the request impossible. PCP's del Prado said that the FOCEP organization was practically nonexistent, and that the candidates offered were unacceptable (DESCO, Resumen Semanal, February 23-29, 1980: 1). Ledesma eventually joined with Villaran's ARS to participate in the election.

10. Opinion polls taken during the campaign showed Belaunde's strength constantly growing, especially in Lima. These polls were so discredited by their methods of population distribution (one-third upper-middle, one-third lower, and one-third pueblos jovenes) that they were throught to exaggerate the AP's popularity. When more complete data is available on the election, it would be instructive to compare the class distribution of turn-out with that used in the polls. (See Caretas, October 22, 1979: 14-17; April 21, 1980: 84-85; and April 28, 1980: 12-21.)

11. Cesar Germana (Sociedad y Politica 3, July 9, 1980: 10) argues that the weak parts of the electoral coalition included social groups which were "ideologically unstable" such as the middle classes and the semi-skilled workers. The middle class he felt preferred the vague plans of AP to the specific formulations of APRA as it allowed them illusions of a return to the "good old days" of gradual modernization and prosperity. He maintains that intellectuals, students, and labor calculated that a liberal regime, "even if bourgeois," would at least provide an atmosphere of respect for democratic liberties and constitutional guarantees under which their activities would be tolerated, which they doubted would be possible under APRA. The urban and rural proletariat, argues Germana, went with Belaúnde out of hope for beneficient government given the failure of the left to offer effective alternatives. See Germana, "Las elecciones de mayo

y sus implicáncias políticas." Even the supporters
of Belaúnde Terry concur in this analysis of the
social bases of Belaunde's electoral coalition, but
rather than seeing the cracks of the coalition, they
see the building blocks of a sturdy foundation
(<u>Realidad</u> 2: May 5, 1980: 97-120).

12. Within the official group there was some sentiment
     toward unity and according to <u>Caretas</u> (No. 636) a
     proposal for amnesty emanated from the bases. A
     secret meeting was held with Villanueva, Townsend,
     Sanchez and Priale attending. Apparently, however,
     the split was deeper than the noteables themselves
     and the National Executive Commission of the party
     would not accept the move toward unity and amnesty.
     This led some to question whether or not Villanueva
     could control his own movement. In addition,
     Townsend, to the disappointment of conciliationists
     like Priale, was skeptical and demanded re-entry
     only with radical reorganization. (DESCO, <u>Resumen
     Semanal</u>, February 1-20, 1981: 4). Thus the point of
     no return had been reached with the factions
     beginning to take on their own life and followers
     even declaring against the personalist tendencies of
     the two leaders. By March 1981 Townsend called
     himself an independent in Congress "supporting
     measures which favor the majorities" and worked with
     a Comando Nacional de Acción claiming 187 bases
     nationwide with 65 in Lima (DESCO, <u>Resumen Semanal</u>,
     March 14-20, 1981: 10).

13. The commission met only twelve times and three of
     those were to deal with the Peruvian-Ecuadorian
     frontier dispute. The majority party apparently
     hoped that the commission would rubber stamp
     proposals from the executive. While this did not
     happen, the sessions were frustrating for
     representatives as Trelles refused to accept
     "motions of the day," that is pronouncements,
     homages, demands, recommendations, protests, etc.
     None of these have the status of law but they do
     have an impact in allowing minority views to be
     recorded. Trelles' action in declaring such motions
     out of order greatly limited the importance of the
     sessions (DESCO, <u>Resumen Semanal</u>, February 1-20,
     1981: 7; March 21-27, 1981: 1; and April 4-10, 1981:
     7).

14. Both factions were maneuvering to select their
     candidates for the post of party secretary-general
     which was to be decided in August 1981 at the
     national convention. But the divisionism was also
     evident in various departmental councils as the AP

leadership in Puno, Ayacucho, Tacna, and Ica was torn apart and replaced after factional struggles, all before they had been in place one year. (DESCO, Resumen Semanal, February 1-20, 1981: 7; March 21-27, 1981: 1; and April 4-10, 1981: 7).

15. Sendero Luminoso is a small group centered in Ayacucho whose founder is said to be a philosophy professor, Abimail Gúzman. Its members are mainly students, teachers, and middle class professionals. They have decided that conditions exist to launch a popular war and on this basis split from the mainstream of the left in Peru--calling them the "electoral left." Although they have organized labor, neighborhood, feminine, campesino, and youth groups, their size is still believed to be under 100 (Latin American Regional Reports, January 23, 1981 and Caretas, no. 629, December 22, 1980: 30).

16. The law defines a terrorist as one who "acts individually or collectively, forming bands or groups to alarm the population or alter the tranquility and public order, employing arms, explosives, and other destructive substances." A person so designated would receive a 10-15 year prison sentence. In addition, mere membership in a group that uses terrorism to achieve their goals could be punished by 2-4 years and leaders of such groups could receive punishment of a six-year jail term. The use of the media to "incite" acts of terrorism could be punished by 4-12 years, even publically apologizing for an act or a terrorist could gain a 3-5 year sentence. The possible abuses in judging organizations as "terrorists," or identifying individuals as such, are so great that one deputy suggested current economic news could not be printed under this act. If modifications are not forthcoming this law's application will be carefully monitored both within and outside of Peru (DESCO, Resumen Semanal, March 7-13, 1981: 2).

3
Mobilization, Austerity, and Voting: The Legacy of the Revolution for Lima's Poor

Henry A. Dietz

The revolutionary government of the Armed Forces attempted to be, and to provide, many things for the citizenry of Peru. Its primary goals, enunciated as the revolution proceeded from 1968 on, included diminishing foreign dependence in general, eliminating the traditional (especially rural) oligarchy, expanding the role of the state in a wide variety of social, economic, and political affairs, and giving the poor increased salience and assistance through redistributive policies. Because of the enormous complexities involved in carrying out these goals simultaneously, and because of errors, miscalculations, and bad luck, the revolution--especially the policy initiatives undertaken during its First Phase under President Velasco Alvarado--suffered drastic setbacks and finally paralysis. Innovative policies that intended to bring the rural and urban poor into the revolution frequently became concerned with control rather than participation, or disappeared altogether as economic pressures overwhelmed any possibility of carrying out the brave slogans with which the revolution had begun. As 1980 arrived, and with it a return to civilian rule, it became all too clear that, so far as the poor were concerned, a host of governmental activities had indeed come to affect them directly, intimately, and also disastrously.

This chapter is a substantially revised and expanded version of a paper (Dietz, 1980b) presented at the 1980 LASA meeting in Bloomington, Indiana. I appreciate comments from a variety of people, both on the original paper and on this chapter. Al Saulniers and Tom Sheetz provided early critical readings, and John Sheahan took much time out to contribute substantial assistance. The final draft, of course, is mine alone. Assistance for research came from the American Philosophical Society (Philadelphia) and from the Institute of Latin American Studies at the University of Texas at Austin.

The purpose of this chapter is to trace the major policies of the revolution as its leaders first attempted to direct events and then, with increasing desperation, tried to cope and finally to survive. By concentrating upon a specific segment of Peruvian society--namely, Lima's poor--the analysis cannot only examine public policy outputs (a largely macro-level concern), but can also provide a parallel, descriptive account of policy outcomes as they affected a certain societal group (a micro-level concern).

THE VELASCO REGIME, 1968-1975

When Juan Velasco Alvarado assumed power and announced the Revolutionary Government of the Armed Forces, many of the major policy initiatives of his regime focused upon the masses--the bulk of the Peruvian citizenry, rural and urban, that was marginal to the modern economy and society of the country. The rural sector quickly assumed dominance for the regime (see McClintock's chapter) and claimed much of the local, national, and international attention. Policies designed to create basic change in Peru's rural areas followed one upon the other: land expropriation and redistribution, new peasant organizations and mechanisms for cooperation and marketing, and the almost total expulsion of long-time oligarchic absentee landowners. While Peru's rural reforms were neither complete nor error-free, fundamental change did reach at least a sizeable minority of Peru's rural poor.

For its urban sectors, however, and especially for those in Lima, the revolution was from the start curiously restrained. Lack of numbers cannot have been the reason; Lima's population, barely 1.5 million in 1961, grew to 3.3 million by 1970, swelled to 4.3 million by 1977, and surpassed 5 million by the end of the decade. This aggregate growth of almost two million people in ten years gave Lima about 30 percent of the nation's total 1980 population of 17 million, as compared to 17 percent in 1961 (Sanchez León et al., 1979; and Collier, 1976: 144-45). It is admittedly difficult to quantify poverty from these data with any precision. But as a rough estimate, Metropolitan Lima in 1977 had ten high poverty districts with 100,000 or more people. Of these, six were predominantly squatter in origin, and four were predominantly high-density, low-income slum rental housing.[1] In total, close to half of Lima in 1981 was in squatter districts, with another quarter in high-density slum areas.

Given this growth in percentages, in absolute numbers, and in poverty, the revolutionary government seemingly had a close at hand (not to say captive) "marginal mass" available as a target for reforms to parallel and complement those implemented in the agricultural sector. Thus, when some moves were made toward the most obvious of Lima's poor, i.e., the inhabitants of its squatter settlements, or pueblos jóvenes ("young towns") in revolutionary parlance, it occasioned little surprise. ONDEPJOV (Oficina Nacional de Desarrollo de los Pueblos Jóvenes) came into being barely two months after the coup, charged with coordinating all governmental activities concerning the squatters. But while its charter gave it a broad mandate and represented a positive view of the squatter settlements (Dietz, 1980a: Chapter 7), ONDEPJOV was a barometer for the urban poor because of what it did not do as much as for what it did.

ONDEPJOV Policies

ONDEPJOV gave new, focused attention to squatters throughout Peru's urban areas, but inevitably spent much of its time and resources on Lima. It created a centralized office for the squatters, and it coordinated various public works projects for neighborhood improvements in many areas, including paved access highways, installation of electricity, and other infrastructural investments. Rumors of comprehensive, meaningful urban reform laws in Lima's press, however, drew continual denials from the Ministry of Housing and other spokesmen. And in fact no such reform laws ever emerged. The only real departure from previous administrations came in the form of a much increased rate of definitive land title distribution in the pueblos jóvenes. Yet even this activity cannot be seen as altering the status quo. Many of the poor looked upon the titles not as a privilege but as a right, and as something that had been promised for years. Acquiring a title, while an important symbolic and legal act, did nothing to alleviate the much more pressing material needs of the poor, and it may have raised expectations that the revolutionary government would supply other desired goods and services.

Such, however, was not the case. Some programs, introduced with much initial fanfare, never lived up to expectations. The so-called caja única was a case in point. Created by Decree Law 19864 in late 1972, the caja única was, in effect, a single provincial treasury for Metropolitan Lima that supposedly had the power to gather together all of the district treasuries for redistributive purposes. Data are sketchy, but in the mid-1970's the city's wealthy districts, while receiving somewhat less than they contributed, still dominated the budget. The five largest squatter districts of the city, meanwhile, each received in 1974 an average of about $2,000 more than they contributed, hardly a significant sum.

It can well be argued from an economic standpoint that large-scale capital investment in housing and infrastructure for the urban poor is a poor use of scarce resources. Yet some far-reaching urban reforms might have come into operation without massive expenditures. Changes in land ownership laws, strong rent contol, enforced taxation, controls over speculative housing development, and a number of other legal and regulatory actions could not only have produced a considerable political harvest for the government, but could have been implemented with relatively little capital outlay, and could have provided some real assistance to the city's poor. Yet such reforms, if ever contemplated, never became law, and thus the urban landowning oligarchy was never eliminated as was (by and large successfully) the rural aristocracy.[2]

It is probably not unfair, in summary, to characterize ONDEPJOV as searching for, and as implementing, minimally acceptable solutions to urban poverty and its manifest problems. Lima's squatter inhabitants came in for a good deal of rhetorical but relatively little material attention. The inhabitants of the turgurios (slums) of the city--at once less numerous, less obvious, and much more difficult to treat without major legal restructuring of basic tenant-landlord relationships--were addressed hardly at all. Overall, no policies attempted to generate structural changes to halt cityward migration and rapid urban growth, or to address the conditions that gave rise to widespread urban poverty in the first place.

SINAMOS and the Mobilization of the Poor

In 1971, ONDEPJOV began to move beyond its activities of providing land titles and other similar assistance into a new and socially much more sensitive area: instructing individual neighborhoods as to how their local community organizations and associations should be organized. ONDEPJOV initiated a standard plan whereby inhabitants of specific blocks would elect a delegate, who together would then elect a council of officers (Dietz, 1980a; Stepan, 1978). This hierarchical arrangement began to be imposed on squatter areas in late 1971. Communities that resisted such a scheme were told that they either would not receive land titles or would not be eligible for future assistance from the government (Michl, 1973).

By 1972, however, the revolutionary government took steps that brought this sort of penetration into local neighborhoods to the fore. First, in May of 1971 a massive land invasion took place in southern Lima, near a pueblo jóven called Pamplona. This invasion caused

considerable embarrassment to the Government, since it
had not been anticipated and since it received
widespread, sympathetic media coverage (Collier, 1976:
104-106; Dietz, 1980a: 151-156). While the invasion
itself rather quickly diminished in salience, its
occurrence played a substantial role in the government's
decision to create a National System for the Support of
Social Mobilization, universally referred to by its
acronym SINAMOS.

SINAMOS was, from the outset, controversial and the
subject of heated debate within the government and across
Peruvian society at large. While relatively few detailed
studies of SINAMOS exist (Woy-Hazleton, 1978a, 1978b,
1979; Collier, 1976; Stepan, 1978: Chapter 5; Dietz,
1980: Chapter 8; Bejar, 1976; Franco, 1975; and Palmer,
1973), most of the evidence suggests that its programs
created substantial ill-will for the government among
Lima's poor. SINAMOS, which incorporated ONDEPJOV and
other similar agencies, had an elaborate, hierarchical
national structure designed to penetrate as fully as
possible into the community life and affairs of the
masses. And while the rhetoric of building "una sociedad
de plena participación social" was used as a rationale
for SINAMOS's existence, its policies quickly assumed a
decidedly corporatist coloration and its strategies
included inclusionary and exclusinary cooptation,
manipulation, and coercion (Stepan, 1978; Dietz, 1980).
Promises of assistance and aid went unmet as SINAMOS
field workers were unable to provide material resources,
and the crucial central contradiction inherent in any
mobilizational policy--the tension between the desire to
control and the desire to encourage autonomous
development and participation--quickly came into focus.
SINAMOS insistence upon participation became, for the
poor, irrelevant, as they realized that participation had
been transformed into an end in itself, rather than a
means to material ends. By 1975, the agency's whole
raison d'etre came under scrutiny, and when President
Velasco was ousted in August of that year, SINAMOS's
future appeared cloudy at best.

THE ECONOMY AND LIMA'S POOR, 1973-1980

ONDEPJOV and then SINAMOS were probably the two
governmental institutions most closely associated with
Lima's poor, especially with the city's squatters. But
while these agencies and their policies were working with
and monitoring this part of Lima's population,
macro-level social and economic changes were occurring
that came to make squatter-specific agencies and policies
a luxury or at least secondary in importance. A variety
of economic difficulties created a national economic
crisis that made any discussion of community organization

irrelevant to the far more pressing issues of unemployment, rapid inflation, and losses in purchasing power.

Sheahan argues that during the 1968-1973 period, "Peru achieved the near miracle of social reform combined with good economic growth" (1980: 3). And while the preceeding discussion might conclude that the nature or the content of the specific social reform policies directed at the urban poor are questionable, it is clear that the revolutionary government up to 1973 at least had the time, inclination, and economic breathing space to devote a good deal of thought (although less resources) to squatter policy-making. If the economy had continued to be in relatively good shape past 1973, SINAMOS and the many other reformist policies that potentially affected at least some of the urban poor (such as the various industrial communities and the introduction of social property) might have been further strengthened, modified, broadened, or in other ways institutionalized as more permanent features of the revolution.[3] But such was not the case.

By 1973, the total consumption of goods and services had begun to exceed the total production of the economy, and in 1975 this excess of expenditures over production reached 10 percent of the gross national product (Sheahan, 1980: Table 2.2). The ability to consume more than was being produced depended upon the ability to borrow abroad to finance the massive flow of imports over exports into the country. From 1972 to 1975, the volume of total imports doubled and their cost in dollar terms almost trebled. In addition, the Velasco government aggressively moved the public sector into the investment picture when private capital failed to increase as rapidly as the government wanted. By 1976, the public sector accounted for more than half of the total investment in the economy (Thorp and Bertram, 1978: 309). To obtain the needed foreign capital, indebtedness rose from $737 million in 1968 to $1,121 million in 1972, $2,170 million in 1974, $4,127 million in 1976, and $8,032 million (85 percent of which was public sector debt) in 1979 (Thorp and Bertram, 1978: 310; and Economia y Politica, I, 2: 6), with a corresponding rise in debt service payments, both in absolute figures and in percentage of gross domestic product and export earnings (Stallings, 1979: 235). At the same time, domestic price and wage stability started to weaken by 1974. Wage increases up to 1973 were positive in real terms, but declined sharply thereafter as government deficits and the money supply both increased rapidly.

By 1976, the necessity of reducing the total of domestic consumption and government expenditures had become only too clear. Cutting back on the volume and value of imports while attempting to boost industrial (as opposed to primary) exports would have been one possible policy: others might have involved increasing interest rates as inflation rose, increasing taxes or reducing exemptions, or reducing the exchange rate. But overall, reductions in government expenditures were essential, and Sheahan points to two major areas that could have been prime candidates for cuts: military expenditures and subsidies to food and oil consumers. While data are at best estimates, military spending in the mid-1970s was approximately equal to almost half of the total aggregate deficit (see ACDA, 1979). During the same period, subsidies "varied between one-fourth and one-half of total domestic expenditures on food and oil products, and from 18 to 25 percent of the total sector deficit" (Sheahan, 1980: 18).

The manifest difficulties, political and otherwise, in implementing reductions in these areas led to increasingly futile attempts by Peru to avoid hard decisions. But the military government found itself unwilling or unable (or both) to pay the now very large debt service payments (about 35 percent of export earnings) that were owed to commercial banks in the United States, Western Europe, and Japan. In 1976, these banks found themselves monitoring Peru's economic performance, a position which, according to some observers (Shapiro, 1976; Belliveau, 1976; Stallings, 1979) they did not really relish. When conditions had still not improved in 1977, Peru once again had to look for financing abroad. This time, however, the banks refused to negotiate without involvement by the Internatinal Monetary Fund. Repeated visits by Linda Koenig and the IMF team led to proposals, refusals, counter-proposals, and (in August 1978) an agreement between Peru and the IMF (LAER, 1978: vi, 28, 30, 32; details in Cabrera, 1978; Caïeses and Otero, 1978: Anexo 4; IMF, 1978). The set of conditions imposed by the IMF were designed to eliminate subsidies to public enterprises; raise gasoline and fuel prices initially by 20 percent and by 3 percent monthly thereafter; devalue the sole by 30 percent with continual mini-devaluations to follow indefinitely; reduce the national budget deficit; raise interest rates by about 40 percent; maintain prices with the inflations rate (in 1978, about 70 percent in Lima); and limit wage and salary increases to 10-15 percent (Caretas, April 5, 1977; Stallings, 1979: 245-248). These restrictions and impositions were accompanied by similar parallel measures by Javier Silva Ruete, Minister of Finance.

The question of whether these policies were the only ones that could have been put together--i.e., whether the IMF and the Peruvian government had any choices in what they did--will be left until later. What is important here is to analyze what happened to Lima's poor as these policies took effect.

Direct Economic Impacts

Perhaps the most straight-forward way to start is by examining some basic changes in un- and underemployment, inflation, the cost of living, and nominal and real wages and salaries. Table 3.1 shows that since 1977 underemployed persons have outnumbered employed, while outright unemployment has risen from 5.86 percent to 8.5 percent (an addition of over 150,000 individuals). But unemployment was not evenly spread throughout society. In 1979, unemployment was 0.3 percent in the agricultural sector and 12.6 percent in the non-agricultural sector. On the other hand, underemployment was 65.4 percent and 39 percent, respectively. It is precisely this fact of two-thirds underemployment in agriculture that gives rise to rural-urban migration, of course, which in turn contributes to Lima's employment difficulties and to its poverty-related problems.[4]

As underemployment and unemployment showed themselves to be stubborn, so also did inflation. According to the Central Reserve Bank (BCR), inflation proceeded from 17 percent (1974) to 28 percent (1975), 48 percent (1976), 77 percent (1977), 95 percent (1978), 68 percent (1979), and was projected to be around 60-65 percent in 1980 (Boletín of BCR, June 1978; Actualidad Económica #27, May 1980: 6). And this severe, constant growth naturally played havoc with consumer prices, the cost of living, and real purchasing power. As Tables 3.2 and 3.3 reveal, the consumer index for all income categories doubled from 1977 to 1978 and again from 1978 to 1979, and showed no signs of abating in 1980. Within Lima, it was the lower-income groups which had to bear the highest rates of increase. Not surprisingly, of course, wages and salaries did not keep pace. Table 3.4 shows that both white and blue-collar workers lost ground starting in 1973, and that salaried workers slipped relative to wage workers. Public sector employees fared the worst; by mid-1980 their real incomes were reduced to 37 percent of their 1973 level. Nevertheless, workers were still the worst off in absolute terms (see also data in table 3.4 on minimum wage[5]).

Data also indicate that the distribution of income within Lima's economically active population became more inequitable during the late 1970s. The Gini coefficient of concentration increased by 7 percent from 1977 to 1978 (.43 to .46); 50 percent of Lima's economically active population at that time received approximately 18 percent of the income, while the top 5 percent was receiving about 25 percent (Ministerio de Trabajo, Dirección General del Empleo: Informe 1978: 1-13).

Table 3.1
Peru's Economically Active Population According to Level of Employment, 1973-1979

Employment Level	1973		1977		1978		1979	
	(000)	(%)	(000)	(%)	(000)	(%)	(000)	(%)
Adequately Employed	n.a.	54.5	2363	46.1	2427	45.9	2484	45.7
Underemployed[1]	n.a.	41.3	2466	48.1	2479	46.9	2489	45.8
Unemployed	n.a.	4.2	297	5.8	381	7.2	462	8.5

Source: 1973: Actualidad Económica (April 1980, No. 26: 11).
1977-78-79: Economía y Política (March-April 1980, I, No. 2: 7).

[1]Persons with remuneration less than minimum salary or with less than 35 hours of work per week.

Table 3.2
Consumer Price Index in Metropolitan Lima

Period	Price Index (1973=100)	Percent Rise
Jan. - Dec. 1975	154.24	24.0
Jan. - Dec. 1976	214.12	44.7
Jan. - Dec. 1977	297.23	32.4
Jan. - Dec. 1978	516.23	73.7
Jan. - Dec. 1979	860.56	66.7
Jan. - March 1980	1043.02	11.8

Source: ONE (1980a): 15-16.

Table 3.3
Changes in Consumer Price Index by Income Strata in Metropolitan Lima (Percent)

Income Level 1976	1976	1977	1978	1979	1980 (Jan.-March)
Low	45.3	33.9	77.2	69.0	13.0
Medium	45.4	32.3	75.3	67.1	12.3
High	47.2	31.9	62.7	64.0	11.9

Source: ONE (1980b): 30.

One of the IMF requisites included instructions to state enterprises to cut expenditures and to adjust rates, prices, and fees. "Pursuant to these instructions, prices for edible oils were increased in May [1978] by 130%, for dairy and wheat products by 40 to 65%, and petroleum products by a weighted average of 60%" (IMF, 1978: 8). This bland statement does not reveal, however, the degree to which basic foodstuffs, for example, rose in price. Table 3.5 shows that food, clothing, and other living expenses climbed 55 percent between April 1979 and April 1980, and that such monthly increases were (as of early 1981) showing no signs of diminishing.

SOCIAL COSTS: DIRECT AND INDIRECT

These economic data, by themselves gloomy and depressing, still cannot paint a full, detailed picture of the social costs of severe austerity and inflation. To note that food prices have risen, for instance, says nothing about what the repercussions were. Did protein or caloric intake diminish? What kinds of food were consumed? Did severe hunger and malnutrition, or infant mortality, increase? Or did strikes, slowdowns, and similar labor troubles increase? Some economic theory holds that such activities are repressed in an economy with high levels of un- and underemployment. Was this in fact the case? Asking these and related questions will move the discussion from macro-level economic policy outputs to micro-level social impact outcomes.

Nutrition

As food prices go up, at least two things can be expected to occur among the poor: certain foods will disappear or at least be less frequent in the diet, and total caloric and/or protein intake will decrease. Taking the latter first, daily caloric intake dropped for Lima's low-income groups from 1,934 calories in 1972 to 1,512 in 1978 (with the minimum recommended being 2,410), while protein consumption fell from 52.7 to 41.2 grams (minimum of 65.1 recommended) during the same period (Fano Rodriguez and Valencia, 1980: 8). Caloric intake thereby decreased 22 percent (1,934 to 1,512) from 1972 to 1979, with the 1979 intake only 62 percent of the recommmended level of 2,410. Thus malnutrition was no longer a problem (as it was in earlier years) found predominantly among the rural poor; rather, it existed in Lima among a significant percentage of the city's population. The calories that Lima's poor did receive in 1978 came principally from bread (15 percent), rice (14 percent), pasta (7 percent), potatoes (6 percent), and the like. Milk as a source of calories fell from 16

TABLE 3.4
Evolution of Average Salaries, Wages, and Minimum Wages in Metropolitan Lima
in Soles Per Month, 1973-1980

Year	Salaries[1]			Wages[2]			Minimum Wage		
	Nominal	Real	Index	Nominal	Real	Index	Nominal	Real	Index
1973	10,338	10,338	100.0	5,150	5,150	100.0	2,400	2,400	100.0
1974	11,088	9,487	91.8	5,670	4,852	94.2	3,000	2,567	107.0
1975	13,977	9,062	87.6	7,184	4,658	90.4	3,540	2,295	95.6
1976	17,087	7,980	77.2	10,749	5,020	97.5	4,500	2,102	87.6
1977	20,458	6,883	66.6	11,850	3,987	77.4	5,400	1,817	75.7
1978	29,007	5,619	54.3	18,251	3,535	68.6	6,900	1,337	55.7
1979	46,711	5,428	52.5	31,316	3,639	70.7	15,000	1,743	72.6
1980	57,731	5,535	53.5	42,336	4,059	78.8	22,020	2,111	88.0

Source: Actualidad Económico, No. 27 (May 1980): 10; Ministerio de Trabajo, Sueldos y Salarios: Encuesta de Establecimientos (January 1980); and Revista Semanal, Ano III, No. 67 (April 19-25, 1980).

[1] White collar employees with all values expressed in 1973 soles.

[2] Blue collar workers with all values expressed in 1973 soles. Both categories are average figures taken from a survey of establishments of more than ten workers.

TABLE 3.5
Cost of Living Percentage Increases in Metropolitan Lima
for Selected Items

Item	Percent Rise (March - Apr. 1980)	Percent Rise (Apr. 1979 - Apr. 1980)
General Index	2.1	55.2
Clothing	4.5	76.8
Sewing Materials	22.0	n.a.
Cotton Dry Goods	10.0	n.a.
Food and Beverages	1.2	58.5
Legumes	12.7	n.a.
Vegetables	8.7	n.a.
Fruit	8.1	n.a.
Tubers, Roots, etc.	-6.3	n.a.
Miscellaneous	2.9	43.7
Education	13.1	n.a.
Textbooks	29.0	n.a.
Kerosene	8.0	n.a.
Potable Water	18.0	n.a.
Real Estate Taxes	12.2	n.a.

Sources: INP/ONE, Consumer Price Index for Metropolitan Lima, April 1980.

percent (1972) to 12 percent (1978), and beef, which had supplied 13 percent in 1972, was no longer listed as a source in 1978. As for protein intake, in 1978 fish (18 percent), chicken (9.5 percent), and milk (7.5 percent) were the only animal-origin sources listed; all other sources (bread, rice, pasta, potatoes of various kinds and bananas) were vegetable in origin. Milk as a protein source fell from 13 percent to 7.5 percent, while beef was again absent in 1978, after having supplied 7.5 percent six years earlier.

In the squatter areas of Lima's "southern cone," families spent 85 percent of their income on food in 1979, compared with 78 percent in 1972, and the consumption of food of animal origin had either decreased drastically or disappeared. A study of 1,500 families in metropolitan Lima found that upper-income families spent 22 percent of their income on food, middle-income 49 percent, low-income 67 percent, and lowest-income 74 percent, and that the latter group spent for food only 55 percent of what the average Lima family spent (Hernandez Perez, 1980: 19).

In a closely related area, Adrianzen and Graham (1974) examined the cost of water in Lima by type of delivery (in-house piped water vs. tank truck deliveries of 55 gallons). The poorest families spent 2.6-2.7 percent of their income for water, while families with in-house services spent about 0.5 percent. In addition, the poor families (i.e., those who depend on truck delivieries) actually spent two to six times more than the economically advantaged families, and for this amount they received as little as one-seventh the volume of water. The unit cost was thus up to 16.7 times greater. Put another way, the advantaged family had to work the equivalent of 125 minutes per month to pay for its consumption of 21.4 cubic meters of water. The poor family worked 423 minutes for its 3.9 cubic meters (Adrianzen and Graham, 1974: 313, 315). In like fashion, low-income families who used candles or kerosene for lighting due to the absence of electrical installations paid about the same actual amount as advantaged families did for electricity. But the sum paid represented 2 percent of a poor family's income, compared with 0.9 percent of the wealthier family's income. Although these data are from the early 1970s, there is no compelling reason to suppose that these differences have changed, except possibly to worsen.

Acute hunger, malnutrition, rising food costs, extreme inequities for basic services, and abrupt changes in caloric and protein sources and consumption levels can have severe short-term and long-term consequences. Infant mortality, chronic and communicable diseases, slowed learning processes: these and a great many more social and individual costs have increased in Peru and

especially in Lima since the mid-1970s. According to
Caretas (#566: August 20, 1980) Peru's infant mortality
rate in 1979 was second only to Haiti's in the Western
hemisphere. And a report by the Ministry of Health
indicated that of all the deaths that occurred in Peru in
1979, half (49 percent) were among children five years of
age or younger (Economía y Política, 1, 2,: March-April
1979: 43).

Housing

Housing quality and quantity have been concerns of
Peruvian administrations since at least the 1920s
(Alexander, 1922; see Collier, 1976, and Sanchez León and
Calderón, 1980, for summary). But by the end of the
1970s, Lima's growth and its way of growing were
qualitatively and quantitatively different from any time
in the city's history. By 1981, half of Lima's five
million inhabitants lived in the pueblos jóvenes, or
squatter areas of the city. This percentage, along with
the increase in absolute numbers it represents, argues
that a large majority of Lima lives in substandard
conditions, since in addition to the squatters another
quarter or so of Lima lives in rental housing generally
described as overcrowded and/or lacking in one or more
basic services (Ministerio de Vivienda, 1978).
    One way in which the Velasco government tried to
confront this massive need was through sites and services
projects and through up-grading existing settlements,
while encouraging the people themselves to build their
own dwellings and to contribute the time, physical labor,
money, and organization for completing neighborhood
infrastructures. Such an approach, however, could not
control the rising costs of building materials every
squatter family requires to move ahead on construction.
In 1973, a 42.5 kilo bag of cement cost s/51 (soles) and
a thousand bricks s/1,750. By 1980, the prices had risen
to s/480 and s/18,000, respectively. Thus a thousand
bricks had gone from the equivalent of two-thirds of a
month's minimum official wage (1973) to three-quarters.
    As for public sector housing, its costs rose as
well. Construction costs per square meter were about
s/1,700 in 1965, rising to s/17,500 by 1978 and to
s/35,000 by mid-1980 (Actualidad Económica, April 1980:
14). With most public housing running about 100 square
meters in size, costs approached s/4 million per dwelling
unit in 1980. Savings and loan associations limit a
family's payments for a housing loan to 20-25 percent of
monthly income; monthly payments generally approximate
s/40,000-60,000, necessitating monthly incomes in the
s/200-250,000 range (roughly $1,000 in 1980). The
Peruvian Housing Bank in 1980 was attempting (with the
assistance of A.I.D.) to make lower-cost, smaller loans

available. But the extremely high rates of under- and
part-time employment generated during the economic crisis
excluded many families from such programs, since
structured monthly payment schedules assume steady income.
    Thus Lima's poor, however identified--by place of
residence (e.g., squatter), by job (employed, under- or
unemployed), or by income level--found the housing
situation increasingly difficult during the late 1970s.
The rises in construction material prices not only placed
commercially available and public sector housing further
out of reach, but also made self-help solutions more and
more expensive for the half or so of Lima's population
with no other alternative.[6]

Paths Not Taken

    The policies implemented in 1978 to cut back on
expenditures had significant and abrupt effects on the
Peruvian economy and its citizenry. The IMF-sponsored
policies produced some desired, immediate goals.
Rollbacks on unsustainable debt service for 1979-80 did
take place, athough future scheduled debt servicing
continued to place Peru's economy in a bind for some
years to come. Exports climbed in value (somewhat less
in volume) beginning in 1978, while imports increased
more modestly (LAER, 1978, 1979), with corresponding
improvements in balance of trade figures. A 1978 $1.025
million deficit became a $547 million reserve surplus by
the end of 1979, with some estimating a $1 billion
cushion by 1981. The influx of new foreign reserves,
especially dollars, meant (among other things) that bank
profits prospered(LAER: February 23, 1979). The IMF
agreement and its austerity measures also served to
indicate that Peru would once more be allowed to borrow
on foreign capital markets since its government would
honor its loans and payment commitments. This state of
affairs, as Frenkel and O'Donnell (1979: 204) note, "is
perfectly congruent with the interests of transnational
finance capital." Specifically, they argue that:

    Increasing demands on the peripheral economies,
    generated by the spectacular growth of foreign
    debt, have led to stabilization programs geared
    fundamentally to guaranteeing the external
    financial solvency of the debtor countries
    (Frenkel and O'Donnell, 1979: 179-180).

    The IMF itself acknowledged that its policies
concentrated upon two macro-level economic disequilibria,
one external (balance of payments) and one internal
(inflation). The IMF's Standby Agreement (IMF, 1973: 20)
put matters as follows:

> With full observance of this program, the
> restoration of balance of payments is apt to be
> the objective of the Peruvian authorities that
> will prove the easiest of attainment. The
> deceleration of inflation is likely to be a
> more elusive objective, mainly because the
> requisite price, wage, exchange, and interest
> rate adjustments are bound to impart new
> inflationary impulses. . . . It is most
> regretable that the sacrificies which the
> combination of contemplated policies is bound
> to exact from the Peruvian public is not likely
> to be rewarded quickly by a resumption of
> economic growth.

And in fact, this prediction was clearly borne out. The
external disequlibrium moderated significantly, to the
financial advantage of the country. But internal, real
economic improvements for the bulk--i.e., the poor--of
the country's population remained a distant goal,
seemingly achieveable (if at all) only through requiring
prior sacrifices by the poor, especially the urban poor.
In an analysis that strongly supports the IMF strategy,
Cline (1979) agrees that the stabilization policies
negatively affected both the organized urban labor force
and especially the informal sector workers. The terms of
trade shifted favorably toward rural areas through
elimination of food subsidies, but this shift in turn
exacerbated the difficulties of the urban poor.
     Neither the IMF nor the Peruvian government
apparently made much effort to cushion the impact of the
stabilization policies on the poor. Economically, the
burden of readjustment could have fallen much more upon
higher income groups (Cline, 1979: 40-41; Sheahan,
personal correspondence). Increases in income and
property taxes and in excise taxes on durable consumer
goods bought mainly by the wealthy could have at least in
part made the austerity visited upon the urban poor less
draconian. To say, as many have, that stabilization
should have been undertaken earlier, or that the IMF was
called in too late to do anything except impose the most
drastic measures, may well be the case. But such
arguments say nothing about why the poor must, it
appears, inevitably pay the highest price for the
mistakes, miscalculations, and subsequent solutions of
the authorities.

LABOR UNREST AND ELECTIONS

     The repercussions of severe austeristy and economic
suffering can be manifested in a variety of ways. Two of
those ways that are especially appropriate and
measureable here are labor unrest and voting behavior.

For instance, the involvement of the workforce in strike activity during times of economic crisis is a debatable topic. On the one hand, high un- and underemployment (it could be argued) will keep down labor unrest since workers are frightened of losing their jobs, and since an abundance of labor is anxious to take any opening that becomes available. On the other hand, when consumer prices, goods shortages, and inflation threaten basic subsistence, it is equally logical that labor unrest from both the organized and the unorganized sectors of the economy will increase. In addition, the relationship between poverty and voting behavior is also unpredictable. The easy assumption that growing poverty produces leftist sympathies has remained unproven in a wide number of intances (Nelson, 1979). Just how Lima's poor manifested their suffering due to the economic crisis either in labor or electoral activities deserves close examination. First, let us focus on the activities of labor organizations.

Labor Unrest

All strike data from Peru indicate that 1978 and 1979 were difficult and costly years (see Scurrah's chapter). Some 364 and 577 strikes were recorded, respectively; more than 1.4 million and 500,000 workers were affected, with 36 million and 7.8 million man-hours lost. The extraordinary bulges in workers and in man-hours in 1978 stem from the nationwide general strike of May 22-23, Peru's first (successful) since 1919.[7]

Distinguishing political from economic causes for labor unrest is at best a chancy business, and one open to differing interpretations. The months-long SUTEP (teachers' union) strike in 1979, for example, could be classified in a number of ways, as could the three-week garbage strike in Lima in April-May 1980. But while some unions have apparently been motivated by political concerns, the first trimester report (January-March) of 1980 from the National Planning Institute showed that remuneraciones (basic wage levels) and alza de costo de vida (cost of living increases) ranked high across this trimester for the past three years as causes listed for labor unrest (INP, 1980b).

In a corollary area, rapid hikes in day-to-day expenses can trigger civil disturbances. The 1978 rise in petroleum prices produced a 33 percent raise in bus fares and subsequent riots that were repressed by a state of emergency decree and a curfew in Lima (LAER: October 20, 1978). And hunger strikes, provoked by dismissals following 1978's general strike, caused a variety of worker-government-employer clashes.

When Fernando Belaúnde Terry assumed the presidency in mid-1980, he confronted a labor movement that had changed dramatically since 1963, the beginning of his first term in office. At that time, APRA had controlled the majority of labor unions as well as the CTP, Peru's national labor confederation. But APRA's shift to the ideological right, its alliance in congress with former labor persecutors, and its strident anti-communism led to the re-emergency in 1968 of a rival confederation, the CGTP, under much more radical leadership.[8] Then in late 1972, the government sponsored its own confederation, the CTRP, in a bid to cut into leftist labor dominance. Nevertheless, the left (splintered as it was) still controlled the largest labor unions in the country, as its ability to call successfully for the May 1978 general strike demonstrated. Thus Belaúnde, whose AP party never had any firm support in organized labor, faced a country that had 40 percent of its economically active population unionized, and two-thirds of that under leftist leadership (Bollinger, 1980: 32).[9] The economic crisis of the late 1970s generated immense pressures for wage increases, and some 100,000 workers--including miners, public health professionals, and state employees-- participated in some thirty strikes during the month following Belaúnde's inauguration (LAWR: August 1, 1980).

The Poor and Electoral Politics

As the economic crisis of 1976-1978 was at its worst, and as IMF-Peruvian negotiations were reaching their acrimonious conclusion, Peru went to the polls to select one hundred representatives to a Constituent Assembly that had been called by the military. Its task was to write a new constitution in preparation for restoring civilian rule in 1980. Then, as scheduled, national elections were held in May of 1980 to elect a civilian president and congress, while local officials were elected nation-wide six months later. Given the backfires that SINAMOS mobilization produced, the extreme deprivations that followed, and the high level of labor unrest, Lima's poor clearly had ample grounds for complaints against the military and against economic policies that caused them to suffer a great deal. Just how all of these difficulties manifested themselves at the polls is our next subject.

The Constitutent Assembly. The strongest, best organized political party to participate in 1978 was APRA. Haya de la Torre, then 83 but still el jefe del partido, led the largest single bloc (37 delegates) into the assembly and was elected head of the assembly. The right-wing PPC party of Luis Bedoya Reyes was second (25 percent), but a somewhat unwieldly coalition of leftist parties and movements together gathered 30 percent of the vote. Fernando Belaúnde and his AP party sat out the

elections, claiming that the military favored APRA. In
Lima, as shown in Table 3.6, results varied somewhat from
the national totals. As it has done historically, APRA
encountered problems in Lima and dropped off 10 percent,
while PPC did, as predicted, better. But the left, to
the surprise (not to say fear) of all groups, received
slightly less than a third of Lima's vote all told, and
in the low-income districts did exceedingly well. The
left took a plurality in all but one of the city's
squatter districts, and an absolute majority in three.
The race in the more traditional barrios populares
(central city slum areas) was considerably tighter all
round, but the left again showed itself at least equal to
the other parties. Based largely on this low-income
strength, the combined left (which after the election was
frequently very much not combined) took a plurality of
the total Lima vote.

This result was, not surprisingly, a cause for great
rejoicing among the left; speeches, manifestos, and
editorials in dozens of leftist newspapers and magazines
proclaimed the new "radicalization of Lima's
lumpenproletariat." But between the assembly elections
and the 1980 presidential elections, several events
occurred that caused crucial changes in the Peruvian
party system and hence in their candidates for the
presidency. In the first place, Haya de la Torre died in
1979. And APRA split bitterly over his successor. At
the same time, Fernando Belaúnde ran as a
centrist-liberal candidate for his AP party. In
addition, the left, for a variety of ideological and
personality motives, splintered badly, and presented five
different candidates and slates in 1980, instead of a
single coalition ticket. Finally, under the rules of the
new constitution, illiterates were allowed to vote, as
were citizens of eighteen (instead of twenty-one) years
of age.

The 1980 Presidential Election. Given these
changes, the 1978 and 1980 elections cannot be compared
directly with one another. The disappearance of the key
personage in APRA, coupled with the reappearance of
ex-president Belaúnde, would have been enough to have
altered the whole political scene completely. But
despite (or because of) these fundamental differences,
the 1980 Lima vote deserves close examination.

Table 3.6 shows perhaps one constant: APRA. The
party fell only slightly in its city-wide total, from 25
to 23 percent, and its performance in the major
low-income districts was approximately the same in both
years. However, as APRA maintained itself, voting for
the other major contenders showed that the Lima
electorate was far from stable. The right, represented
by PPC, lost half of its percentage total (falling from

TABLE 3.6
Low Income District Voting Results in Percentages for Lima for Two Election

	1978 Constituent Assembly			1980 Presidential			
	APRA	PPC	LEFT[1]	APRA	PPC	LEFT[2]	AP
Squatter Districts							
El Agustino	25.4	16.0	48.3	18.4	6.4	25.7	52.3
Comas	25.2	12.0	54.6	21.9	4.8	27.4	50.3
Chorrillos	22.6	35.2	33.2	20.7	15.5	16.9	
Independencia	19.8	8.6	63.8	19.9	3.3	32.2	49.6
San Juan de Miraflores	24.4	21.6	44.3	20.8	8.7	22.9	50.6
San Martin de Porras	25.8	20.7	43.5	24.2	8.6	25.6	46.8
Villa Maria del Triunfo	21.7	17.6	51.4	18.1	5.0	25.2	53.0
Slum Districts							
Lima Cercado	20.0	34.9	30.4	25.4	15.9	17.7	44.5
La Victoria	27.4	32.7	30.4	24.7	13.8	17.4	47.1
Rimac	26.4	27.9	33.3	26.5	12.6	19.2	45.4
Surquillo	35.5	5.1	48.0	23.4	3.6	17.8	47.8
Lima Total	25.4	29.7	32.4	23.2	15.3	18.2	47.1
Peru Total	35.4	23.8	29.3	27.6	9.4	17.2	45.4

Source: Realidad (1980).

1 Includes FOCEP, PCP-U, PSR and UDP
2 Includes UNIR, PRT, UDP, UI and FOCEP

about 30 percent to 15 percent) and took a maximum of 15 percent among the poorer districts of the city. The left did virtually as badly overall, but its most devastating losses came paradoxically from Lima's poor. The left fell anywhere from thirteen (Lima Cercado and La Victoria) to as much as thirty-one percentage points (Independencia). And it must be stressed that these represent the combined totals of five leftist parties. Individually, PRT scored the higest, taking 4.3 percent of Lima; its highest district total was in Independencia, with 11.7 percent. The left was, in a word, shattered by its inability to maintain a coalition.

All of the PPC and leftist losses, of course, seemingly went directly to Belaunde and AP, whose triumph in Lima was resounding. Belaúnde took well over 40 percent of Lima's poor vote and 47 percent of the city (out of a total of fifteen parties). His victory clearly carried across all income groups; he surpassed 45 percent in thirty-five of Lima's thirty-nine districts, and 50 percent in seventeen.

The 1980 Municipal Elections. Six months later, Peru held local elections throughout the nation for mayors and for local and provincial councils. While such elections are rare in the twentieth century (the last two were in 1919 and 1966), they obviously offer the electorate the opportunity to show candidate and party preferences as they concern local issues. In Lima, the electoral process is a complex one, since a mayor and a multi-member council are elected both for Greater Lima and for each of the city's forty-five districts (see note 1).

The left, obviously disappointed by its individual and collective showing in May, pulled itself together under the IU (Izquierda Unida) banner, hoping to improve its showing. All polls showed that Eduardo Orrego, the AP candidate, would win, and they were right. However, Orrego's total of 36 percent placed him well behind Belaúnde's 47 percent. The left, behind Alfonso Barrantes Lingan, gathered 27 percent, while PPC with 21 percent and APRA with 17 percent (its lowest ever in Lima) followed behind. The distribution of members in Lima's municipal council mirrored this vote almost exactly.

Within Lima itself, AP gathered in the lion's share, taking the mayorality in twenty-seven districts. Again, AP's range of support was broad; the party not only swept upper and middle-class strongholds such as San Isidro, Jesús María, and Pueblo Libre, but also poor areas, including Rimac, La Victoria, Surquillo, Independencia, Villa María del Triunfor, and San Juan de Miraflores. While PPC and APRA took only three between them (Miraflores and Cieneguella, and Brena, respectively), and four independent candidates won, the left did in fact better its showing by carrying Agustino, Comas, San Martin de Porras, Ate/Vitarte (an indistrial, blue-collar-to-poor district, and Caraballo.

Overall, the left gained some of the ground it had lost between 1978 and 1980. The meaning of the local victories, however, remains difficult to sort out. From one perspective, AP clearly overwhelmed the left by better than five to one in mayoral races, and took several districts in which the left had triumphed in 1978. And the staying power of the IU coalition has yet to be demonstrated. But from another angle, outright wins in five populous barrios populares cannot help but encourage the left, and perhaps serve as an influence for coalition-building in the future. As for the practical benefits to the left of holding local offices, there may be serious drawbacks. In terms of power, all local authorities in Peru have little real chance to undertake major programs or projects, since their financial bases are so limited. Thus a mayor of any party or persuasion who makes extravagant promises will find that keeping them (especially in a poor district) becomes extremely difficult, if not impossible.

CONCLUSION

1970 to 1980 were clearly years of vicissitudes and trauma for Lima's poor. During the decade, the city's population grew from 3.3 million to 5 million, with a disproportionate share of that growth composed of poor people. Cooptive manipulation and penetration marked the earlier years of the decade, but as the 1970s reached their mid-point and beyond, this growing number of poor became demonstrably poorer. Reformist policies were discarded for austerity programs designed to cope with macro-level external economic disequlibria by placing much of the burden upon the poor.

That such a strategy was finally adopted in 1978 should, however, cause little surprise. Few Latin American governments in recent times have been able or willing to risk the enormous political pressures that inevitably arise when middle or upper-income groups in society feel threatened, and the Peruvian military was apparently no exception. Whether or not the government felt any compunction about the impact of its policies on Lima's poor is perhaps impossible to say; that they knew what the impact would be is impossible to doubt.

Forecasting what repercussions that impact would in turn produce--i.e., whether mobs would turn out into the streets, whether the military would have to use force to maintain order, whether the poor would turn electorally en masse to leftist ideologies or solutions--might have occasioned some debate. Short-term street demonstrations over price increases for bus fares or for food staples, while predictable, caused little real difficulty for the government. The large-scale general strikes, on the other hand, frustrated and embarrassed the military, and were quite possibly a final blow to their legitimacy and to their ability to govern effectively (Bollinger, 1980: 27)

The relationship between the existence of wide-spread, deepening poverty and broad-scale leftist voting behavior by the poor, however, is much more problematic. The nature of the linkage--whether it exists or not, whether it is direct or indirect--has occupied the attention of many Third World scholars, but evidence is contradictory. Empirical studies (i.e., Walton and Sween, 1971; Martz and Baloyra, 1976; Perlman, 1976; for Lima, Powell, 1969; Torres, 1980; Roncagliolo 1980) taken as a whole suggest that direct, causal relationships seldom appear--that is, that poverty per se does not provoke leftist voting tendencies. Several intervening variables must generally be present before the connection appears. For intance, Castells (1972), in an examination of Santiago, found that the location and size of neighborhood, socio-economic homogeneity, degree of migrant population, class structure, and history of the neighborhood all play influential roles. Handleman (1975), also looking at Santiago, identified two other factors as vital for explaining leftist voting among the poor: a high degreee of group consciousness or solidarity, and strong linkages to external political actors.

Data are not available to test these hypothese in Lima. But it would appear that along with those variables operating in the Chilean context, others may have to be included to explain the behavior of Lima's poor in 1978 and 1980. Whether a leftist coalition existed was an obvious, important factor in all three elections. In the 1980 presidential vote, Belaúnde's personal appeal as a strong, established centrist candidate who intentionally geared his campaign and his platform to appeal to as broad a spectrum of the citizenry as possible played a crucial role. On a somewhat broader, societal level, two additional factors stand out: the largely non-institutionalized nature of the party system itself, and the fluidity of the electorate. Only APRA had a solid, rigid organizational structure and a traditionally fervent party loyalty and identification. Even so, in 1980, ironically, these characteristics may have worked against the party's success both nationally and in Lima, where 30 percent and 13 percent, respectively, of the electorate voted for the first time. That is, new voters (primarily illiterate or the young) may have found it easy to vote for an established figure such as Belaúnde, who promised to be "a president for all." APRA, on the contrary, with its long, controversial history as the party constantly on the outside and in opposition, and with its sometimes self-righteous "we versus the rest of Peru" image, encountered difficulty in persuading the undecided and first-time voter over to its side. The left was unable to keep itself together for the 1980 presidential vote, and was seemingly absorbed in ideological hairsplitting that at times left the poor either nonplussed, bored, or unconvinced. Bollinger (1980: 30) quotes first a worker and then a leftist leader, both disillusioned at the splintered left:

> The Left has no business coming into our neighborhoods asking us to choose between a dozen revolutionary candidates for President.

> I don't cry for the rupture of a friendship, but rather for our failure to carry out the responsibility we had assumed. History will judge us, but as usual it will be the masses who will pay dearly for this failure.

Predicting the circumstances of Lima's poor in the 1980s unfortunatly presents a few difficulties: they will continue to expand numerically and to be poor. Predicting their behavior is quite another matter. While it can be argued that the poor manifested their discontent (not to say desperation) by participating in labor disputes and by certain tendencies (still somewhat unclear) toward leftist voting behavior, the role of poverty per se remains difficult to assess. In the first place, clearly not all labor unrest stems only from the existence of poverty or from the presence of large numbers of poor people; just as clearly only a minority of Lima's poor are actively involved in organized labor. And secondly, no coherent patterns emerge from the results of the three elections linking poverty and leftist voting. If the authorities (civilian or military) perceive the urban poor as moving uniformly to the left, reaction could be a mix of responses: repression, inclusion through carrot-and-stick strategies, exclusion, or honest efforts at assistance. But whatever the response, the safest assumption would be that fundamental improvements will continue to be evanescent.

Notes

1. The number of districts in Lima, and indeed the
   exact meaning of Lima, are both problematic. For
   our purposes, Metropolitan Lima includes the
   province of Lima and the Constitutional Province of
   Callao. These two together have 45 districts:
   twenty-five are urban, seven suburban, and seven
   beach resort, while six are within Callao. Greater
   Lima and Metropolitan Lima are used synonymously
   with just "Lima," although the latter is an
   ambiguous term: "Lima" by itself can refer to a
   district, a province, a department, or the
   metropolitan area (see Sanchez Leon et. al., 1979:
   9, 162, and 163). The six squatter districts are
   Comas, Chorillos, Independencia, San Juan de
   Miraflores, San Martin de Porras, and Villa Maria
   del Triunfo; the slum districts are Lima Cercado, La
   Victoria, Rimac, and Surquillo. El Agustino is an
   additional, sizeable (100,000 plus) district that
   contains both types of housing.

2. Indeed, by allowing rural landowners whose lands
   were expropriated to reinvest their indemnities in
   urban sector activities, the revolutionary
   government encouraged new money into Lima, but did
   nothing to insure its fair distribution or to avoid
   its investment into real estate.

3. The question of whether the social reforms
   themselves might have caused or intensified the
   1975-1976 economic breakdown is a difficult one.
   Sheahan characterizes the reformist-oriented
   structural changes as having a complex and mixed
   effect on the economy. He concludes, however, that
   the social reforms do not _explain_ the breakdown,
   although they might have contributed to it (Sheahan,
   1980: 10-11).

4. On underemployment in Peru and its definitional and
   conceptual problems, see Maletta (1978) and Avances
   de Investigacion (March, 1980: entire issue).

5. The number of people who earn the minimum wage or
   less in Lima can only be guessed at. Santos (1979)
   estimates that 50 percent or more of Lima's street
   vendors are self-emloyed, but estimating the average
   wage of this group of workers is extremely
   difficult. Presumably earnings vary widely.

6. New housing laws announced in 1979 were designed to
   promote construction. Although at least 40,000
   units are needed yearly to keep up with demand,

house construction fell by 15 percent in 1978. But one of the main measures invoked by the government to spur new investment was permission granted to landlords to raise rents by up to 30 percent during 1979 (<u>LAER</u> April 13, 1979).

7. Two other attempts at general strikes (July 1977 and January 1978) were less successful.

8. The CGTP was originally estblished under the influence of José Carlos Mariátegui in 1929, but disappeared under later anti-Communist persecution. It received official recognition from the military government in 1971.

9. The labor movement, however, has its strength among the quarter of a million or so workers who work for the largest 5 percent of all firms but who produce three-quarters of Peru's manufacturing (Sulmont, 1980: 143). Union strength is much more fragile and dispersed among the urban un- and underemployed and independent artisans, who are the lowest wage-earners and the poorest of Lima's workforce.

4
The Condition
of Organized Labor

Martin J. Scurrah
Guadalupe Esteves

When General Juan Velasco succeeded Fernando Belaúnde as president of Peru through a coup d'etat in late 1968, among most political observers there was a sense of disappointment and frustration at the unfulfilled or only partially fulfilled promises of the reformist civilian government. Few suspected that the new government would differ significantly from the previous status quo oriented military regimes in Peru.

Perhaps fittingly, almost 100 years after the War of the Pacific, which had such a profound effect on Peru's political and economic life and upon the national psyche, the Velasco government embarked Peru upon a roller coaster ride of boom and depression, liberation and oppression, revolution and reaction. After twelve years of intense political conflict, of the rise and fall of political mobilization never previously experienced, Fernando Belaúnde is once again president, leading a team of ministers largely resurrected from the sixties and determined to govern, to the extent possible, as if the military interregnum had never occurred.

For some, the twelve years of military rule were a nightmare to be forgotten, an attitude perhaps best symbolized by La Prensa which, like all other newspapers, was returned to its previous owners by a stroke of the pen on the first day of the new civilian government and then continued its numbering from the day before it was expropriated in 1974. For others, it was an historical opportunity lost, an attempt to profoundly restructure Peruvian society bungled by the military and their advisors, defeated by forces beyond the government's control or quixotic and doomed to failure from the beginning. The halls of congress which were filled with peasant leaders for the founding convention of the Confederación Nacional Agraria (CNA) in 1974 now rang

We thank Edgardo Cardenas who prepared the tables and diagrams.

once again with the rhetoric of senators and congressmen, many of whom had returned to the seats they occupied in the sixties. Thus, one was tempted to question whether anything was really changed by the military-led revolution. In this chapter we address ourselves to this question in one specific area: the experience of the Peruvian organized working class.

MAJOR TRENDS IN LABOR ORGANIZATION SINCE THE 1960S

The condition of organized labor underwent a variety of changes in different economic sectors both immediately before and during the revolution. This was true for both urban and rural workers. During the sixties there were a series of governmental measures aimed at promoting social mobilization and/or controlling popular movements. In conformity with its populist ideology and in collaboration with the APRA party, in 1964 the Belaúnde government issued the Cooperatives Law and the following years saw a dramatic increase in the number and variety of cooperatives formed in Peru. The Velasco government inherited a rapidly expanding but not yet consolidated cooperative movement and used this model to form the rural enterprises to which the lands adjudicated under the agrarian reform were transferred. However, during the seventies the rate of growth in cooperatives declined and the emphasis changed from the formation of service cooperatives to the creation of production cooperatives. To what extent, then, was the cooperative sector inherited by the Belaúnde government in 1980 quantitatively different from that in 1968?

The first Belaúnde government (1963-1968) also saw a dramatic increase in the number of labor unions officially recognized and, presumably (since figures are not available), of the proportion of the work force affiliated to unions. However, when the military assumed power only one national union confederation, the APRA-controlled Confederación de Trabajadores del Perú (CTP), existed. Although the military government introduced a number of reforms and created a number of new institutions aimed at circumventing the unions and undermining their support, there was an even more dramatic increase in the number of unions recognized; industrial conflict reached record levels (including the most successful national strike since the strike for the eight-hour day in 1918); and three new national union confederations were formed: the Confederación General de Trabajadores del Perú (CGTP), controlled by the Peruvian Communist Party, the Confederación Nacional de Trabajadores (CNT), controlled by the Christian Democrat Party, and the Confederación de Trabajadores de la Revolución Peruana (CTRP), controlled by SINAMOS and the Ministry of the Interior. Faced with four rather than

one confederation with a much larger number of affiliated
unions, and without any union aparatus linked to Acción
Popular's party structure, to what extent did the
Belaúnde government face in 1980 a union movement
quantitatively and qualitatively different from that
which it left behind in 1968?

When the military government assumed power in 1968,
the major forms of working-class organization were the
unions, peasant communities and leagues and, to a much
lesser extent, cooperatives. With the Industrial
Communities Law of 1970 the government began to sponsor
the creation of so-called labor communities (including
Industrial Communities), to be found in industry and
mining and, to a lesser extent, in the telecommunications
and fishing industries. In their initial formulation,
these were to create an evolutionary process by which the
organized workers in each firm would progressively
increase their share in the ownership, management, and
profits of their firms until a situation of fifty-fifty
co-participation with management was attained. After
several years of intense criticism and fierce resistance
by businessmen, this scheme was modified in 1977,
replacing collective share ownership by a form of
peoples' capitalism whereby the labor community would be
weakened, shares would be individually owned, and the
participation by workers in management restricted to a
minority role. Although these measures served to defuse
the situation and break the potential deadlock in favor
of capital, the conflicts surrounding the labor community
led to the creation of many new unions and increased the
level of political and economic awareness of many
workers. The labor communities, though weakened,
represented a limit to managerial prerogatives and a
useful potential ally for unions. To what extent, then,
did they represent a gain in economic and political power
and an additional organizational weapon for the working
class in 1980 in comparison with the situation in 1968?

One of the tendencies within the military government
which maintained a tenuous hegemony during several years
under President Velasco had proposed that the structural
reforms being implemented be directed toward the creation
of a fully participatory social democracy, a form of
self-managed socialism based on the social ownership of
the means of production. With this end in view, in 1974
the Social Property Law was issued. Under this law
priority was to be given in the creation of new firms to
those which would be worker owned and managed. Through
heavy state support, these firms would grow and multiply
until they became the prodominant enterprise form in the
economy. Furthermore, these firms would be articulated
in such a way as to form their own economic sector which
would compete with and, presumably, displace the private
capitalist and state sectors in the future, transforming

the economy into one based on social property and worker self-management. Not surprisingly, this measure was opposed by private industry, which managed to prevent the transformation of all existing private capitalist firms into social property enterprises; by the state-owned companies, which managed to block a 1976 measure aimed at converting a substantial number of state companies into social property enterprises; and by the cooperatives, which successfully resisted their conversion into social property enterprises or delayed the formation of a "social sector", into which they would be incorporated. Nevertheless, by 1980 over fifty social property enterprises existed and the social property sector had been created. Although its long-term viability still remained to be tested, it represented a possible threat and more radical alternative to the cooperatives and a potential model of working class economic and political organization, and yet another piece in the vastly more complex mosaic of working class organizations facing the Belaúnde government in 1980.

It is evident from this brief introduction that the panorama of working class organizations was much more complex after the military government than before. There were many more organizations and there was a much greater variety in them. However, it was not so clear to what extent this was a legacy of the military government and its measures, and to what extent it was the result of other forces that had been operating over the last decade. Certainly, the influence of the many left-wing political parties and organizations should not be overlooked. Furthermore, it was not necessarily the case that more, and more varied, organizations meant that the working class was more powerful and better organized in 1980 than it was in 1968. An element that was unquestionably new was that there were organized forms of economic power in the hands of workers that did not exist in 1968, and that these could complement the political power achieved by workers through unionization. However, just as the various union confederations have been unable to merge in the cause of working class unity, so also the vision of creating a popular economic sector based on the various forms of self-managed organizations seems at the present time remote. Nevertheless, the simple raising of such possibilities would not have been possible in 1968.

In what follows, we shall attempt to trace the evolution of these various forms of working class economic and political organization from the period of the first Belaúnde government through the military governments of Generals Velasco and Morales Bermúdez to the present. Our definition of working class is rather wide and, some would argue, imprecise, as we will include both urban and rural wage earners, small peasant and marginal urban proprietors, and the salaried middle

class. In general, the distinction we make is between
employers and large property owners, on the one hand,
and wage earners, small property holders, and the
self-employed, on the other. Equally imprecise,
unfortunately, and often times incomplete are the data we
will employ to illustrate the changes and tendencies we
have detected. Those familiar with official statistics
and data gathering in Peru (and in Third World countries
in general) will appreciate the difficulties encountered.
Finally, we have made a selection, to some extent
arbitrary, in the organizational forms considered.
Political parties, for example, have been excluded both
because of the difficulty in determining exactly to what
extent they represent different class interests and
because of the lack of available data on their numbers
and strength. Furthermore, we have not included barriada
organizations even though they, too, could be said to
represent predominantly urban working class interests.

Finally, we will not consider peasant organizations,
rural unions, or agrarian cooperatives or SAISs in any
detail as their experience will be analyzed in the
McClintock chapter. We shall first consider the
evolution in the labor union movement. This will be
followed by a similar study of the cooperative movement.
From there we will pass to the labor communities and the
social property enterprises. Finally, we will try to
draw some conclusions concerning the present state of
popular oganization in Peru, both in comparison with the
past and with a view to the future, and the extent to
which this can be considered to be a "legacy" of the
Peruvian revolution.

THE UNION MOVEMENT

The origins of unionism in Peru are associated with
anarcho-sindicalism and the group surrounding the
Peruvian intellectual Gonzalez Prada in the early years
of this century (see Sulmont, 1977). When Haya de la
Torre emerged on the national stage in 1918 with the
university reform and the struggle for the eight-hour
day, this nascent movement received an additional
impulse. During the 1920s the labor movement was
associated with both Haya de la Torre and José Carlos
Mariátegui, two intellectuals and politicians whose ideas
have profoundly influenced Latin American political
thinking within the social democratic and marxist
perspectives, respectively.

With the death of Mariátegui in 1930 and the
foundation of the Peruvian Communist Party led by Eudocio
Ravines, a competition began with the APRA Party, founded
by Haya de la Torre, for influence within the working
class movement. In this competition, APRA emerged as a
clear and early winner, enabling it to found the

Confederación de Trabajadores del Perú (CTP) in 1944. After a brief democratic interlude between 1945 and 1948 when a large number of unions, linked to the CTP, were formed, the CTP was banned, unions repressed, and their leaders persecuted under the dictatorship of President Odría (1948-1956). Under the conservative government of Manuel Prado (1956-1962), elected with APRA support, union organizing activities were once again allowed. But owing to APRA's alliance with the Prado administration and the resurgence of new political groups on the left, its control over the union movement loosened and marxism began to re-emerge as a viable and attractive alternative political ideology within the working class, although it was clearly no longer dominated exclusively by the Moscow-oriented Peruvian Communist Party. By the mid-1960s under the Belaúnde government there was a new burst of union activity, characterized by an intense competition between the Aprista-controlled CTP, whose hegemony was not threatened, and the new Peruvian left. This competition resulted in the formation of the Confederación General de Trabajadores del Perú (CGTP), controlled by the Communist Party, in 1968. In Table 4.1 we present figures showing the number and type of union organizations officially recognized from 1960 until 1978, the most recent date for which figures are available. Indices have also been included in order to give a greater sense of the tendencies and relative rates of growth. In Table 4.3 and in Figure 4.1 we show the rate of union recognition during the governments of Presidents Belaúnde, Velasco, and Morales Bermúdez. This nineteen year period saw the most important growth in labor unions in the history of Peru. Moreover, this occurred under both civilian and military governments, breaking a previous pattern whereby military governments (especially those of Benavides and Odría) were associated with the repression of union organizations.

From 706 recognized union organizations in 1960, the number grew to 4,589 in 1978; over six times as many. If we examine the period between 1963 and 1968 (the first Belaúnde administration) we find that the number of union organizations increased by 71 percent (from 1,362 to 2,318). This growth was most marked in blue-collar (83 percent) and mixed white and blue-collar unions (71 percent), and somewhat less in white-collar unions (50 percent). Union federations and confederations which are organized on a sectoral and regional basis, respectively, had somewhat slower growth rates (57 percent and 25 percent, respectively). The "other" category includes "unions" organized by small businessmen and the self-employed (e.g., taxi drivers and bus operators, stallholders in municipal markets, etc.). This pattern of growth seems to reflect two phenomena: first, the more radical new left's attempt to gain influence among

TABLE 4.1
Officially Recognized Unions by Type and Year

Year	Total No.	Total Index	White-Collar No.	White-Collar Index	Blue-Collar No.	Blue-Collar Index	Mixed No.	Mixed Index	Federations No.	Federations Index	Confederations No.	Confederations Index	Others No.	Others Index
1960	706	100	83	100	359	100	94	100	23	100	4	100	143	100
1961	849	120	105	126	442	123	124	131	27	117	4	100	147	102
1962	1093	154	141	169	593	165	171	181	30	130	4	100	154	107
1963	1362	192	149	203	783	218	204	217	35	152	4	100	167	116
1964	1670	236	195	235	1000	278	247	262	39	169	5	125	184	128
1965	1854	262	214	258	1118	311	279	296	42	182	5	125	196	137
1966	2025	286	223	269	1235	344	309	328	48	208	5	125	205	143
1967	2172	307	243	293	1321	367	333	354	53	230	5	125	217	151
1968	2318	328	253	305	1430	398	350	372	55	239	5	125	225	157
1969	2436	345	263	316	1511	420	364	387	59	256	5	125	234	163
1970	2635	373	286	344	1649	459	390	414	63	273	7	175	242	169
1971	3021	427	336	404	1903	530	460	489	69	300	8	200	246	172
1972	3432	486	380	457	2168	603	548	582	80	347	8	200	248	173
1973	3806	539	426	513	2391	666	641	681	91	359	8	200	248	173
1974	4150	587	491	591	2577	717	729	775	96	417	8	200	248	173
1975	4284	620	529	637	2714	755	782	831	102	443	8	200	248	173
1976	4510	638	543	654	2780	774	828	880	102	443	8	200	248	173
1977	4538	642	547	659	2796	778	836	889	102	443	8	200	248	173
1978	4589	650	560	674	2820	785	848	902	104	452	8	200	248	173

Source: Sectoral Planning Office of the Ministry of Labor; and Realidad, No. 5 (July 1979): 9.

TABLE 4.2
Unions and the Economically Active Population

Year	Economically Active Population		Unions		Average Workers Per Union		Wage Earners	Wage Earners Per Union
	Number	Index	Number	Index	Number	Index	Number	Number
1960	3,417,500	---	706	---	4,840	---	---	---
1961	3,462,600	---	849	---	4,078	---	---	---
1962	3,512,400	---	1,093	---	3,213	---	---	---
1963	3,569,400	100	1,362	100	2,620	100	---	---
1964	3,633,500	101	1,670	122	2,175	83	---	---
1965	3,704,700	103	1,854	136	1,998	76	---	---
1966	3,783,000	105	2,025	148	1,868	71	---	---
1967	3,868,400	108	2,172	159	1,781	67	---	---
1968	3,960,900	110	2,318	170	1,708	65	---	---
1969	4,060,500	113	2,436	178	1,666	63	---	---
1970	4,167,300	116	2,635	193	1,581	60	---	---
1971	4,281,000	119	3,021	221	1,417	54	---	---
1972	4,401,700	123	3,432	251	1,282	48	1,760,700	513
1973	4,534,300	127	3,806	279	1,191	45	1,842,700	484
1974	4,672,900	130	4,150	304	1,126	42	1,914,900	461
1975	4,817,500	134	4,384	321	1,098	41	1,973,600	450
1976	4,968,000	139	4,510	331	1,101	42	2,024,900	448
1977	5,124,700	143	4,538	333	1,129	42	2,048,100	451
1978	5,287,100	148	4,589	336	1,152	43	2,059,800	448

Source: Realidad, Number 5 (July 1979): 7.

FIGURE 4.1
Unions Recognized by Year

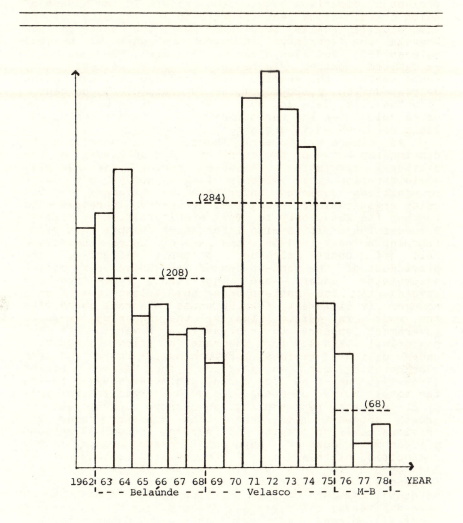

blue-collar workers and, second, the fact that in the early stages of union organizing it is easier to organize blue-collar than white-collar workers. In Table 4.2 we present a comparison between the growth in the number of union organizations and the growth in the size of the economically active population over the same period. Whereas the workforce increased by only 11 percent between 1963 and 1968, as we have seen the number of recognized unions increased by 71 percent and, consequently, the average number of workers per union decreased from 2,620 to 1,708 (a fall of 35 percent). Unfortunately, data are not available which would enable us to calculate the variations in the proportion of the labor force which is organized.

As Figure 4.1 clearly shows, it is necessary to distinguish between the First and Second Phases of the military revolution, because during the Velasco administration the already large number of union recognitions achieved under Belaúnde (average of 208 union organizations recognized per year) increased even further (to 284), only to fall off sharply under Morales Bermúdez (68). It is also interesting to note that after reaching a peak in 1964, the rate of union recognition fell off under Belaúnde, probably reflecting the playingout of the pent-up demand for union organization accumulated under --and inherited from-- previous governments. The pattern under the Velasco government, however, is different, forming amost a normal curve with the mode in 1972. Finally, the Morales Bermúdez government appears to represent a reversion to the historical tendency for the rate of union recognition under military regimes. Returning to Table 4.1 and concentrating our analysis on the Velasco period (1969-1975) we find that during this seven year period the total number of recognized union organizations grew by 80 percent, representing an average annual rate of growth somewhat less than that achieved under the previous civilian regime (10 percent versus 14 percent per annum). However, there was a marked change in the composition of this growth. White-collar unions grew by 101 percent in this period (versus 50 percent under Belaúnde), blue-collar unions by 80 percent (versus 83 percent), combined white- and blue-collar unions by 115 percent (versus 71 percent), federations by 73 percent (versus 57 percent), confederations by 60 percent (versus 25 percent), and "others" by 6 percent (versus 35 percent). In terms of average annual growth rates, during the Velasco government, mixed blue- and white-collar unions increased fastest (12 percent), followed by white-collar unions (11 percent) and blue-collar unions (10 percent). As a result, at the end of the Velasco period the distribution of unions had changed considerably in comparison to the earlier period.

Most notably, there was a shift toward white-collar unionism during this period, mainly at the expense of unionization among small, independent proprietors and the self-employed. Referring to Table 4.2, we see that during the seven years under consideration the work force increased by 757,000 people (19 percent) whereas, as we have seen, the number of union organizations recognized increased by 80 percent and the average number of workers per union organization declined from 1,666 to 1,098 (34 percent). Furthermore, between 1972 and 1975 (the only years for which we have data) the number of wage earners increased by 212,900 (12 percent) and the average number of wage earners per union organization declined from 513 to 450 (12 percent). Stephens (1980: 177) captures the importance of union organizing during this period by noting that, of all unions recognized by 1975, almost half (48 percent) were recognized between 1968 and 1975.

How do we explain these tendencies during the First Phase of the Peruvian Revolution?[1] Evidently, the radical rhetoric expounded by government spokesmen was such as to create an environment favorable to popular mobilization in general and union oganization in particular. As we shall see later, government measures such as the creation of labor communities and the passing of the job stability law in 1970, despite the intention to eliminate class conflict, create harmonious class relations, and eliminate the need for unions, tended to promote conflict and the formation of unions. Further evidence in support of this argument is provided in Table 4.4 where the number of strikes are shown to have increased from 345 in 1970 to 788 in 1973 (an increase of 128 percent). This argument is further confirmed by Table 4.5 which shows that manufacturing industry (where most Industrial Communities were to be found) accounted for the major proportion of strikes in this period and was the major source of the increase in their number.

Another factor which played an important role in increasing the number of unions during this period was the formation and recognition of new national union confederations. In January 1971 the Communist Party-controlled Confederación General de Trabajadores del Perú (CGTP) was officially recognized; in July of the same year the Christian Democrat-controlled Confederación Nacional de Trabajadores (CNT) was also recognized and in December 1972 the government organized and recognized its own confederation, the Confederación de Trabajadores de la Revolución Peruana (CTRP). In 1977 SINAMOS produced a classifed study of the four national union confederations and of the unions affiliated to them. The results of this study were made generally available in the magazine Realidad (No. 6, August 1979). Although the accuracy of these figures is very questionable, no other comparable figures are available. The figures in

TABLE 4.3
Average Annual Percentage Increase in Number of Recognized
Unions by Government Period and Union Type

Government Period				Type of Union			
	Total	White Collar	Blue Collar	Mixed	Feder- ations	Confeder- ations	Others
Belaunde (1963–1968)	14	11	16	13	11	4	7
Velasco (1969–1975)	10	11	10	12	9	8	1
Morales Bermudez (1976–1978)	2	2	1	3	1	0	0

Source: Calculated from Table 4.1

TABLE 4.4
Measurements of Labor Conflict, 1968-1978

	1968	1969	1970	1971	1972	1973	1974	1975	1976	1977	1978
No. of Strikes	364	372	345	377	409	788	562	779	440	232	367
Workers Affected (thousands)	107	9	110	161	130	416	347	617	258	387	1398
Man-hours lost (millions)	3.4	3.9	5.8	10.9	6.3	15.7	12.5	20.2	6.8	4.6	36.1

Source: Instituto Nacional de Planificacion, "Indicadores económicos y sociales
        para la planificacion global y sectorial," and; Julio Montenegro A. and
        Zoila Perez S. (1980), Estabilidad laboral y empresa, p. 72.

113

TABLE 4.5
Percentage Distribution of Strikes by Economic Sector, 1970-1978

Sector	1970	1971	1972	1973	1974	1975	1976	1977	1978
Agriculture, Livestock Forestry, Fishing, etc.	14.2	6.9	5.4	2.9	3.3	1.5	2.2	4.9	1.6
Mines and Quarries	20.6	25.4	9.8	11.4	11.5	13.4	9.0	25.8	28.5
Manufacturing Industry	39.4	48.8	63.3	54.8	55.4	54.3	54.0	46.4	50.2
Construction	3.8	4.8	5.9	7.2	6.1	5.2	11.1	9.3	2.7
Utilities and Health Services	1.7	0.3	0.7	1.0	0.0	1.0	0.6	1.3	0.8
Commerce, Banking, and Real Estate	14.5	8.2	8.3	10.4	13.1	14.1	10.4	8.0	8.7
Transport and Communications	2.6	1.6	1.2	3.9	3.5	3.3	3.1	4.0	3.2
Services	3.2	4.0	4.9	6.3	5.9	6.1	7.5	2.2	11.2
Unspecified	---	---	0.5	1.9	0.5	0.7	1.5	2.2	3.8

Source: "Las huelgas en el Perú," Analisis Laboral, 2 (1978): 18.

Table 4.6 show, for example, the relative decline in the
CTP and the rapid growth of the CGTP and CTRP. The
figures for the CTRP are almost certainly overstated as
it is generally recognized that the CGTP is the largest
and most important confederation today. In organizing
the CTRP, SINAMOS and the Interior Ministry concentrated
their efforts on smaller firms, especially in the
provinces. It would not, therefore, be surprising if the
number of unions affiliated to the CTRP exceeded the
number of those affiliated to the CGTP. However, the
size of the unions affiliated to the CGTP is in general
larger than the size of those affiliated to the CTRP,
with the exception of the fishermen's union, suggesting
that the figure for the number of workers connected with
the CTRP may be overstated. It is believed that
political and bureaucratic pressures led to the creation
of a number of "phantom" unions, once again leading to
overstatement. Finally, it is probable that with the
dissolution of SINAMOS, a large number of these unions
have disappeared or become inactive. However, taking
into account these considerations, it is evident that the
Velasco government's tactical alliance with the CGTP and
its own organizational efforts gave an important impulse
to the creation of new unions during this period.

From 1974 onward the Peruvian economy began to enter
a period of crisis which some have described as the most
serious in this century. As Table 4.7 shows, real wages
fell dramatically; from an index number of 100 in 1973 to
50 in 1979 for white-collar workers, and from 100 in 1973
to 71 in 1979 for blue-collar workers. Thus, in real
terms, the wages of white-collar workers fell more
sharply than those of blue-collar workers and this
undoubtedly stimulated the relatively more rapid growth
of white-collar and mixed unions. The creation of labor
communities and the conflicts between workers and owners
arising therefrom united white- and blue-collar workers
in a common struggle in many firms, leading to the
creation of mixed unions. Finally, as indicated above,
earlier unionizing efforts tended to eliminate the pool
of easily organized blue-collar workers, leading to
greater efforts aimed at organizing white-collar workers
during this period. After 1976 under the Morales
Bermúdez government, union recognition dropped off
dramatically and strikes were frequently met with force.
But the labor movement remained active. Overall then,
the second Belaúnde administration in 1980 faced a
larger, better organized, and more "clasista" union
movement than in 1968. However, in 1977 SINAMOS
estimated that only 18 percent of the work force was
organized. Nevertheless, this low figure needs to be
considered in the light of unemployment and
underemployment in 1978 of 6.5 percent and 52.2 percent,
respectively (Actualidad Economica, No. 25, March 1980).

TABLE 4.6
Number and Type of Unions by National Confederation Affiliation and
Total number of Affiliated Workers, 1977

Confederation	No. Workers	Federation	Unions	Committees	Associations	Total
CTP	83,000	21	205	23	12	262
CGTP	152,000	29	642	30	6	707
CNT	10,700	7	111	4	1	123
CTRP	192,000	42	876	230	115	1,263

Source: SINAMOS data, presented in Realidad, No. 5 (July 1979).

TABLE 4.7
Indices of Real Income Trends, 1973-1979

Year	Salaries	Wages
1973	100	100
1974	92	94
1975	88	90
1976	77	98
1977	67	77
1978	54	69
1979	50	71

Source: Actualidad Económica, No. 25 (March 1980).

Moreover, the union movement was more unified than it had been since the early days of CTP hegemony. The leftward swing in the APRA Party (though divided and weakened), the failure of the CTP to create a counterforce to the CGTP by forming a block comprising the CTP, CNT and CTRP, the national strike supported (for the first time) by all four confederations under CGTP leadership in January 1981, the incorporation of a number of important Maoist-oriented unions in the CGTP, and the close coordination on the political front with the Izquierda Unida all pointed to a growing consolidation and unification of the union movement.

THE COOPERATIVE MOVEMENT

Although cooperatives have been known in Peru since the beginning of this century (Van Ginneken, 1974), it was not until the 1960s that the cooperative movement began to expand rapidly. The birth of what is considered to be the "modern" cooperative movement in Peru began in the late 1950s when a U.S. Maryknoll priest began to form savings and loan cooperatives in the department of Puno and later extended his activities to Lima and other parts of the country. However, from its beginnings the APRA party included the cooperative as an important element in its preferred economic model, and the Christian Democratic Party, with its concept of the "communitarian enterprise" (very akin to the cooperative model), has also provided an ideological justification for cooperatives. Finally, the Acción Popular party has found it easy to accommodate cooperativism within its pragmatic ideological framework. Thus, the cooperative movement has in general encountered relatively little ideological opposition from the various political parties, except those from the marxist left.

During the 1960s a combination of a positive disposition on the part of the major political parties and outside economic support, especially from the U.S., for a type of non-communist, humanitarian development alternative, which the cooperatives were able to present themselves as, provided a favorable environment for the development of the movement. In this context an important event was the passing of the Cooperatives Law in 1964 with APRA and AP bipartisan support that provided a legal and normative framework for their creation, as well as a number of tax incentives.

Despite this bipartisan origin and current multipartisan support, the party that has given a greater impulse to the creation of cooperatives and received more political support from them has been APRA. Party members seem to control a large number of the cooperatives and federations, and much of the cooperation and linkages, as well as the conflicts and cleavages, between them can be traced to this hidden network among party members. This, in turn, seems to reflect the predominantly lower middle class membership of the cooperatives which tend to serve the needs of this sector of the population, providing savings mechanisms for the purchase of consumer durables and the provision of some common services. As Table 4.8 shows, the number of cooperatives has grown from 540 in 1963 to 2,881 in 1979, an increase of 2,341 or 334 percent in seventeen years. However, when this rate of growth is broken down by periods some interesting differences emerge, as Table 4.9 indicates. The rate of growth declined continuously throughout the period, being 19 percent under the Velasco administration and 3 percent under the Morales Bermúdez administration. Thus, while growth continued to be positive throughout the period, it was continuously declining. When we examine the figures for second and third level cooperatives and federations, a similar pattern emerges except for the Velasco period. In general, these figures reflect prevailing economic and political conditions. The annual growth rates follow very closely overall economic conditions, rising during years of rapid economic growth (1960-1965 and 1969-1973) and falling during periods of economic crisis (1967-1968 and 1974-1977). The Belaúnde government was, in general, favorable toward cooperatives, sponsoring the cooperatives law and granting tax concessions. The military regime, however, with the exception of the creation of agrarian production cooperatives as part of the agrarian reform process, paid little attention and was at times highly critical. Tax incentives were abolished and alternative, more "radical" models, such as social property, were given preferential treatment. The increase in higher level organizations during the Velasco regime may be attributed in part to its activity in creating second level cooperatives in the agrarian sector and to the formation of federations as political and economic defence mechanisms within the rest of the cooperative movement.

Another measure of cooperative growth is financial: paid up capital. However, Table 4.10 should be treated with caution, especially the final column of figures for 1978. Taking into account that these figures do not necessarily represent complete coverage for each year, and that the rate of omissions per year is unknown, we can make the following observations. Between 1970 and 1974 the fastest rate of growth in capital was experienced by service cooperatives, followed by communal, fishing, and savings and loan cooperatives. However, overall the largest cooperatives in financial terms in 1974 were the savings and loan cooperatives, followed by agrarian, housing, and service cooperatives.

In assessing the evolution and current state of cooperatives in Peru, several comments may be made.

TABLE 4.8
Number of Cooperatives by Year and Type, 1963-1979

Type	1963	1964	1965	1966	1967	1968	1969	1970	1971	1972	1973	1974	1975	1976	1977	1978	1979
Agrarian	22	30	92	120	152	193	231	298	349	478	636	758	879	951	990	1005	1037
Savings and Loan	254	303	352	385	411	435	485	518	525	516	526	525	522	519	524	535	534
Communal	0	0	2	3	4	9	19	22	30	42	54	53	53	51	51	54	54
Consumer	120	129	154	167	181	191	207	223	220	208	212	215	215	211	208	204	205
Educational	2	2	2	3	3	3	3	5	6	8	10	12	15	18	21	23	25
School	0	0	1	1	1	1	1	1	0	0	1	1	1	1	1	1	1
Fishing	5	6	10	11	11	12	12	12	19	28	30	31	29	27	26	26	26
Prod. and Work	4	5	11	14	18	22	35	51	74	86	118	133	148	143	147	152	158
Service	7	7	21	28	33	42	55	70	79	110	160	184	208	206	239	283	301
Transport	11	22	37	45	51	55	65	74	75	71	79	80	82	82	86	90	96
Housing	115	140	190	227	265	290	327	374	397	392	419	420	425	426	436	440	444
SUB-TOTAL	540	644	872	1004	1130	1253	1440	1648	1774	1939	2245	2412	2577	2635	2729	2813	2881
HIGHER LEVEL	4	4	5	5	7	9	10	19	21	27	33	38	40	53	55	58	58
RATE OF GROWTH (%)	19.1	35.3	15.1	12.7	11.0	14.9	15.0	7.7	9.5	15.9	7.6	6.9	2.7	3.6	3.1	2.4	
Period Averages			18.63							11.04						2.94	

Source: Research and Statistics Unit, General Directory for Cooperatives, Ministry of Labor

TABLE 4.9
Percentage Rates of Growth for Cooperatives by Type and Government
Administration, 1963-1979

Type of Cooperative	Belaunde Administration	Velasco Administration	Morales Bermudez Administration	Total
Agrarian	64	24	4	32
Savings and Loans	11	3	0.5	5
Communal	42	33	0.5	28
Consumer	10	2	-1	4
Education	10	27	14	18
Fishing	21	16	0.8	14
Production and Work	45	32	2	29
Service	56	26	10	31
Transport	42	6	4	17
Housing	21	6	1	9
Higher Level	19	26	11	20

Source: Calculated from data in Table 4.8.

TABLE 4.10
Cooperatives' Paid-up Capital by Year and Type (in thousand $US)[1]

Type		1969	1970[2]	1971	1972	1973	1974	1978
Agrarian	Amount	1,555	32,767	33,510	36,528	40,808	46,625	4,237
	Index	5	100	102	111	125	142	13
Savings and Loan	Amount	59,527	58,867	71,942	107,685	142,483	181,679	66,932
	Index	101	100	122	182	242	308	113
Communal	Amount	18	66	75	156	224	308	120
	Index	26	100	113	236	339	419	181
Consumer	Amount	1,167	2,044	2,125	3,823	3,632	4,485	2,701
	Index	57	100	104	187	178	219	132
Education	Amount	n.a.	n.a.	n.a.	n.a.	n.a.	n.a.	6,805
	Index	n.a.	n.a.	n.a.	n.a.	n.a.	n.a.	n.a.
Fishing	Amount	n.a.	43	54	73	130	137	18
	Index	n.a.	100	125	171	303	319	43
Production and Work	Amount	1,118	1,332	1,397	1,265	2,279	2,866	1,529
	Index	84	100	105	95	171	215	115
Service	Amount	676	1,340	1,364	1,964	15,638	22,498	9,450
	Index	50	100	102	147	1,167	1,678	705
Transport	Amount	645	1,002	1,099	1,219	1,735	1,624	487
	Index	66	100	110	122	173	162	49
Housing	Amount	14,515	22,980	24,338	29,406	33,410	34,072	18,613
	Index	63	100	106	128	145	148	81
Sub-total	Amount	79,936	120,443	135,803	182,119	240,339	294,265	104,094
	Index	66	100	113	151	199	244	86
Higher Level	Amount	n.a.	3,111	3,128	3,832	5,801	5,407	20,375
	Index	n.a.	100	101	123	186	174	655
Total	Amount	n.a.	123,554	138,931	185,951	246,140	299,672	124,469
	Index	n.a.	100	112	150	199	242	101

Note: The paid-up capital for the years 1969-1974 is underestimated because not all cooperatives presented their balance sheets to SINAMOS. In 1978, only 44 percent of the 2,871 cooperatives in existence as of December 1978 filed returns.

[1] Based on the average exchange rate for each year.

[2] Base year 1970

Source: Research and Statistics Unit, General Direction for Cooperatives, Ministry of Labor.

First, while cooperatives are by nature self-managed, a distinction can be made between production cooperatives (which are governed by their workers) and user or service cooperatives which are governed by their clients. The former may be considered as falling more legitimately within the definition of a working-class movement than the latter. Unfortunately, available data collected in Peru makes no clear distinction between these two categories of cooperatives. However, it seems probable that over time the composition of the movement has shifted slightly toward production cooperatives. Table 4.11 shows the distribution of cooperatives by type among the various departments, which suggests that the cooperative movement has not been especially strong in the poorest of the highland regions (excluding the essentially working-class agrarian cooperatives).

A second and related comment refers to the real beneficiaries of the cooperative movement. As noted previously, cooperatives in general tend to be a petty bourgeois rather than working-class movement, though this comment would not apply to agrarian, production, and work cooperatives. Cooperatives, therefore, tend to be more moderate in their ideologies and demands on society. Thus, in fact, a large part of the cooperative movement serves to tap and channel resources (especially private savings) from lower social groups to private capitalist industry, especially that engaged in the production and sale of consumer durables. In fact, savings and loans cooperatives have been remarkably reluctant to make loans to production cooperatives.

Third, while growth has been positive among all types of cooperatives over the past twenty years, the growth rates have fallen steadily until under the Morales Bermúdez government they became stagnant or even turned negative. Does this mean that the cooperative in Peru has exhausted its potential as an organizational and developmental model? The fact that the movement has continued to grow, even if at declining rates, during a fairly long period of government neglect and, in recent years, economic crisis, suggests that this would be a premature conclusion. The new civilian government announced that it would revise the Cooperatives Law and devise new incentives for them, and these promises sparked a renewed optimism and enhanced level of political activity among cooperative leaders. Thus, the cooperative movement survived and grew. Although it was not a "favorite child" of the military revolution, it was larger both numerically and financially in 1980 than in 1968.

TABLE 4.11
Number of Cooperatives by Location and Type as of June 1980

Department	Agro	Savings & Loan	Com-munal	Con-Sumer	Educa-tional	School	Fish-ing	Produc. & Work	Ser-vice	Trans.	Housing	Higher Level	Total
Amazonas	23	2	0	1	0	0	0	0	0	0	0	0	26
Ancash	35	15	3	10	0	1	4	21	18	2	2	3	114
Apurimac	27	1	1	1	0	0	0	0	0	1	1	1	33
Arequipa	40	21	0	17	0	0	2	10	7	13	52	2	164
Ayacucho	17	6	2	2	0	0	0	1	8	4	3	1	44
Cajamarca	80	14	1	3	0	0	0	0	4	0	1	2	105
Callao	2	34	0	9	0	0	6	6	17	10	33	1	118
Cuzco	80	11	1	7	1	0	0	5	2	1	24	3	135
Huancavelica	15	3	0	1	0	0	0	0	6	1	0	0	26
Huanuco	28	7	0	4	1	0	0	0	0	0	1	2	43
Ica	85	9	0	14	3	0	4	1	8	2	24	4	154
Junin	54	16	8	9	0	0	0	4	16	8	11	5	131
La Libertad	93	15	0	14	1	0	0	15	5	5	10	1	159
Lambayeque	49	21	0	4	3	0	2	2	1	0	11	1	94
Lima	133	314	0	76	14	0	2	63	182	39	247	18	1088
Loreto	19	4	0	3	0	0	2	1	2	0	1	0	32
Madre de Dios	6	0	0	1	0	0	0	1	1	0	0	0	9
Moquegua	3	3	2	2	0	0	0	1	1	1	3	0	14
Pasco	21	5	16	5	0	0	0	4	0	2	0	1	54
Piura	124	17	17	8	1	0	4	1	6	2	11	9	200
Puno	41	2	5	3	0	0	0	19	21	0	1	3	95
San Martin	27	4	0	2	0	0	0	1	0	0	2	0	36
Tacna	19	3	0	2	0	0	0	1	3	5	5	1	39
Tumbes	14	1	0	1	0	0	0	0	0	0	0	1	17
Ucayali	7	9	0	2	1	0	0	1	2	0	1	0	23
Total	1042	537	54	201	25	1	26	158	310	96	444	59	2953

Source: Research and Statistics Unit, General Direction for Cooperatives, Ministry of Labor

LABOR COMMUNITIES

Whereas in agriculture the military regime carried out a frontal attack against the rural bourgeoisie with a view to replacing it by other social groups, in industry government measures sought to ameliorate class conflict by means of a mechanism for promoting labor-management collaboration within the context of a progressive sharing of power within the firm. The chosen instrument was the labor community or Industrial Community, composed of all workers in the firm, to which 25 percent of each year's profits would be transferred: 10 percent in cash to be distributed among the workers and 15 percent in shares to be held collectively by the community. The community would also have the right to attend shareholder meetings and to have a minimum of one seat on the board of directors. Later legislation extended this concept to telecommunications, fishing, and mining firms; in the latter two cases establishing a compensation community which would receive a portion of the profits to be redistributed, both in shares and dividends, from the wealthier to the poorer firms' communities.

In its earlier version, the labor community was required to act collectively, both in voting on the board of directors and in holding its shares, at least until the community achieved 50 percent of the ownership and 50 percent of the seats on the board of directors. The community was conceived as a complement to and eventual substitute for the union, since it was believed that as workers gained experience in exercizing their ownership rights the union, as an instrument of the class struggle, would no longer be necessary. As we have seen, this did not occur. With government backing, communities were rapidly organized, especially in the larger firms, despite the opposition of owners. This owner resistance took a variety of forms and an increasing number of communities found themselves in a situation of conflict rather than harmony. In some cases, a struggle ensued between the owners and the union for control of the community. In other cases, when appeals to the Ministry of Industry proved fruitless, the community sponsored the creation of a union to provide it with a more effective weapon in the struggle with the owners (Pasara and Santistevan et al., 1973). Finally, in 1975 special courts were established to handle the vast number of disputes concerning labor communities.

Business opposition was fierce and persistent, centering on the threat to managerial prerogatives posed by the community rather than on the principle of profit sharing. Finally, in 1977 under the Morales Bermúdez government a new law was passed substantially modifying the previous one. The collective aspect of the community was de-emphasized. Of the 15 percent of each year's profits assigned to the community (apart from the 10 percent distributed in cash dividends), 1.5 percent was to cover community administration expenses. Of the remaining 13.5 percent at least one-third was to be distributed among the individual workers (not collectively to the community) in the form of labor shares, which were later made transferable. The 9 percent remaining could be used to buy more labor shares, bonds issued by the firm, bonds issued by the Industrial Bank (never implemented), or savings certificates to promote social programs within the firm. Besides being individually held and transferable, the labor shares were not to exceed one-third of the shares in the firm, thus preventing the workers from ever gaining a majority on the board of directors.

In the early 1970s under the Velasco government the labor community was seen as a potential means of worker mobilization and organization at the margin of the union movement, which was already controlled by the political parties. With this in view the National Industrial Communities Confederation (CONACI) was formed. However, sectors of the armed forces feared that CONACI might easily get out of hand and a combination of bureaucratic infighting within the government and factionalism within CONACI itself kept it divided and relatively ineffective (Pasara et al., 1974; Stephens, 1980: 145-168). In the case of the Mining Compensation Community (COCOMI), however, an alliance was struck with the mining unions which enabled government intervention to be kept at a minimum while the struggle between the workers and ownership was concentrated within the unions.

To what extent did the labor community serve to strengthen the working class? The community was limited to those firms with six or more workers. Even with such a low limit, this meant that the majority of firms (though not necessarily the majority of workers) were excluded from its scope. As Table 4.12 shows, by 1980 a total of 3,831 industrial communities had been organized with a membership of 308,664 workers. However, it should be pointed out that these "workers" included all salaried employees, from the general manager to the doorman. Furthermore, they represented only about 12 percent of the modern sector workforce.

Reports filed by 557 firms with the Statistics and Registry Office of the Ministry of Industry in 1976 (the most resent year for which data are available) provide a composite picture of the distribution and relative performance of labor communities. It is not surprising to find that the majority of communities (80 percent) were in Lima and that the greater part of the capital was concentrated there (61 percent). By the end of 1976 the communities owned on average 23 percent of their firms, indicating that within a further 10 to 15 years the

TABLE 4.12
Number and Membership of Industrial Communities Recognized, 1970-1980

Year	Number of Industrial Communities		Number of Members	
	Total	Percent	Total	Percent
1970	594	15.51	63,634	30.50
1971	2,348	61.29	115,425	55.32
1972	204	5.32	13,226	6.39
1973	206	5.38	3,137	1.50
1974	183	4.78	6,733	3.23
1975	164	4.28	3,370	1.62
1976	102	2.66	1,908	0.91
1977	5	0.13	338	0.16
1978	16	0.42	486	0.23
1979	7	0.18	197	0.09
1980	2	0.05	100	0.05
Total	3,831	100.00	208,664	100.00

Source: General Direction of Participation, Ministry of Industry; and
Analisis Laboral, No. 4 (June 1977).

TABLE 4.13
Formation of Social Property Enterprises by Year and Economic Sector

Economic Sector	1974	1975	1976	1977	1978	1979	Total
Consumer Goods	1	3	1	1	0	0	6
Intermediate Goods	0	3	2	3	0	0	8
Capital Goods	0	9	6	1	0	0	16
Agriculture and Forestry	0	7	8	1	0	1	17
Fishing	0	1	1	1	1	0	4
Mining	0	1	1	0	0	0	2
Construction	0	1	1	0	0	0	2
Com., Transport and Others	0	2	0	0	0	0	2
Total	1	27	20	7	1	1	57

Source: Statistics Office, National Social Property Fund.

majority would probably have reached 50 percent
ownership. It is interesting to note that in the low
priority (and presumably more profitable) firms, in terms
of the legislation granting incentives to industry, the
community had advanced further (39 percent) than in the
high priority basic industries (10 percent), largely in
the hands of the state. However, we need to note that
these figures came from a small and not necessarily
representative sample (15 percent) of the approximately
3,800 communities existing in 1976. We would expect the
larger and more profitable firms to be over represented
in this sample.

Similar problems are to be found concerning the data
for mining communities. In the first year of the law's
operation (1973), 65 communities were registered and by
1979 this number had risen to 83. Reporting to the
Ministry of Energy and Mines was so uneven and incomplete
that it was impossible to get figures comparable from
year to year concerning the number of workers involved,
though they were somewhere between 40,000 and 50,000.
According to ministry figures, the cash distribution of
profits to the miners increased from 41 million soles in
1971 to 2.3 billion soles in 1979, indicating the greater
relative profitability of mining and the greater economic
importance of the community to miners.

The available data, despite their shortcomings,
indicate that the labor comunity did represent a
respectable transfer of ownership to the workers. It
enabled them to increase their bargaining power through
the leakage of information to unions and it gave
community representatives the opportunity to
participate--in a minority position--on the board of
directors. The degree of business opposition also
suggested that the community represented a real threat to
their interests in the medium and long term. Finally, it
served to increase the level of industrial conflict and
politicize and radicalize many workers. However, these
gains in working class organization were not without
their limits. Many communities were dominated by
management or cowered into submissiveness. Coordination
between communities was weak and interest representation
at the national level ineffective. Those gains that had
been achieved were seriously undermined by the
modification of the community in early 1977. In its
current form the community is basically a form of
"people's capitalism" with a combined profit and stock
sharing mechanism designed to supplement wage earnings,
promote savings, and introduce workers to the intricacies
of the stock market. Its more lasting effects in 1980
were to be found in heightened worker consciousness and
increased union formation.

SOCIAL PROPERTY ENTERPRISES

Perhaps the potentially most far-reaching reform introduced under the Velasco government was the creation, after a long debate and on the basis of a critical analysis of previous experiences, of the social property sector. Through perhaps the most carefully designed of the reforms, it was introduced at the moment when the Velasco government reached its "radical" high point and began to decline. With an internal organizational structure not too dissimilar to that of the cooperative, the major innovative aspect of the social property enterprise was its sectoral design. All social property enterprises were to belong to a social property sector and the ownership of the firms would reside in the sector rather than in the individual worker or groups of workers. Firms would be grouped into regional units for planning or coordination purposes and these units in turn would send representatives to the sectoral assembly which, together with the National Social Property Commission (CONAPS), a government agency, would set policy for the sector as a whole. Financing for the sector would be channeled through the National Social Property Fund (FONAPS), a government financed, worker-run financial institution responsible for financing the social property firms, redistributing income between them and fomenting capital accumulation in the sector as a whole with a view to financing the creation of new firms.

This innovation was viewed with suspicion by both the state and private sectors. The latter was mollified by legal requirements making it extremely difficult to convert existing private firms into social property enterprises, and the former by giving government ministries considerable say in the initiatives for the creation of new firms and by placing the responsibility for initial financing in the hands of the Development Finance Corporation (COFIDE). COFIDE was a public enterprise in which most functionaries were known to be skeptical of the idea. After an initial debate over whether the social property sector was to be "predominant" or a national "priority," it was decided in favor of the latter. And with the replacement of Velasco by Morales Bermúdez as president in 1975, the social property sector lost much of its original dynamism and support. The crucial point came in mid-1976 when most of the remaining First Phase generals were ousted from the government and a proposal to convert a large number of state enterprises into social property firms was rejected. The jewel which was to have been the set piece defining the new "fully participatory social democracy" was left on the shelf as a somewhat embarrassing rhetorical left-over from the First Phase. Nevertheless, despite much government rhetoric, intervention, and mismanagement (and in the face of the severe economic crisis) the firms and sector survived with the help of state subsidies. With the advent of the civilian government, efforts were made to reorganize and consolidate the firms, reduce the role of government functionaries, and set up the sectoral mechanisms (finally under worker control) which would give the firms and sector a fighting chance of surviving independently.

When measured against early, exaggereated claims that the sector would displace both private and state firms and absorb cooperatives and other associate enterprise forms, the social property sector was a dismal failure. However, when measured against the amount of support received and the economic and political conditions faced, there is room for cautious optimism. Table 4.13 shows that after an early burst of activity during 1975-1976 when 47 firms were established, in the remaining three years (1977-1979) only 9 new firms were created as efforts were devoted to "consolidating" existing firms in the face of the economic crisis. The result was that at the end of 1979 there were only 57 social property firms, of which 30 were in industry, 17 in agriculture and forestry, and the rest spread among the other activities. Table 4.14 shows that these firms employed a total of 7,573 workers, of whom 31 percent were in industry and 46 percent in agriculture and forestry. The average firm employed 132 workers, with the largest firms being in commerce and transport, and a relatively small average size (77) for firms in industry. The total investment in these firms up to 1979 was the relatively small sum of $13.6 million, with a little under half going to industry. The average financing per firm was only $238,965, with the investment per worker ranging from a low $747 for intermediate goods firms to $6,231 for consumer goods. These figures indicate the low level of investment of public funds in these firms and the relatively labor-intensive nature of most of them.

Before closing this section, mention should be made of a slightly smaller group of firms administered by their workers (EATs), many of which are grouped around the Committee of Firms Administered by their Workers (CEAT) and whose exact number is unknown.[2] These are generally small firms that were forced into bankruptcy during the economic crisis or closed by their owners with a view to reopening with new, lower paid workers. Many were taken over by their workers to be administered initially by the industrial community or the union, though some were also sold to the workers. Under evolving Peruvian legislation, in case of bankruptcy the workers are given first option to buy the firm, usually with their retirement benefits, and the firms are required to eventually convert themselves into work and

TABLE 4.14
Situation of the Social Property Enterprises by Economic Sector, 1979

Economic Sector	Enterprises		Workers		Workers per Firm	Total US$ Investment	Investment per Firm	Investment per worker
	Number	Percent	Number	Percent				
Consumption Goods	6	10.6	421	5.6	70	2,617,139	436,190	6,231
Intermediate Goods	8	14.0	1,028	13.6	128	765,252	95,657	747
Capital Goods	16	28.0	876	11.5	54	2,469,329	154,320	2,858
SUBTOTAL	30	52.6	2,325	30.7	77	5,851,720	195,057	2,533
Agriculture	17	29.8	3,516	46.4	206	3,822,916	224,877	1,092
Fishing	4	7.0	353	4.7	88	1,324,055	331,014	3,762
Mining	2	3.5	120	1.6	60	132,068	66,034	1,101
Construction	2	3.5	62	0.8	31	125,929	62,964	2,031
Other[1]	2	3.5	1,197	11.5	598	2,364,329	1,182,164	1,977
TOTAL	57	100.0	7,573	100.0	132	13,621,017	238,965	1,810

Source: Centro de Estudios Superiores del Sector Social.

1 Includes transport and commerce.

production cooperatives. However, many operate as
limited liability companies owned by the workers
themselves or continue in a legal limbo administered by
their industrial communities. Most are small and under
capitalized, short on working capital, and eke out a
marginal existence owing to the fierce loyalty and
determination of their workers. (For a more complete
description of these firms, see Berenbach, 1979.)

The social property enterprises, supposedly the
ideal economic base for building a new society predicated
on work and worker power, have clearly not lived up to
their early expectations. The sectoral inter-firm
mechanisms, intended to cope with the problem of survival
and development within an unfavorable and predominantly
capitalistic economic system, have proved insufficient
without a massive commitment of funds and political
support from the government. Nevertheless, over 50 firms
and a sectoral apparatus controlled by workers do exist
and show signs of surviving. They are part of the
country's complex economic and political scene and
represent a base for worker economic and political power.

CONCLUSIONS

In this final section we will attempt to make an
assessment of the overall implications of the military
revolution for Peru's organized urban working class and
suggest the likely labor relations that will unfold in
the near future. Our discussion on this point, however,
must avoid the error of assuming that the multiple
changes in the conditions of Peruvian labor at the close
of the revolution were necessarily or directly the result
of the policies of the military. Other forces
independent of who controlled the state apparatus also
contributed to the increasing complexity of organized
labor.

As we have seen, the Velasco government either
directly (in the case of the CTRP) or indirectly (through
its rhetoric or the conflicts surrounding the labor
communities) fostered the creation and recognition of
labor unions. The Morales Bermúdez government, however,
slowed down this process considerably and, in any case,
the pattern of union creation and recognition was not so
different from that experienced during Belaúnde's
civilian government in the sixties. Similarly, we have
seen that, despite government policies during the
seventies that were in general rather unfavorable, the
cooperative movement continued to grow as it had during
the sixties, although at a slightly slower pace and with
a greater emphasis on production cooperatives.

When we consider the labor communities and social
property enterprises, however, we are on surer ground in
assigning paternity to the military revolution. The

problem is, however, that these became "unwanted children" as the armed forces' honeymoon with popular social movements ended and a remarriage with the urban industrial bourgeoisie and their foreign mentors was negotiated.

These reflections lead us to the following conclusions concerning the impact of the military revolution on the organized urban working class. First, it is important to emphasize that much of the urban working class within the formal or "white" economy was already organized before 1968. Previous tendencies toward the organization of this sector of the workforce continued during the seventies. Second, much of the military government's mobilization efforts were directed toward creating parallel organizations (such as SINAMOS and the CTRP) which it was hoped would form clientelistic relationships with government agencies and undermine existing working-class organizations (especially unions) controlled by political competitors (especially APRA and the Communist Party). These efforts were not very successful and were largely abandoned during the Second Phase led by President Morales Bermúdez. While these measures may have weakened working-class organization and unity during the early seventies, the mobilization and conflict they created, the failure to achieve the objectives set for them, and their abandonment under Morales Bermúdez created the structures and conditions for later, more autonomous organization and unity. Third, there was a small net positive impact attributable to the revolution both directly, through the creation of social property enterprises, and indirectly, through the emregence of independent worker-administered firms and production cooperatives. In comparison with the rural sector, where the agrarian reform was both earlier and more radical, and its legacy more permanent and visible, these measures appeared toward the end of the Velasco government and lost government support before they could really get off the ground. Finally, just as the agrarian reform essentially ignored the majority of the rural population to be found in peasant communities and among landless peasants, government measures aimed at mobilizing (and/or controlling) the urban working class essentially ignored the majority of this population to be found in the informal or "black" economy without stable employment: the "real" urban poor. It would thus be a wild exaggeration to claim that the military revolution succeeded in bringing about a profound transformation in Peruvian society. The political pendulum continues to swing between military and bourgeois civilian governments. Political and economic power continues to be centralized in Lima whose population is still growing at a rapid rate. The differences between rural and urban, traditional and modern sectors described by Webb

(1977) still characterize the economy; underemployment still hovers around 50 percent; and income and capital continue to accumulate in the hands of a minority of the population.

Does the reelection of the Acción Popular government and of Fernando Belaúnde as president represent a return to the status quo antes of the 1960s? We think not. In part because of, and in larger part in spite of, the military revolution the politics of the 1980s are more complicated than those of the 1960s. There are more political actors to be taken into account and their veto power has increased. Many of these new actors came from the organized working class. As we have noted, as many unions were formed and recognized in the seventies as in the whole previous history of Peru. Unionization has expanded toward white-collar workers, the number of confederations has increased from one to four, and the hegemony over the union movement has passed from the relatively conservative, APRA-controlled CTP to the more radical, Communist Party-controlled CGTP. Unions have become more politicized as the number of solidarity strikes has increased, and there have been more national strikes (with varying degrees of success) in the seventies than in all previous decades together.

All this seems to presage a greater degree of coordination between unions and an increased articulation of union demands and strategies with other popular movements, including the left-wing political parties and the two major peasant confederations. This challenge is being met by the government with a new "model" of industrial relations. The Acción Popular party has almost no direct influence within the union movement and the government seems to have discarded the option of creating government-sponsored organizations. There has also been an abandonment of the "European" approach of creating new participatory structures through legislation. Faithful to its fundamental belief in the advantages of the free market economy, the government is fostering direct negotiations at the firm level with minimum government interference within the framework of wage and price guidelines set by a national tripartite agreement between labor, capital and the government.

This is the first time this approach has been tried in Peru and although the experiences of other countries seem to suggest that agreements reached through these arrangements tend to be ephemeral, initial indications are positive. Both labor and capital have cooperated and--most important--the Minister of Labor seems to have the confidence of both parties. What is significant in this approach, however, is that it involves the implicit recognition of an important degree of unity within the labor movement and a sufficient amount of political clout to require that its views be considered on a par with

those of captial. Thus, we are witnessing the initiation
of a new stage of union organization within Peru which
could   lead   either   to   its   bureaucratization   and
domestication,   or   to   its   institutionalization   as   a
powerful force for social and political change in Peru.
Clearly, the government is hoping for the former, rather
than the latter, result.

The   cooperative   movement,   for   its   part,   was
initially ecstatic with the return to civilian politics
and had great expectations of increased government
support. These hopes seem to have faded as it has become
increasingly clear that, while some concessions and
little hostilities can be expected, private enterprise
enjoys a privileged position on the government's list of
priorities. Thus, one can expect a renewed emphasis on
consumer rather than production cooperatives, and a rate
of growth that keeps them at the margin of the national
economy.   Even   the   castrated   version of   the   labor
community left   by   the   Morales   Bermúdez   government
appeared to be too much for the Belaúnde government and
new legislation was prepared eliminating the concept of
the   "community"   altogether,   though   retaining   the
profit-sharing   arrangements   in   modified   form.   These
proposals served to revitalize the labor communities and
their leadership as they saw their very existence being
threatened. As of early 1981 it was difficult to foresee
what the precise outcome of this confrontation would be,
but the net result will surely be a further weakening of
the   labor   community   as   a   form   of   working-class
organization.

This brings us, finally, to the revolution's
step-child.   Ideologically, the social property sector
seems to have moved closer to the union movement and
further away from the cooperatives. However, Acción
Popular has sought to extend its influence among
enterprise managers and technicians, widening the breech
between the workers and their representatives in the
sector assembly, on the governing board of FONAPS and in
the national union (FENATEPS), and the managers.   It is
estimated that about one-third of the firms are in danger
of bankruptcy but, while government rhetoric implies they
will   have   to "sink   or   swim,"   it seems   that   further
financing will be forthcoming.   Legislation is being
prepared to convert "social" property into something more
akin to the "group" ownership of cooperativism and, given
the sector's weak leadership and ill-defined ideology, it
is probable that the social property enterprise will
evolve into a sort of left-wing version of the
traditional cooperative.

It seems, therefore, that the economic and political
potential of the 5,719 self-managed organizations with an
estimated five million members (INDA, 1979: 9) is more a
statistician's dream than a likely reality, given their

ideological diversity and organizational weaknesses. A greater force for organizing and mobilizing urban labor will likely be the 5,000 registered unions, especially if recent trends toward cooperation between the union confederations and unity among the left-wing political parties are maintained.

Notes

1. A good, brief account of unionism in Peru in the 1970s is contained in Angell (1980).

2. CEAT mentions figures varying between 60 and 70 firms. A survey carried out by INDA was able to get rudimentary information about approximately 30.

5
Post-Revolutionary
Agrarian Politics in Peru

Cynthia McClintock

During Fernando Belaúnde Terry's first term as president of Peru (1963-1968) agrarian problems weighed heavily among the difficulties confronting the civilian government. As a presidential candidate, Belaúnde had pledged agrarian reform; in office, however, he failed to overcome the resistence to his reform program from a coalition of opposition parties. Peasant unrest grew, and Belaúnde surrendered to landowners' pressures and authorized violent repression of the peasant movements. Amid political uncertainties and meager agricultural investment, the nation's agricultural product dipped at an average of 1.3 percent annually during 1965-1968 (Cabieses and Otero, 1977: 210). In 1968, peasants did not protest Belaúnde's overthrow.

In 1980, when Belaúnde was elected to his second presidential term, were agrarian problems still very serious ones for the government? Did peasant unrest remain as great a threat to the Belaúnde government as in the 1960s? To answer these questions, this chapter will first review the key features of rural Peru's political economy during the 1960s, then consider the nature of the agrarian reform program implemented by the military government between 1968 and 1980, and, finally, examine the policy issues facing the Belaúnde government today.

The chapter advances several arguments. I suggest that the military government's agrarian reform proved a major economic and political benefit to a significant sector of the peasantry. The peasant beneficiaries seem much less likely to undermine the Belaúnde government now than in the 1960s; they have more to lose economically, and they have been woven into the tapestry of power in Peru.[1] However, the chapter will also emphasize that, in part because of Peru's demographic problems and in part because of the dependently developing "dual" character of its rural economy, the nation's agrarian reform did not help a majority of the peasants. Moreover, the non-benefited sector of the peasantry was

the same sector which, in the 1960s, had been most
assertive in its demands.

Perhaps most important for the nation's political
economy as a whole, the agrarian reform did not spark a
major increase in agricultural production. Agrarian
reforms rarely do spark such an increase--indeed, in the
short-run decreases are often expected as a result of
economic dislocation and political uncertainties.
However, production increases were necessary because of
Peru's growing population and rising demand for food.

Thus, despite the considerable advances achieved via
the agrarian reform, rural problems still loomed large
before Belaúnde at his second inauguration. The record
of Belaúnde's first few months in office suggested that
solutions to these problems would not be forthcoming
soon, if at all. Solutions for Peru's countryside are
not easy to devise.

AGRARIAN STRUCTURE AND POLITICS BEFORE THE REVOLUTION

Land tenure was an explosive issue in Peru during
the 1960s. In various highland regions, peasant unrest
was intense. Approximately 300,000 peasants from some
350 to 400 rural communities invaded hacienda lands
between 1960 and 1965 (Handelman, 1965: 121). The land
seizures were effectively stopped by police repression,
but at the cost of an estimated 8,000 lives (Villanueva,
1969: 47; and Jaquette, 1971: 146-147).

Land was an explosive issue because it was both very
scarce and very unequally owned. Although Peru is the
third largest country in Latin America, most of its land
is desert, mountain or jungle that cannot be used
agriculturally. In 1967, available crop land per capita
was .48 hectares, only about half the amount available in
such countries as Bolivia, Chile, and Ecuador (Valdez
Angulo, 1974: 2; and World Bank, 1978). Peru's
population has been increasing rapidly--from about 11.5
million in 1965 to 16.2 million in 1977 (Wilkie, 1980:
40), further exacerbating pressures on the land.

In 1965, about half of Peru's economically active
population lived off the land (Wilkie, 1980: 40).
However, a tiny fraction of these families owned most of
the best land. Astiz (1969: 9-10) estimates that only
1.4 percent of landowners--or 3,000 people--controlled
over 62 percent of the productive land in 1961. For the
same year, Peru's Gini index of land distribution was the
most unequal among fifty-four reporting nations (Taylor
and Hudson, 1972: 267).

The nature of the large landholdings varied
considerably between Peru's major agricultural regions,
the coast and the highlands. On the coast's fertile
river valleys there emerged efficient, capital-intensive
haciendas producing such goods as sugar and cotton for

export. In the vast, arid pastures of the high Andes, the haciendas were primarily livestock enterprises, typically consolidated in the early 1900s through encroachment on the lands of indigeneous peasant communities. In most highland areas, peasant community members (called comuneros) always saw the hacienda's holdings as illegitimate, and continued to hope for the return of the lands to the peasant communities. As the haciendas expanded and peasant population increased, most peasant community members barely eked subsistence livings from tiny plots and/or small herds of sickly sheep, and often had to migrate to the coast or upper jungle regions for temporary work.

Peru's haciendas employed a small number of permanent workers--no more than 10 percent of the economically active agricultural population, in contrast to the 40 percent or so living in peasant communities.[2] Especially on the coastal haciendas, these permanent workers tended to constitute a peasant elite. The "typical" permanent workers on a coastal hacienda in the 1960s earned approximately double the income of a "typical" peasant community member.[3]

However, the hacienda worker was more controlled than his peasant community member counterpart. Landowners discouraged workers from seeking an education, from traveling to the cities, and from listening to radios (McClintock, 1981: Ch. 3). Unions were violently repressed; the extent of unionization was low relative to other Latin American nations, and most unions were rather docile ones on the prosperous cotton and sugar haciendas of the coast (McClintock, 1981: Ch. 3).

In the early 1960s, the example of the Cuban revolution and the rhetoric of the Alliance for Progress began to rekindle aspirations for agrarian reform. A number of guerrilla leaders, including Hugo Blanco, sought to mobilize the peasantry, especially in the highland Cuzco area. In 1962 and 1963, Fernando Belaúnde campaigned with unprecedented vigor in remote rural areas, invariably promising land reform. Many thoughtful middle-class professionals were attracted to Belaúnde; younger and less politically compromised than his rival Haya de la Torre, the architect seemed to offer the better hope to end what many middle class groups saw as the stranglehold of a traditional rural aristocracy on Peruvian society.[4]

As indicated previously, Belaúnde was unable to fulfill his promise of agrarian reform. In the legislature, a coalition of opposition parties worked against the enactment of a dramatic reform, and the law that emerged in 1964 was weak. Landowners could easily evade its regulations through loopholes in the law or through judicial manuevers in the implementation process. Hacienda workers, however, did not protest the failure of

the reform; they remained fearful of the hacendado, who
could always fire activist workers. But in any case the
union movement was growing somewhat, and workers'
salaries were also increasing (McClintock, 1981: Ch. 3).

In contrast to the hacienda workers, the highland
peasant community members acted boldly during the early
years of Belaúnde's first administration. Some comuneros
may have believed that Belaúnde, sympathizing with the
peasants' cause, would allow them to retain seized lands;
others may have felt disillusioned by Belaúnde's failure
to carry out agrarian reform and acted in protest. In
any case, the goal of virtually all the peasant movements
was a simple, direct one--land (Handelman, 1975:
216-245). Peru's peasants had not developed a more
radical or revolutionary vision, in the sense of an
aspiration for a socialistic transformation of Peru's
political economy, and the Belaúnde government's violent
repression of land invading peasants cowed them rather
quickly.

THE MILITARY'S AGRARIAN REFORM

In 1968, Peru's military leaders apparently espoused
various goals for the agrarian reform program (see
McClintock, 1980b). Critical of the historical role of
Peru's "oligarchy," the officers hoped to undermine the
traditional landowning aristocracy. The officers feared
future peasant agitation that could conceivably spread
from the highlands to the coast; and, form relatively
humble families themselves, they also desired a more just
agrarian order. Clearly, too, Peru's mushrooming
population required greater agricultural production, and
during the 1960s Peru's haciendas had not been performing
particularly well economically.

However, the achievement of these goals was
obstructed by the character of Peru's traditional
agrarian structure, as described above. Peru's dualistic
rural economy, characterized by a "modern,"
capital-intensive sector that occupied the best land and
produced most of the agricultural output, but employed
few Peruvians, stood alongside a "traditional,"
labor-intensive sector that held the worst lands,
produced relatively little, but employed most of the
peasants. A comprehensive reform that encompassed all
the peasantry was necessary on egalitarian principles,
but risked total disruption of the efficient,
export-oriented enterprises.

Although various government policies indicated that
the military remained concerned about the plight of
peasant community members and landless, temporary rural
workers, by and large the officers decided that their
reform program should not endanger the "modern,"
capital-intensive enterprises. The military's reform

swept away Peru's hacendados as completely as any Latin
American reform save the Cuban, but the beneficiaries of
the reform were the relatively small number of permanent
workers on the haciendas, not the more impoverished
peasant community members or landless seasonal workers.
    The discrepancies in benefits from the reform emerge
clearly from the data on the land transfer process. By
1979, land generating roughly 60 percent of Peru's
agricultural income--some 8.5 million hectares--had been
adjudicated to a minority of Peru's farm families--some
375,000 families or 20 to 25 percent of all farm
families.[5] Moreover, at most only half of these
"beneficiaries" gained dramatically. Most of the "big
winners" were the ex-hacienda workers who became members
of cooperatives, either the Agrarian Production
Cooperatives (CAPs) or Agrarian Social Interest Societies
(SAIS). Typically, the CAP was simply one reformed
ex-hacienda, a geographically integral cooperative in
which each worker became a member. In contrast, the SAIS
comprised not only at least one ex-hacienda but also the
nearby peasant communities, and a "member" of the SAIS
was each peasant comunity plus the ex-haciendas, not
individual families. CAPs were adjudicated on the coast
and in the highlands, but SAISs almost exclusively in the
highlands (as peasant communities were almost exclusively
in the highlands). Benefits to ex-hacienda workers
versus peasant communities varied from SAIS to SAIS, as
will be discussed below, but by and large the ex-hacienda
workers did better. Ministry of Agriculture data do not
separate ex-hacienda workers from peasant community
members in the SAIS, and so the exact number of
ex-hacienda beneficiaries cannot be computed. About
110,000 farm families benefited from the reform as
members of CAPs. Among the 60,954 who benefited from
SAISs, perhaps 10,000 were ex-hacienda workers (Matos Mar
and Mejia, 1980: 67).
    Even among the CAPs, gains from the reform varied
widely, in accordance with location, capital stock in the
hacienda, depletion of the enterprise capital by the
hacendado at the moment of the reform, and other factors.
Thus, for example, whereas the average value per family
of adjudicated CAP property was about 82,000 soles
(approximately $2,000) as of November 30, 1974, the value
was about 100,000 soles in the fertile coastal zones of
Chiclayo, Trujillo, and Lima where haciendas had been
well-capitalized, but only 6,312 soles in the Cuzco
region.[6] Even in the same area, discrepancies were
great. In the Puno region as of December 1973, the
average value per family for adjudicated CAP property was
about 88,000 soles across eleven CAPs. However, the
value was over 100,000 soles in three CAPs and under
50,000 soles in four.[7] The biggest winners were
families in CAP Huaycho, where the value per family was

246,187 soles. In contrast, the value for each family in CAP San José was a mere 1,136 soles (Padrón Castilla and Peace García, 1974: 47).

The discrepancy in benefits was even greater between CAP families and peasant community families, who comprised somewhat over one-third of all beneficiaries (Matos Mar and Mejía, 1980: 67). Most peasant communities "gained" only through the addition of some hacienda pasture land to their communities and the end of some feudalistic services to hacendados. The value of this land was typically small. Whereas the average value per family of adjudicated property in CAPs was noted above to have been about 82,000 soles in November 1974, the average value per family of the property adjudicated to peasant communities was merely 7,800 soles (Ministry of Agriculture, 1974: Table I).

Other peasant communities gained through membership in the SAIS. Figures on the number of peasant communities in SAISs are not available. Once again, benefits from SAIS membership varied a great deal. For example, in the central highlands near Huancayo three large SAISs were established--Cahuide, Pachacutec, and Tupac Amaru. All three were developed from a number of prosperous, well-capitalized ex-haciendas and the with-interest adjudication value of all three was similar, ranging only from 215,464,393 soles for Pachacutec to 237,416,956 soles for Cahuide (Padrón Castillo and Peace García, 1974: 47). However, whereas Pachacutec included only 9 percent communities with a total of 850 comuneros, Cahuide included 29 percent with a total of 3,249 (Caycho, 1977: 39). As each peasant community in a SAIS was to receive one share of the enterprise's profits annually, the peasants in Pachacutec would gain more from their SAIS than their counterparts in Cahuide (assuming that the enterprises continue to operate as profitably as before). Large SAISs often established "Development Divisions" for technical and social services in the peasant communities. Again, given an equal capital base, the SAIS with fewer communities could presumably help each one more. In practice, of course, the actual amount of assistance received by a community depended a great deal on the diplomacy of its leadership in the political networks of the SAIS.

These large SAISs of the central highlands were in a position to help peasant communities more than many SAISs. The adjudication value of SAIS Huancavelica, for example, was only about 10 percent that of the central highland SAISs, but it too was supposed to help ten peasant communities with 3,285 families (Padrón Castillo and Peace García, 1974: 47; and Vela, 1980). The dualities of the land transfer process were not modified by egalitarian credit, investment, or pricing policies. Although the government provided significant support for the reform sector, it favored the "modern" coastal enterprises.

In current soles, Agrarian Bank loans better than quadrupled between 1970 and 1976, to 22 million soles. In real terms, the increase would be approximately double. As inflation jumped, interest rates became negative.[8] However, the increase in credit was still considered insufficient by many analysts for various reasons. First, after 1968 private banks withdrew their credit from the cooperatives; second, cooperatives were obliged to pay the "agrarian debt" to the government;[9] and, third, the loan processs at the Agrarian Bank was slow and clumsy. Approximately 65 percent of the Agrarian Bank's short-term loans were extended to cooperatives.[10] Increasingly, Agrarian Bank loans were allocated to the cultivation of export crops such as sugar, cotton, and coffee grown primarily on larger coastal cooperatives. In 1970, 40 percent of loans were for such export crops; in 1974, about 45 percent; and, by 1978, approximately 50 percent.[11]

Government investment in agriculture increased at a real average rate of over 40 percent between the 1968-1970 biennium and the 1974-1976 biennium, and its share in total public investment rose from 6.3 percent to 15.9 percent during this period.[12] However, the major emphasis of the government's investment program was large-scale irrigation projects on the coast, such as the Chira-Piura, Majes, and Tinajones projects. Eguren (1980: 41) calculates that large-scale irrigation projects absorbed 64 percent of all government investment in agriculture during 1978 and 1979. The massive Majes project alone received over a quarter of the agriculture investment allocation in the 1978-1982 five year plan (The Andean Report, December 1980: 222). World Bank and other economists criticized the military's emphasis on large-scale irrigation projects, arguing that other programs would be more cost-effective and egalitarian.

The impact of the government's food pricing policy on different peasant groups was difficult to assess. The policy was to maintain low prices, ostensibly to check inflation and help the urban poor. From 1969 to 1974, the index of food prices rose only at the same rate as the cost of living generally (Fitzgerald, 1976: 67). After 1974, prices for agricultural goods were allowed to rise, often at a rate greater than inflation (see McClintock, 1981: Ch. 10). Yet, the price of the commodity most important to disadvantaged peasants, the potato, increased less than the price of other foods, and less than commodities more typically produced in well-capitalized enterprises, such as sugar, meat, and milk (McClintock, 1981: 358; see also Avances de Investigación, February 1979: 17).

THE POST-REFORM POLITICAL ECONOMY OF PERU

For most ex-hacienda workers who became members of cooperatives with an average or better-than-average capital endowment, the reform signified a major advance, economically and politically. Although these peasants did not represent a major threat to the Belaúnde government in the 1960s, as long as the peasants remained vulnerable to the abuses of the hacendados, a social class that insisted on its traditional social and economic privileges,[13] a revolutionary alliance between hacienda workers and peasant community members was a possibility. That possibility no longer existed after the revolution.

This conclusion is based on both data compiled by other analysts and my own data from three agrarian cooperatives that I studied from 1973 through 1980. The three enterprises are two smaller crop Agrarian Production Cooperatives in the Viru valley near Trujillo, with the pseudonyms Estrella and Marla, and one large livestock Agrarian Social Interest Society in the highlands near Huancayo, SAIS Cahuide. Cahuide is very large; my research focused on one ex-hacienda within it, which I name Monte, and three peasant communities within it which I name Varya, Patca, and Rachuis. The key criterion in site selection was the availability of pre-reform survey data. Together, the three sites are about as representative of Peru's reformed agrarian sector as of 1973 as any three sites could be (see McClintock, 1981: Ch. 4 for further information).

In the cooperatives, members' wages and quality of life improved, often dramatically. In the three cooperatives I studied, workers' wages approximately doubled in real terms between 1973 and 1980.[14] Data from other enterprises, although less comprehensive and less up-to-date, also indicate a sharp jump in wages. Fringe benefits and the overall quality of life also improved markedly in the three cooperatives studied, and by all accounts did so too on most other enterprises with similar capital endowments. "Fringe benefits" included access to small parcels in the enterprise, profit shares, and extra pay for more "specialized" jobs in the enterprise. Promotion from blue-collar to white-collar jobs with much better pay was also considerable over the decade. On visits after a year or two away from a cooperative, I would find new housing, additions to the school, special kindergartens, more children at secondary school in the provincial capital, better transportation services, and even television antennas. My 1974 sample survey also indicated a positive assessment of the cooperatives by CAP members, and a majority of CAP respondents reporting that they were "better off now than five years ago" (see McClintock, 1981: Chs. 4 and 10).

With respect to production rather than consumption on these cooperatives, the record is difficult to assess,[15] but overall the enterprise seemed to be at least as productive as before the reform. In a nationwide sample of 23 cooperatives, Horton (1974: 108-109) concludes that production increased in about half the enterprises, stayed the same in roughly 20 percent, and declined in merely 30 percent. Among the three cooperatives I studied, I believe on the basis of observation and interviews that production rose dramatically in Estrella, stayed approximately the same in Cahuide until the construction of a large irrigation canal enabled production increases in 1979 and 1980, and fell in Marla.

Although profits are not a perfect indicator of enterprise performance because members preferred wage increases to profits, they provide some insight into the economic viability of the cooperatives. However, available data are scant. For the year 1977, CEDES (1980: 13) reported that, of 611 cooperatives for which information was available, 60 percent showed a profit, and that the profits in these 60 percent were an absolutely greater sum than the losses in the other 40 percent. In the three cooperatives I studied, the profit record was mixed.[16] CAP Estrella shone, making excellent profits between 1970 and 1974; the CAP's profits for 1975 and 1976 amounted to more than its total agrarian debt (calculated without interest). SAIS Cahuide's record was erratic. The SAIS turned a profit of almost 10 million soles in 1973 and 1974 but, plagued by corruption and peasant conflict, lost an average of almost 7 million soles a year between 1975-1978. After conflicts subsided and the new irrigation canal was completed, however, Cahuide returned to the black in 1979 and 1980, showing profits of over 35 million soles each year.

Only Marla, the smallest enterprise with the least capital stock and the furthest from the main highway, performed consistently poorly. Marla's losses during the 1970s may surpass 50 million soles. Other cooperatives began under less auspicious circumstances than Marla, and for the most part these did not fare well either. For example, of fifteen cooperative enterprises studied in the remote, disadvantaged area of Andahuaylas, in the department of Apurimac, only one showed a profit for the fiscal year 1976 (Huamantinco Cisneros, 1979: 74).

Despite the fact that Peru's cooperative members owed their new advantages to a military government, they did not align themselves with this government. My sample survey research revealed that a smaller percentage of Estrella and Marla residents perceived the Velasco government as "helpful" in 1974 than in 1969, and a smaller percentage of respondents from these cooperative

(McClintock, 1980b: 22). The military government failed
to secure cooperative members' loyalty for various
reasons. One reason was the nation's economic crisis,
and the fact that cooperative members blamed the military
government for this crisis. But this perception was
widespread in Peru and was probably more important to the
alienation of poorer peasants from the government, and so
will be discussed later.

A reason especially important for the military's
failure to win political support from the cooperative
members was the threat to their new prerogatives posed by
"the progressive tendency" in the military government in
1972-1974, and the overall incoherence of agrarian
policy. Despite an image as a unified, hermetic "command
force," Velasco's government was seriously factionalized
(Peace García, 1977). In 1973, when more prosperous
cooperatives had just been consolidated, the most
progressive officers in Velasco's coalition were
prevailing, in particular in the policies and personnel
of SINAMOS, the social mobilization agency. SINAMOS
officials were concerned about the dualistic impact of
the agrarian reform and aspired to make the reform more
egalitarian by cajoling the cooperatives to admit more
temporary workers as full members, and by building new
large-scale cooperatives (centrales) to rationalize and
equalize investment and capital among them. These
initiatives enraged many cooperative members, who became
frightened that they would lose the property that they
had only just gained (McClintock, 1981: Ch. 9; and van
den Berghe and Primov, 1977: 198-200).

The "progressive tendency" also stood behind the
establishment of the National Agrarian Confederation
(CNA). The CNA was a nationwide peasant confederation
with four tiers, launched in 1974 under the primary
auspices of SINAMOS. In many respects, the CNA was to
take the place in the countryside of a Velasquista
political party, transmitting the government's analysis
of events and responding to peasant concerns in a
coherent way. Despite some initial interest in the CNA
among peasants, the confederation confronted serious
obstacles (see McClintock, 1981: Ch. 9). Disadvantaged
highland peasant communities were the dominant group in
the organization while coastal cooperative members were
increasingly disinterested in, or even opposed to, the
peasant community concerns voiced by the CNA.

During the late 1970s, the concern of cooperative
members was to consolidate their gains. These peasants
did not participate to any extent in the strikes that
many highland peasants supported during these years. (In
Estrella, the main preoccupation during the nationwide
strike of August, 1977 was what to do with the milk that
could not be transported to Trujillo and sold. The
solution was making cheese.) In the early 1970s,

cooperative members had still smoldered in resentment against the hacendados as a class, and had sought revenge indirectly by making life especially difficult for technicians--reducing their salaries and, in a great many cases, firing them. But by 1980, cooperative members seemed to have resolved their anger and held a new respect for the expertise of the technicians. A sense of group identity had emerged as the cooperative members worked out political and economic issues in the meetings of the enterprises over the course of seven or eight years, or longer (McClintock, 1981: Chs. 5 and 6).

These cooperative members believed they had seen a revolution and gotten what they wanted: the patrón was gone. They did not want further reforms that might threaten their new prerogatives. In the wake of the economic crisis, which many cooperative members attributed to the "radical" policies of the Velasco government (see below), these peasants now endorsed the principles of private enterprise. Of Estrella respondents in 1980, 74 percent thought that some division of cooperative lands, devolving them to individuals, would be a good idea (see appendix 1). The major concern of the peasants was not agrarian structure or any political issue, however, but water. Virtually the entire coast of Peru, including Estrella, was suffering from a serious drought, and needed new irrigation facilities. Seventy-two percent of Estrella respondents cited water facilities as their greatest problem in 1980.

The great majority of cooperative members were enthusiastic about the 1980 elections and favored "centrist" parties, Acción Popular or APRA, over the left. Although Estrella was strongly pro-APRA and was disappointed by the party's loss, a few weeks after the election 80 percent said the elections had been a good idea, 60 percent said the elections had been carried out "correctly," and 92 percent hoped the political parties would "work harmoniously" with each other. In the coastal provinces where well-capitalized cooperatives are numerous, the approximate vote for the leftist parties was only 24.15 percent in 1978 for the Constituent Assembly, well below the 33.88 percent national average; and 18.70 percent in 1980 for the senate, also below the 21.20 percent national average.[17]

Cooperative members are only a small percentage of the rural population, however, as the previous section indicated. Most of Peru's peasants did not gain from the military's agrarian reform, and for many living standards had fallen. In 1980, it was clear that once again Peru's disadvantaged peasants hoped Belaúnde would provide them land and prosperity, but it was not clear to what extent they were willing to commit themselves to political protest if once again Belaúnde failed to fulfill their hopes.

My assessment of the economic and political position of disadvantaged communities is based primarily upon one case, the peasant community Varya in the department of Huancavelica.[18] Varya is not one of the worst-off peasant communities in Peru. Since the 1960s it has enjoyed a secondary school, and it became a member of SAIS Cahuide, which as noted above is a well-endowed enterprise. However, as in most peasant communities, the meager potato crops and sickly sheep of Varya's families barely provided subsistence livelihoods. Varya is very remote, almost a day's journey from Huancayo, including a two-hour walk after the end of the road. SAIS Huanca contributed some funds for the construction of a road through to Varya, but in 1980 the road was still not completed. Without a road, Varya peasants remained very dependent upon exchange with unscrupulous intermediaries. The community had no portable water, no medical post, and no electricity. Varya peasants live in a region that has traditionally advanced its land demands against the haciendas aggressively; Varya is contiguous to the peasant community Huasicancha, which launched a large land invasion against the hacienda Tucle in the 1960s (Smith and Cano, 1978; and Long and Roberts, 1980).

During the 1970s, Varya's living standards certainly did not improve and may have even declined. One of the reasons was government policy: as noted above, highland agriculture had received virtually no public investment and the price of the potato had been kept low. Moreover, the economic crisis ravaging Peru during these years hurt the poor highland peasant. Although not as woven into the national economic tapestry as the urban dweller, the highland peasant did confront skyrocketing prices for transportation and petroleum-based fertilizer. Weather conditions had also been poor. Finally, although Varya was a member of SAIS Cahuide, the SAIS did not help Varya much; profit shares were low (only about $30 per family even in the profitable 1972-1973 year), and Varya's leaders did not get the community its fair share of the technical assistance available (Haldelman, 1979: 38; and Caballero, 1976) In the 1980 survey, 84 percent of Varya respondents said that, since the inauguration of the SAIS, Varya's progress had been "bad."

The stagnation of Peru's highland peasant communities bred anger, frustration, and a greater interest in the programs of the left. Peasants had become more politically active during the 1970s; many had heard about the National Agrarian Confederation and the Marxist CCP (Peruvian Peasant Confederation), and some even participated in land invasions, rallies, and conferences endorsed by these organizations. Reliable figures on membership in these organizations are not available. Handelman (1979: 3) reports that "hundreds of delegates" attended the CCP's fifth national congress in Chacón in 1979. Whereas in the early 1970s the CNA and the CCP had been divided along pro-government and anti-government lines, in 1978 the Morales Bermúdez government had become frightened by the increasingly militant stance of the CNA and officially abolished its top tier. Subsequently, the CNA and the CCP have worked more closely together, and even merged in some areas.

In 1980 illiterates voted for the first time but many peasants had qualified to vote earlier in the 1978 Constituent Assembly elections. The returns suggested that many peasants opted for leftist parties at the poles. In 1978, leftist parties won an average of 48.9 percent of the vote in eight departments where impoverished peasant communities dominate (Apurimac, Ayacucho, Cajamarca, Cuzco, Huancavelica, Junín, and Puno), versus 33.9 percent nationwide (Bernales, 1980). The percentage fell to 25.8 percent in the 1980 Senate election, but this decline stemmed partially from the fractionalization of the leftist parties. Nevertheless, a significant number of unbenefited peasants resorted to direct actions outside the electoral arena.

Many communities similar to Varya, although not Varya itself, tried to seize ex-hacienda lands during the months after Belaúnde's election. As of February 1981, of the three major SAISs of the central highlands, both Pachacutec and Tupac Amaru had been invaded, and only Cahuide had not been. Blood spilled in Cerro de Pasco, where comuneros invaded 120,000 hectares of the Central. These cooperatives aimed to turn back the invasions, but meagerly endowed cooperatives dissolved in the face of the comunero pressure. Two large SAISs, Huancavelica and Tupac Amaru II, had disintegrated by the end of 1980.

Although the peasants' desire for land was intense, it was unclear that they saw this specific grievance in any broader ideological context. In 1980, Varya peasants seemed resigned, even cynical, about the chances for far-reaching political change. Many thought that they had seen a revolution, and that it had not worked. Peasants were very critical of the performance of the leftist parties between 1978-1980, and some felt let down or even betrayed by leftist leaders. The former guerrilla leader Hugo Blanco, the political star of the left in 1978, was perceived to have spent much of his time thereafter enjoying life in Europe. Already divided into six parties in 1978, the left continued to quarrel over the next two years, presenting ten party lists at the polls in 1980. Many Varya peasants denounced the leftist leaders as "arrogant," "ambitious," "quarrelsome wranglers" and "liars" who "deceive the people." Also, although Varya had gained little from the SAIS, several Varya peasants had served as SAIS leaders. Not surprisingly, Varya respondents criticized these leaders; some peasants suggested that ambition and opportunism among political leaders was virtually inevitable. In other words, Varya's peasants had seen their community forgotten by "their own kind," and had less faith in peasants as politicians.

Perhaps most important, despite the land invasions of 1980, the land reform brought stratification changes in the countryside that should act as a check against full-scale rural warfare. To gain land, the comuneros now must fight not hacendados but other peasants, often their own kinfolk.

It is important to indicate, too, that for both ex-hacienda workers and peasant community members, the reforms of the Velasco period had been interpreted as a failure for the nation as a whole; as a process that had culminated in perhaps the worst economic crisis in Peru's history. For the peasants, the crisis coincided with a serious drought that ravaged coastal agriculture. Many peasants, perhaps most, interpreted the crisis as a vindication of conservative ideas. Despite the fact that bad luck--the failure to find as much oil as had been expected, the disappearance of the anchovy, declines in the prices of other key commodities--was a major factor in the economic crisis, Peru's peasants rarely acknowledged the luck factor. Rather, peasants felt that the crisis was the logical, inevitable culmination of the reform process. In 1979, I asked the question "Why do you think there is an economic crisis in the country?" All but one respondent blamed the military government (either because it was corrupt or had made bad decisions); not one blamed "bad luck" or "international forces such as the IMF," even though these latter two explanations were explicit alternatives mentioned. In 1980, much more frequently than in the early 1970s, peasants would say that Peru cannot "get away" with hostility toward the United States; that farms cannot do without technical expertise; that individual intitiative is the key to progress.

The overall economic legacy of the agrarian reform is difficult to assess.[19] A sound evaluation would require a rather long time span, but as time passes new variables complicate the analysis. Probably the most important new "variable" by 1980 was the three-year drought of 1978-1980. The data for the agrarian cooperatives provided previously in this section and official data for overall agricultural production suggest, however, that the agrarian reform had no dramatic impact on production, positive or negative. Table 5.1 indicates that Peru's agricultural production was slightly up in the 1970-1977 period over the 1965-1968 period. However, this record was not good enough, for various reasons. First, Peru's population

TABLE 5.1
Peru's Agricultural Product, 1960-1978

OUTPUT (In billions of soles at 1963 prices)	1960	1967	1970	1975
Export/Industrial Crops	5.6	5.0	5.0	5.4
Food Crops	3.8	5.8	6.3	5.9
Livestock	1.8	2.3	2.4	4.5
Total	12.6	13.8	13.8	15.8

ANNUAL PERCENTAGE INCREASES
(based on 1970 prices)

1965-68	1970	1971	1972	1973	1974	1975	1976	1977	1978
-1.3	7.8	3.0	0.8	2.4	2.3	1.0	3.3	0.1	-2.4

Sources: For Output, the Sectoral Planning Office of the Ministry of
Agriculture, as presented in FitzGerald (1979: 73); for Annual
Increases, figures are from Matos Mar and Mejia (1980: 90).

grew at about 3 percent annually, and food demand at over 4 percent (Fitzgerald, 1977: 71). Second, during the 1970-1975 period, food crop production did not fare as well as export, industrial crop production, or livestock production. As a result, Peru's food imports skyrocketed; whereas food accounted for about 15 percent of Peru's imports in 1972, it accounted for approximately 25 percent in 1974, only two years later.

The production shortfall was exacerbated by the 1978-1980 drought. The three-year drought was the longest and worst that Peru had suffered in seventy years. Agricultural production declined by approximately 4.7 percent in 1979 and 5.3 percent in 1980.[20] The production of rice and sugar, both of which require abundant water, was devastated; production may have declined by as much as 30 percent in 1980. For the large agro-industrial sugar cooperatives that were particularly important and lucrative, and had thus been the object of greater official attention, the drought was perhaps only one new problem among many others (such as government fraud and interventions). But for most cooperatives, in particular the rice-producing enterprises, drought was the only problem perceived as serious (see Marka, February 21, 1980: 15). [21]

THE BELAUNDE GOVERNMENT AND PERU'S AGRICULTURAL PROBLEMS

The legacy of the military's agrarian reform was mixed. For a minority of peasants, the reform brought significant economic and political gains, and these peasants became concerned primarily not with reform or revolution, but with cultivating their gardens (or, more specifically, improving their irrigation facilities). The majority of peasants had, however, gained little from the reform. Although these peasants were perhaps more ideologically skeptical of "revolution" in 1980 than in 1968, many were yet ready to try again to secure plots for their families through land invasions or a vote for the left. Political expediency and social justice seemed to require programs to benefit these peasants. Programs to increase agricultural production were also crucial.

As of early 1981, the programs of the Belaúnde government seemed unlikely to resolve the urgent agricultural problems. At a time when many agrarian cooperatives, such as Huanca, Estrella, and Marla, seemed to be gaining institutional coherence, the government's new Agricultural Promotion Law threatened the reform sector. Moreover, at a time when agricultural investment, especially for small-scale irrigation and water control projects, seemed crucial, the government failed to advance significant help along these lines.

The Belaúnde government hoped to promote private enterprise and initiative in agriculture. The new

Minister of Agriculture was Nils Ericsson Correa, a cousin of Belaúnde's wife and himself a rice producer. A graduate of the agricultural university La Molina, Ericsson had received fifty hectares of land in the Chiclayo coastal area under the agrarian reform program, and had achieved an excellent production record on his farm. In an interview with the weekly Caretas (December 2, 1980: 36-39), Ericsson criticized the agrarian reform on various scores, charging that it had "satanized" the patrón and undermined the technician, and that the cooperative system should not have been compulsory. Ericsson's beliefs were reflected in the Agricultural Promotion Law, passed in November 1980.[22] The law retained landholding maximums in the coastal and highland regions, but paved the way to the dissolution of the cooperatives and the return of private capital. Whereas agricultural land had been non-negotiable under the 1969 reform law, and could not be offered as collateral for credits, the new law allowed land to be bought, sold and mortgaged. The stated aim was to encourage private bank loans to farms, but the result may be to return cooperatives that cannot pay their debts back to private hands. Further, the law authorized the Ministry of Agriculture to "restructure" cooperative enterprises at its own discretion, unilaterally, and permitted enterprise members to restructure or parcel cooperatives if they so chose. The law also provided generous incentives for private investment in the jungle; facilities for soft loans from abroad were promised, and landholding maximums were as high as 10,000 hectares.

Not surprisingly, the new law was condemned by the two major peasant federations, the CNA and the CCP. Both federations feared the reconcentration of agricultural land in large private landholdings. Presumably, the law would also stir a great deal of organizational confusion and uncertainty in the important coastal cooperatives and in the highland SAISs. As the previous section indicated, many landless highland peasants chose not to debate the problem but to invade the land.

Government investment in agriculture did not promise to be sufficient for the need. Despite considerable rhetoric about the priority of agriculture, its share of the government budget fell from 5.40 percent in 1980 to 2.42 percent in 1981 (Resume Semanal, December 6-12, 1980: 6). Although some agricultural projects were passed to a new budget sector (Regional Development Organizations--ORDES), many analysts feared that porkbarrel politics in the regions would harm the projects.

Also, the Belaúnde government's investment and loan priorities were not the ones believed most appropriate by World Bank analysts and most agronomists. For several years, these economists have argued that large-scale irrigation projects, aiming to bring new coastal land under cultivation, are not cost-effective. They have recommended instead programs to recover already irrigated but currently saline land on the coast, and small-scale irrigation projects in the highlands (Fitzgerald, 1970: 70; and The Andean Report, December 1980: 221-224). Although various Peruvian economists were making similar arguments to Belaúnde, by early 1981 no specific program had been elaborated to reallocate funds away from Majes and the other large-scale irrigation projects.[23]

Agriculture was scheduled to receive considerable support from foreign sources in 1981 and 1982, in particular from the United States Agency for International Development (AID). AID loans and grants to Peru increased from 22.9 million dollars in 1977, to 70.7 million in 1979, and were planned to increase further in 1981 and 1982 (AID, 1980: 59; and AID, Congressional Presentation Fiscal Year 1982, Annex III: 244). However, approximately twenty to thirty percent of these funds was to be allocated for coca eradication programs in high jungle areas (AID, Congressional Presentation Fiscal Year 1982, Annex III: 241-244). Such programs were not priorities in most economists' eyes.

In early 1981, the Belaúnde government introduced new price and credit programs. The likely effect of these programs on agriculture, compared to the military's programs in these areas, was difficult to assess. State subsidies for milk, sugar, pasta, bread, rice, and other foods were sharply reduced, allowing prices for these items to rise 20 percent to 65 percent (The Andean Report February, 1981: 23). Although the hope was that these price increases would benefit the producers of these goods, commercial intermediaries play a key role in Peruvian agriculture, and they may prove to be the big winners from the new policy.

With respect to agricultural credit, the government was planning to increase the total amount of credit available, but to channel the credit primarily to the private sector, and to private sector initiatives in the upper-jungle and jungle areas in particular. The agricultural potential of these areas is, however, uncertain at best. Moreover, in January 1981 interest rates were hiked from about 30 percent to roughly 50 percent for most types of agricultural loans (The Andean Report, April 1981: 63). Although these rates were still below inflation, the sharp jump presumably made many agriculturalists uneasy.

CONCLUSION

The problems of Peruvian agriculture are difficult ones. It seems uncertain that Peru's mountains, deserts, and jungles could ever be the "breadbasket" that Peru's mushrooming population requires. The rate of increase in agricultural production lagged well behind the rate of population growth not only in the 1970s but also in the 1950s and 1960s (Carroll, 1970: 10). Land scarcity is so severe that, if all the land were to be redistributed equally among peasants, plots would be miniscule, and the possibility for higher living standards for all still distant. Well intentioned agricultural policies, such as the new price policy of the Belaúnde government, are often frustrated in implementation by the remoteness of many communities and other factors. In the highlands, the conflict between rural enterprise workers and comuneros has persisted for decades. The SAIS was perhaps the best possible effort at a compromise, but yet in many regions the conflict persisted.

However, the previous section indicated that, despite the severity of Peru's agricultural problems, the initial policies of the Belaúnde government apparently erred in various respects. The government's emphasis on private agricultural enterprise seemed a hasty u-turn, likely to create confusion in the countryside. After the catastrophic three-year drought, the need for investment in small-scale irrigation projects and for the recovery of saline lands was much clearer than ever before, and yet the government did not move quickly and aggressively ahead on these projects. Nevertheless, at least in part because of the political and economic effects of the military's agrarian reform, the Belaúnde government was given time for the development of a more effective agrarian policy.

APPENDIX 1: THE SURVEYS

I.   The 1969 and 1974 Surveys: Random surveys in all sites except Varya and Patca. See McClintock (1981: Ch 4.) for details.
II.   The 1975 Survey: Non-random surveys in Estrella (N=38), Marla (N=22) and Rachuis (N=28) for a total "N" of 88. Survey heavily male.
III. The 1977 Survey: Non-random surveys in Estrella (N=17), Marla (N=16), and Patca, Varya, and Rachuis (N=15 in each community) for a total "N" of 78. Survey heavily male.
IV.   The 1979 Survey: Non-random surveys in Monte (N=15), Estrella (N=15), Marla (N=15),and Varya (N=15) for a total "N" of 60. Survey heavily male.
V.   The 1980 Survey: Non-random surveys in Estrella (N=25), Varya (N=25), Agustin (N=30), and Pampas (N=51) for a total "N" of 131. Survey heavily male.

Notes

1. Scholars of agrarian reform have generally argued that the long-run effect of agrarian reform upon beneficiaries is stablizing, conservatizing, and to some extent even "democratizing." See especially Huntington (1968: 374-380); Tai (1974; 433-441); Powell (1971); Seligson (1980: 104-155); and Landsberger (1969: 1-61).

2. Exact figures for the different groups in Peru's rural population are difficult to calculate. See Cleaves and Scurrah (1980: 35) and McClintock (1981: Appendix 2).

3. Exact figures are not available. My calculation is frcm Webb (1974: 2-34) and OIT (1975).

4. The aristocracy was pejoratively referred to as "the oligarchy" and "the forty families." See Gilbert (1977).

5. See Matos Mar and Mejia (1980: 67) for figures on Peru's reform and McClintock (1981: Ch. 2) for percentage calculations. Percentage of families benefitted is uncertain because the Ministry of Agriculture counts family beneficiaries, not individual beneficiaries. Figure on percentage of agricultural income in the reformed sector is from OIT (1975: 7-33).

6. Calculation from data in Matos Mar and Mejia (1980: 67).

7. Calculated from data in Padron Castillo and Pease Garcia (1974: 47). Two CAPs that had fewer than 35 members were excluded from the calculation. Value figures include interest.

8. Data from Peru's Agrarian Bank. See also annual World Bank reports.

9. The "agrarian debt" was the sum to be paid by the reform beneficiaries to the hacendados via the government for their new property. The debt was officially "condoned" by Decree Law 22748 of November 1979, but debt due through that date must still be paid.

10. Data from Agrarian Bank. See also World Bank reports.

11. See Marka, Vol. 2, No. 26 (February 19, 1976: 14) for 1970 and 1974 figures; see Eguren (1980: 41) for 1978 figures.

12. Data from Rodolfo Masuda Matsura, Ministry of Agriculture, Lima, May 26, 1980. See also World Bank reports.

13. The persistence of abusive and arrogant behavior by hacendados through the 1960s is well documented. See Greaves (1968), McClintock (1981: Ch. 3), and Van den Berghe and Primov (1977: 197) for portrayals of such hacendados.

14. See McClintock (1980b: 11-12) for details. Workers' wages increased from approximately 50-60 soles a day in 1973-1974 to between 470 and 676 soles a day in 1980. The inflation rate for the period 1973 through the first quarter of 1980 was officially 275 percent; the U.S. dollar was worth about six times as much in March 1980 as in the 1969-1975 period. (Sources for these figures may be found in McClintock, 1980b: 29). Note too that over this same period administrators' salaries fell in real terms (McClintock, 1980b: 13).

15. Available Ministry of Agriculture statistics do not separate the cooperatives from other agricultural entities. Accurate pre-reform data are rarely available, especially for smaller enterprises, and sudden changes in product mixes and price levels seriously complicate analysis of the cooperatives. See also difficulties mentioned below with respect to the analysis of Peruvian agriculture as a whole.

16. Data are from the Memorial Anual and budget publications for Cahuide, and mimeographed sheets on the Balance in Estrella and Maria. See McClintock (1980b: 12) for comprehensive information.

17. My calculation for 1978 is from Bernales (1980) and for 1980 from DESCO data. Departments are Ancash, Ica, La Libertad, Lambayeque, Lima provincias, and Piura. The 1978 "leftist" parties are PCP, FNTC, ARS, UDP, PSR, and FOCEP; 1980 "leftest" parties are PRT, PAIS, FOCEP, APS, UNIR, UI, OPRP, PSP, FNTC, and UDP.

18. I am also grateful to Dr. Catherine Allen, anthropologist at George Washington University, who studied a remote community in the Cuzco area 1975-1976 and returned there in 1980, and shared her insights with me.

19. Comprehensive, accurate figure-keeping is difficult when so much production is self-consumed in remote areas, when many peasants were trying to avoid selling their products through state channels, and when cooperative enterprises were tempted to doctor their figures up in some circumstances and down in others. Also, determination of the "value" of agricultural production is unclear when prices were kept artificially low. Given all the difficulties of figure-keeping, it is not surprising that critics of the government charge that its figures are optimistic. (They have not yet, to my knowledge, specified in exactly what respects.)

20. On the severity of the drought, see Peru Agrario, Vol. 4, No. 15 (February-March, 1980): 10-11. Figure for 1979 from Agro Noticias (June 18, 1980): 5; figure for 1980 from Resumen Semanal (March 14-20): 8.

21. On the many problems of the sugar cooperatives, see Marka (February 21, 1980): 16-18; and Latin America Regional Report (February 29, 1980): 3.

22. The law is the Ley de Promoción y Desarrollo Agrario, Legislative Decree #2, published in El Peruano (November 25, 1980). The law is discussed in The Andean Report (November, 1980): 207-209; the Latin America Regional Report (December 12, 1980): 2-3; and Quehacer, No. 9 (January-February 1981), 23-28.

23. See the interview with Nils Ericsson in Caretas, No. 644 (April 13, 1981): 22-24, and The Andean Report (December 1980): 221-224.

6
Peru's "New" Military Professionalism: The Failure of the Technocratic Approach

Victor Villanueva

From the very moment of Peruvian independence, the armed forces have been intimately involved in national politics. Between the 1820s and the 1870s the military--which was little more than an incoherent group of poorly trained adventurers--dominated the executive to the total exclusion of civilian politicians. After a tumultuous period of war and social upheaval between the 1870s and the 1890s, a more or less stable civilian political order was institutionalized and the nature of military involvement in politics changed. Even so, the military remained an important political actor.

Progressively after 1914--with the gradual weakening of the civilian political order--the military emerged as a politically independent and institutionally more coherent force. It was now substantially free from its previous dependence on provincial supporters and had become somewhat more professional in the sense that its leaders were no longer the products of civil wars and political intrigues. The intervention of the armed forces in politics steadily took on the appearance of "protecting" the constitutional order or guaranteeing the "honesty" of elections. In practice, this meant protecting the political and economic prerogatives of the upper classes against the growing challenges from the popular classes. This required, however, that the military assume control of the state for protracted periods from time to time. Thus, between 1930 and 1968, civilians ruled for twenty years while the military ruled for eighteen years. This was an unmistakable measure of the increasing debility of the praetorian or elitist political order, as well as an indication of the increasing mobilization of the masses. In 1968, however, the nature of military involvement in politics underwent yet another change; this time more rapid and profound.

Translated and revised by Stephen M. Gorman. This chapter is based on an earlier paper by the author entitled "Doce años bajo la cruz y la espada."

Perhaps sensing the nearly complete bankruptcy of the prevailing system of political domination by the upper classes (in conjunction with an openly repressive military establishment), the armed forces' political intervention in 1968 dramatically departed from earlier experience. This time the generals proclaimed that their seizure of the state apparatus represented a revolution, and that power would not be relinquished until society had been completely reordered along new, more equitable lines. Many observers, most notably Alfred Stepan (1973), reacted to this new axis of military intervention in politics by attributing it to a changed outlook on the part of the officer corp, sometimes referred to as the "new professionalism" of the armed forces. However, in spite of the professed motivations and unique rhetoric of the military in 1968, the intervention still appears in retrospect to have been part of a general and prolonged pattern of military politicization in Peru. The Peruvian military has never abstained from politics. In 1968 it simply acted on the basis of changed perceptions and therefore out of seemingly different motivations, but not necessarily out of any "new" professionalism.

In what follows, we will attempt to explain why the military intervened as it did in 1968, what it sought to accomplish, and, finally, what the outcome for Peru has been. Certainly the actions of the military on the surface were new for Peru, but the underlying rationalizations were consistent with a long history of political activism. And when faced with crisis decisions, the military displayed a fundamental conservatism.

CAEM AND THE MILITARY'S PERSUIT OF POWER

The military officers who overthrew the government of Belaúnde Terry in 1968 were not the old caudillos of the past century, nor even the institutionalist officers who carried out the 1962 coup. They were revolutionaries of a new type, who did not come out of the barracks simply to "defend" the constitution or wave the old banner of electoral supervision. In 1968 the military spoke in different terms, no longer using a strictly military vocabulary but rather a universal language more appropriate to academicians than soldiers. They did not promise to restore respect for the constitution or supervise new and supposedly more honest elections. They proposed nothing less than the creation of a new society (see Velasco, 1973).

This new orientation resulted from the formative experiences of the officers who overthrew the government in 1968. Most of them had either studied at the Center of High Military Studies (CAEM) or, more commonly, served in the intelligence services of the military (Stepan,

1978: 135-136). The former had completed theoretical
studies on the Peruvian reality; studies which dealt with
the problems of the country and proposed norms for
resolving them. Those from the intelligence services,
who were more pragmatic, had penetrated the world of the
campesino and had seen, lived, and even suffered what
others had only glimpsed from a distance. This was
especially true during the period of campesino unrest and
guerrilla activity that swept the Peruvian highlands
during the mid-sixties. These two groups--the
theoreticians from CAEM and the veterans of the
counterinsurgency activities of the sixties--came
together in the coup of 1968.

CAEM was founded in 1950 and modeled after the war
colleges of North America. Its spirit gradually came to
penetrate the mentality of many of the higher ranking
officers in the armed forces (Villanueva, 1973b: Ch. 1;
and Einaudi, 1971). The logic that guided the directors
of CAEM was simple: Since the end objectives of the
institution was to produce officers to direct and
preserve the national defense, it was also necessary to
prepare these officers for intervention in the general
politics of the state where the roots to the problem of
national defense were to be found. This outlook served
as a powerful stimulus for military officers to seek
increased participation in politics through collaboration
within the highest organisms of the state. Thus, CAEM
cooperated with the technical departments of the
ministries--the offices designated as "direcciones" where
laws were formulated and debated.

The leaders of CAEM argued that with this
intervention the armed forces would be in a position to
control not only public expenditures and eliminate
misappropriations, but also everything relevant to
national development, which was viewed as basic to
national defense. Therefore, it was compelling to
intervene in the country's development to insure that
government was conducted in a harmonious fashion that
benefited the national defense, and that all individuals,
without exception, participated in one way or another.
At the very bottom of CAEM's argument was the notion that
in the event of international conflict the armed forces
would have to assume control of practically the totality
of national life--as the ultimate act of the drama--in
whose functioning the military would have neither
experience nor understanding without prior involvement.
That is to say, in the event of war the military would
have to assume responsibilities that it could not
discharge unless it had previous experience in directing
government (Philip, 1978: 42).

CAEM succeeded with these arguments in legitimizing
a new military intervention in politics, defining such
activity as the maximum expression of patriotism. This

is what in other terms has been referred to as "The New Professionalism" which in Peru, as we are trying to demonstrate here, is really as old as the army's institutional existence.

On the basis of this academic endorsement propounded by CAEM, the army began to plan openly for the necessity to invade the field of general politics of the state. To intervene in politics, therefore, was not considered a transgression, but a legitimate and patriotic act. The other armed institutions--the navy and air force--adopted this same legal opening to politics in order to make themselves part of the scheme and justify analogous behavior. That is, they adopted this position to secure the same right and legitimacy to intervene in politics that the army had created for itself.

The belief that national development was an integral part of national defense grew up slowly during the fifties and sixties. Alfred Stepan and Jorge Rodriquez (see Stepan, 1978: 130-133) have shown that only about one percent of the articles appearing in the Revista de la Escuela Superior de Guerra up to 1957 concerned themes related to what has been termed the new professionalism (e.g., internal war, national industrialization, etc.). That which was included mostly concerned road construction and colonization of the hinterland. Between 1958-1962, with the victory of the Cuban Revolution and the assumption of power by Fidel Castro (or in other words from the moment at which the communist threat became a concern in the Western hemisphere) the number of articles in the military's journal concerned with guerrilla warfare rose to 30 percent. When guerrilla activities actually broke out within Peru between 1963-1967, the preoccupation of the military with this theme caused the same journal to devote up to 50 percent of its space to such topics. A review of other military publications reveals the same trend. The "new professionalism" was assimilated theoretically by the military elite. Further along in this study we will be able to see how this concept colored the subsequent evolution of the Peruvian armed forces.

The Military in Power

Upon taking power and assuming tasks quite alien from its own professional formation, the army encountered great difficulties in overcoming the administrative and technical problems associated with a developmentalist approach to governance. Therefore, the military opted to assume control of only those positions that directly concerned decisionmaking, leaving the more technical positions in the hands of trained civilian bureaucrats. This dependency on civilian state employees was accepted as the only alternative until the military could form its own corp of experts to take on the full range of public administration functions. Nevertheless, because of the military regulation requiring most officers to rotate positions once a year, many military personnel who served a year of apprenticeship in a particular governmental post were unable to remain in their respective positions and apply their recently acquired skills. For this reason, one virtually never found military personnel experimenting in the execution of their public functions. Instead, they opted more often than not for following the advice of tradition-bound civilian advisors who came from a wide range of political ideologies, but were experts in some function of public administration. Nevertheless, this was not the desired solution. Military officers felt belittled in the presence of the knowledge of these civilians in matters of public administration. The military officer felt an obligation to master the intricacies of technocratic roles because of the enlarged responsibilities assigned to the armed forces by the teachings of CAEM.

To alleviate this situation, the high command decided to send a certain number of officers to universities and professional schools each year to develop skills comparable to those of the civilian advisors. With this objective in mind, an agreement was signed with the University of San Marcos for the formation of programs in economics, social science, and administrative science designed for military personnel. Some of the programs of study created under this agreement required as many as five years to complete, which signaled quite clearly that the military did not intend to surrender power anytime soon. In any case, the idea was to obtain scientific and intellectual autonomy for the military in the diverse fields related to governing the country, and thereby reduce the role of civilian professionals in public administration. The goal was to create professionals with a military mentality who would operate within the disciplinary and ideological parameters of the armed forces. At the same time, the document signed with San Marcos stipulated that the military would dictate certain courses to be taught in the university on national defense, which revealed the armed forces' desire to "militarize" Peruvian higher education. To some Peruvians, this appeared as merely the first step in a larger plan to militarize the entire society. "Militarization," in this context, refers to the intention of the armed forces to indoctrinate the population as a whole in the values and ethics of the armed forces to the complete exclusion of competing or incompatible norms.

Two hundred officers were originally selected to pursue courses of study at San Marcos and elsewhere

ranging from four months to five years. But the programs
did not flourish because it was difficult to recruit a
sufficient number of additional officers to fill all the
vancancies. Few younger officers were willing to
sacrifice the career they had elected for another that
seemingly offered them a less promising future. The
thinking was that more strictly military assignments
would enhance their prospects of promotion. Moreover,
there appears to have been some disagreement over the
payment of honoraria to the extra professors required by
this arrangement which the university said it could not
afford, and which the Ministry of War also did not want
to pay.
      There is little question that this initial program
was intended to be the beginning of a much broader
project aimed at implanting military values in the civil
society in order to militarize it and instill discipline,
so that once the country was "united"--which is to say
without political parties--it would be possible to
manipulate it like a military regiment. It must be
recognized, however, that if the new professionalism
could not be legitimized and implemented in the
theoretical field of the universty, it was nevertheless
pragmatically applied over the course of twelve years in
the field of governmental policy. But as is well known,
practice falls into many errors when it is not guided by
a basic theoretical framework or grounded in scientific
principles. This is what happened during the military
dictatorship; this was the principal source of the
military's failure to carry out socialist reforms in a
purely capitalist society. The military never truely
succeeded in establishing an indepedent set of
theoretical precepts to orient its transformation of
society. Thus, its policies were subject to the
contradictory values and outlooks of civilian "experts."
Perhaps the only real and persistent ethics of the
military were honor and patriotism, which indeed did
influence the military's behavior in power.

Revanchismo: The Motive of Revenge

      Although this subject may be very speculative, it
cannot be entirely ignored as one of the important
factors that motivated the armed forces to take power in
1968 and oriented their behavior thereafter. Just as
faith is the supreme law that orients the lives of
priests, for the military officer it is patriotism. Love
of God or love of country; the cult of saints or the cult
of heros: these are the principal ideological lines that
guide the Church and the military, respectively. If
heaven is the referent and the conduct of Saints is the
paradigm of the priest, for the soldier it is glory
exemplified by the conduct of heros. But heros, like

saints, don't come along every day. Above all, military heros can only be created in the process of war, and in Peru there have been no real wars for almost a century. The glory acquired on the field of battle is, therefore, almost unobtainable for the contemporary Peruvian officer, which has caused a certain frustration that the military has strived to overcome.

It is over one hundred years since the outbreak of Peru's bloody war with Chile which resulted in complete Chilean victory and the loss of Peruvian territory. The Peruvian officer, by some unknown psychological mechanism, came to consider himself dishonored by this, or more correctly was made to feel dishonored by society (beginning with the works of González Prada). This inculcated him with a desire for revenge. In the ruling class this sentiment is explained as a necessity to preoccupy the military with preparing for a war to regain lost territories, which in turn lessens the military's interest in politics (or, at least, so it was thought in the past). But the upper class was always careful not to give the military sufficient resources to undertake such a war. The military thus saw itself as impotent to reconquer lost territory, as the bourgeoisie seemingly encouraged it to do. The lost territory in question was rich in minerals whose exploitation had signaled the beginning of Chilean prosperity late in the last century. Thus, any real interest the bourgeoisie had in recapturing this lost territory was material, while the military's interest was moral and therefore more imperative.

Most Peruvian officers came to perceive two alternatives for overcoming the frustrations that arose from this irredentism. The first was to persevere in a strictly military career, seeking promotion to ever higher rank until reaching the rank of general. This personal success, however, was small compensation compared to the anxiously desired glory that only victory in war could provide. The second alternative was to become active in politics, take power, and from there direct the resources of the state (which the military felt were poorly allocated anyway) toward strengthening national defense. This would enlarge the war machine and place the armed forces in a position to recapture their dignity through war.

As was suggested earlier, the Center of High Military Studies evolved social and political courses of study, eventually creating a rudimentary theory of the necessity for the army to intervene in the politics of the state. In this fashion, political activity by officers was re-legitimized in military circles, and although it remained just as illegal as before it came to represent a patriotic obligation. When the armed forces took power in 1968, one of the first objectives they pursued (although naturally not stating so openly) was to increase military enlistment, training, and technical sophistication. The military also began to acquire modern armaments beyond the levels possessed by Chile.

Given the high cost of modern armaments such as sophisticated supersonic aircraft and computerized air defense systems with surface-to-air missiles, it was understood that it would not be possible to significantly strenghen national defense over the short-run by relying on national resources alone. It was therefore decided to borrow heavily abroad, which eventually imposed severe sacrifices on other important sectors like industrial development, housing, education, etc. Since the United States government refused to sell sophisticated weapons systems to Peru, the military turned to other markets like France and the communist bloc whose armaments were more expensive, but were much more easy to obtain. The Soviet Union, in particular, became an important source of arms and related technology over time. Peruvian dependency on Soviet arms was encouraged when Moscow extended easy credit with low interest rates and lengthy grace periods to the military regime. The army and air force took full advantage of this credit to acquire some of the most modern equipment that existed in South America. Indeed, the Peruvian air force became perhaps the most powerful on the continent, according to some evaluations, including those of Argentina and Brazil (for a comparison see Gorman, 1978a: 52-53). The navy, for its part, rejected Soviet credits for ideological reasons, turning instead to England and Italy, inter alia, for its air and sea material.

Technical training improved in the armed forces as a consequence of the modernization program, while an ideology of revanchismo was interjected even more than before into the training of officers and recruits. The officer corp had been educated in revanchismo since the early 1950s, but after 1968 this sentiment was stimulated even further with the steady acquisition of weapons that suggested the actual possibility of winning a victory over Chile in an armed conflict. At one point in 1974 it was determined that the correlation of forces between Peru and Chile favored Peru, with the exception of naval power where the two countries were at parity. It has also been rumored that during the same year the Peruvian military actually considered initiating hostilities against Chile, but that the navy succeeded in obtaining a delay until the delivery of new vessels which were under construction in Germany and Italy. But when Morales Bermúdez assumed power in mid-1975 additional weapons orders were placed with the Soviet Union and a new and accelerated round of arms buildup began.

After the first year of the Morales Bermúdez government, the prospects for a Peruvian assault on Chile had diminished for several reasons. Most importantly, the military regime in Chile had overcome some of the international isolation which had followed the violent overthrow of Allende, and Peru found itself increasingly preoccupied with domestic economic and political difficulties. Although the Morales Bermúdez regime began seeking more cordial relations with Chile, tensions remained high between the two countries. But when an extensive Chilean spy network directed against top secret Peruvian air and naval installations was uncovered in 1978, the reaction was relatively mild. One Peruvian soldier was executed and a number of individuals connected with the Chilean Embassy were expelled from the country.

Even as the military acquired the material necessary to strengthen the national defense, the real power of the Peruvian armed forces became threatened on two fronts. First, the popularity of the military plummeted and the country exhibited debilitating political cleavages. Second, the morale of the upper echelon of the military declined as corruption became widespread.

Under Morales Bermúdez, the economic crisis that had set in with Velasco in 1974 deepened--having been accelerated in large part by increased spending for defense, the construction of large and extravagant government buildings, and the corresponding escallation of the external debt that these and other expenditures stimulated. With inflation and the resulting devaluation of the sol, the price of basic commodities rose dramatically and repeated protests broke out among the working class and urban poor. Since the devaluations of the sol ordered by the IMF in the late 1970s were periodic, so too were the strikes which were called in protest against the effects of the devaluations. Such strikes were intended to obtain wage increases which would keep salaries more or less in line with prices, but where increases were granted they lagged far behind the real rise in the cost of living. Understandably, strikes became more frequent and militant, and the military was forced to respond with ever greater force--placing Lima under what at times appeared to be a state of military occupation.

The labor disturbances eventually culminated in three nation-wide general strikes, one of which lasted three days and semi-paralyzed the country. The military regime lost political ground to the unions since it had already lacked popularity to begin with. This moral crisis increased with the revelation of corruption among high government functionaries; generals and ministers were accused publically of committing various political and common crimes, the most usual being involvement in contraband which had reached enormous dimensions by the late seventies. None of the accused was ever legally prosecuted. Even when an air force general was caught in the act of transporting cocaine abroad, the government contented itself with merely forcing him into retirement. Ministers of state caught participating in contraband were simply removed from their posts, with no effort whatsoever to bring the offenders to trial. The pervasiveness of corruption fundamentally injured the pride of the armed forces, and weakened the military so much that no other escape was seen than to surrender power to civilians at the earliest possible opportunity.

THE OPENING TO DEMOCRACY

By 1977 the economic crisis of the country had produced a moral and institutional crisis within the military. Corruption was pervasive in the barracks and the honesty of even the highest military chiefs was questioned by the people, whose skepticism was expressed in the left-wing press. Under the avalanche of embezzlement, fraud, contraband and other crimes, President Morales Bermúdez took refuge in a curious mysticism, adopting the cross as the "guide and symbol of the Peruvian Revolution," and calling on the people to pray for Jesus to "illuminate the way to govern better." All of his public discourses during this period ended with a similar invocation to the almighty. Finally, Cardinal Landazuri felt compelled to ask the president in the name of the Peruvian Episcopacy to leave Jesus in peace and not involve him in the government's political problems. The public invocations quickly ended.

Deprived of the popular support which he had failed to mobilize, lacking the more charismatic style of Velasco, and with his backing within the armed forces based solely on patronage (and therefore unstable and unreliable), Morales Bermúdez found himself in a difficult political position. In spite of his efforts, the president had been rejected by all the social classes, including the bourgeoisie which had not been granted everything it demanded and the petty bourgeoisie which began to feel the effects of the deepening economic crisis. Finally, Morales Bermúdez was confronted with serious divisions within the armed forces and growing anarchy as discipline in the ranks deteriorated. It seems clear that the president concluded that there was no other alternative than for the military to relinquish power in order to save itself as a viable institution. It was decided that power would have to be transferred as soon as possible, but that the military's withdrawal from formal authority would have to be orderly and well structured in order to protect the military from any future recriminations for its conduct during the docenio.

The Military and APRA

It was determined to hold elections for a Constituent Assembly which would formulate a new constitution. Once the new document was promulgated, general elections would take place to select a president and the members of the parliament, who would then assume power in 1980. The schedule for the transfer of power proposed by the military and accepted by virtually the entire population and a good part of the political parties unfolded in a climate of repression and suspension of legal guarantees. The government made use of a State of Emergency to impose periodic curfews and press closures (especially of independent left-wing publications). While all this was taking place, an agreement was negotiated between the military government and Haya de la Torre's Aprista party to smooth the transfer of power to civilians. The pact signed by Haya de la Torre with Morales Bermúdez provided, inter alia, that the military would assist APRA in winning the general elections in return for APRA's coorperation in restraining the political pressure that was mounting against the military rulers. Haya de la Torre at first denied that any accord had been reached between APRA and the military, but later admitted the existence of a pact (to the embarrassment of other party leaders) while traveling abroad.

The pact had many ups and downs because of the opposition of some Aprista followers and the pragmatic interpretations applied to it by both sides from the outset. The Apristas were naturally pleased to find themselves close to gaining power after nearly half a century of frustration, but it was an embarrassed pleasure since the pact was not considered an honorable accord, but rather a clandestine and elitist arrangement. The pact signaled that the military had finally overcome its long-standing institutional antipathy for the Aprista party. The new officers did not belong to the generation that had suffered the Aprista rebellion in Trujillo in 1932. By 1977 the military was composed of officers who saw in APRA an ideologically farsighted organization, with analogous ideas to the military--the rejection of communism in particular--and an admirable mystique that created devotion among the party's followers. Morales Bermúdez had tried in vain to create a similar mysticism within the army. Most military officers also admired APRA's widespread reputation for iron discipline, its authoritarianism, its cult of hierarchy, and its vertical organizational structure.

The scheduling of elections for the Constituent Assembly for 1978 ignited enthusiasm among the parties of the right, who's leaders believed that the military would insure their victory at the polls. The leaders of the

revolutionary left, in contrast, were loath to concede
the importance of an assembly in which their
representation would likely be kept to a minimum. Under
the best of circumstances, the left hoped that the
assembly would convert itself into a democratic enclave
within an otherwise thoroughly totalitarian country. But
even if that were possible, it would not really promote
liberty. President Morales Bermúdez moved quickly to set
the parameters for the new assembly, stating that it
would convene for the specific purpose of writing a new
constitution. If it attempted to arrogate to itself
other functions, "the government would dissolve the body
and terminate its history." The president also added
that the military was willing to turn over the government
to civilians, but it would continue to hold the real
power in its own hands. This was an unfortunate
statement since it revealed the entire reality of the
military's surrender of "formal" power.

As if to show that the Second Phase of the
revolution had nothing to envy of the First Phase, only
fifteen days before the election for the Constituent
Assembly the government rounded up and deported a large
number of politicians, labor leaders, repoters and
left-leaning retired military officers. They were placed
on an airplane and flown to Jujuy in Argentina where they
were held under the custody of the commander of the local
infantry batallion (without any intervention by
immigration authorities). They were turned over to the
Argentines without passports or other personal papers,
and were not released until after the voting ended in
Peru. This notwithstanding, various members of the group
were elected to the Constituent Assembly to the chagrin
of the Morales Bermúdez regime.

The assembly was installed under the presidency of
Haya de la Torre who arrogantly declared that the body
represented the supreme power of the state and,
therefore, no one could restrict the themes with which it
concerned itself. He also declared that the assembly
would never recognize any power above it. Nevertheless,
soon afterward the assembly had to bite the bridle and
meekly submit to the military government's ability to
dictate the body's sphere of competence. By decree, the
government made important changes in the Code of Military
Justice which provided for trial by military court for
all soldiers <u>and civilians</u> charged with the offense of
"ultraje" (slander) against the military or police.
Although there were demands from certain members of the
Constituent Assembly for a review of the government's
action on this matter, the assembly's leadership refused
to address the question because it was outside that
body's jurisdiction. As such, the decree was certified
as legal by the Aprista leaders in the assembly, since
the assembly did not in their opinion have the authority

to contravene the government's decree. Thereafter, there were no further delusions about the real power of the Constituent Assembly.

While the assembly worked on a new constitution, Morales Bermúdez concentrated on dismantling most of the remaining reforms and programs left over from the Velasco period, and returning many state industries to private hands. The Apristas, for their part, worked asiduously to contain the political reactions of the population to the counter-revolutionary policies of Morales Bermúdez.

The Transfer of Power

The twelve years during which the military enjoyed absolute power were characterized by poor management of public funds, misappropriations, unnecessary and expensive acquisitions, and construction of public buildings without competitive bidding. Nepotism was pervasive in both phases of the revolution and corruption (which had always been common in earlier governments) reached new and unprecedented levels. Generals in both military and political posts dedicated themselves completely to various businesses, from the most filthy and reprehensible such as drug trafficking, to smuggling contraband or the submission of false expense accounts to cover personal expenditures. Military planes and vessels were routinely sent abroad to return full of merchandise on which no duty was ever paid. The wives of many high ranking officers had veritable department stores in their homes where they sold almost everything imaginable without the least precaution or shame. Everyday new luxury hotels, exclusive bars, and expensive restaurants opened in Lima where a huge amount of money exchanged hands--money that came from various illegal activities. Meanwhile, the country suffered severe economic recession so that surrounding this insolent luxury walked an infamished people, without work or working only occasionally or part-time in the best of situations. With long lines in front of hospitals that had no more room for the sick, long lines of job seekers in front of factories with no more jobs to fill, and long lines of women in front of prisons looking for a missing son or husband, the population began to lose its morale. But at the same time the masses became increasingly susceptible to political mobilization against the military government. The impoverished masses, whose condition grew worse by the day and who suffered most severely and directly from the collapse of the economy, became politically activated between 1976-1979. Either in demanding better wages or fighting against the police in the streets or seized factories, the people underwent an education and training in struggle which increased their revolutionary potential. They no longer ran when the

Civil Guard was turned out, preferring instead to hold
their ground and fight back with stones, molotov
cocktails, and other rudimentary weapons. The people
demonstrated great solidarity in these protests and
stikes. During the national protest strikes, Lima was
converted into one huge restaurant when kitchens were set
up on practically every corner to feed the strikers; a
development that revealed an increasing capacity for
popular organization.

The commanders of the armed forces paid considerable
attention to these events, and the intelligence services
kept close watch on developments. They came to the
conclusion that the human and even class solidarity that
were being forged by the national strikes—coupled with
the aggressive behavior of the police—were creating a
typically pre-revolutionary training period for the
masses. It was concluded that popular armed action could
easily breakout at any moment. From this it followed in
the analysis of the intelligence services that the
military should retire from power as soon as possible.
But in such circumstances the surrender of power, the
abdication of the responsibility to govern, could also be
very dangerous in the judgement of the generals. The
Aprista party, which had been designated to take over the
government, was beginning to show unmistakable signs of
misconduct and the existence of more or less serious
structural defects that had been obscured by the previous
secrecy that had always surrounded the party's
activities. (The secretiveness of APRA had been acquired
during extended periods of persecution and clandestine
existence in the past.) The single most important
development was the death of Haya de la Torre in 1979 who
was to stand as his party's presidential candidate.
Initially, the military had seen in APRA the perfect
ideology and organizational structure to take over the
state. After Haya's death, APRA did everything it could
to abide by the agreement that had been made by Haya with
Morales Bermúdez. Never was a critical word spoken
against Morales Bermúdez, and APRA was not afraid to face
the censure of the left and come out in defense of the
dictatorship every time it was necessary. Through the
CTP, which is APRA's instrument for manipulating the
working class, the party obstructed protests and strikes
during the last three years of the military government.
APRA worked against the marches and other manisfestations
called to defend workers' rights, blocked the campaign to
gain the reinstatement of teachers who had been fired
from their positions for political reasons, provided
individuals to break a teachers' strike and, in short,
did whatever was in the party's power to avoid provoking
the anger of President Morales Bermúdez. Nor did APRA
criticize other members of the military, since they too
were viewed as friends and allies.

Nevertheless, the electoral advantages that APRA thought it was gaining through its adhesion to the military were lost in the actual election campaign for the presidency and parliament. Although APRA enjoyed the unrestricted support of the political authorities and police (that is, the support of the repressive forces who looked the other way whenever an Aprista committed an offense), as well as the blind and unquestioning support of the state-controlled mass media throughout the early campaign, the party lost the election. This was partly the consequence of the aggressive and bullying attitudes of the Aprista shock troops officially called "disciplinarians", but more often referred to by the people as "buffalos." The behavior of these groups, together with the conduct of the police, awakened old resentments from the period between 1945-1946 when the buffalos had more authority in some areas of Peru than the police. It recalled the crimes committed by Aprista terrorists to punish supposed traitors or avenge imaginary offenses. The people remembered all of this and foresaw what would occur if APRA returned to power.

After APRA's defeat, all the internal rivalries and power contests within the party were awakened and its carefully maintained image of unity was shattered. A party incapable of maintaining order and unity within its own ranks would have been much less capable of implanting these qualities in the entire country where there existed much larger contradictions. APRA's internecine conflicts, on the other hand, pointed to the party's ideological debility which translated into incoherent action. That is to say, APRA was incapable of putting a barrier around communism which continued to make advances in Peru. As if this were not enough, during the campaign the government intelligence services began to detect a slippage in attendance at Aprista rallies as many older party members began to feel deceived by their party leaders, while others turned to more stable political tendencies. Clearly, APRA's ideological thrust proved less dynamic, and its organizational structure less viable, than the military had anticipated. Toward the end of the campaign, the generals began to look about for another promising political party to back.

The situation subsequently changed so much that just a few days before the election Aprista leaders were forced to complain about the new treatment they were receiving from state entities, especially the press and TV which were accused of ignoring APRA campaign events in order to concentrate exclusively on what Acción Popular (AP) was or was not doing. The protests were well founded. The government had changed its position in favor of former president Belaúnde Terry's Acción Popular party, and was now withholding help from APRA. The party of Belaúnde Terry, which the military had thrown out of power twelve years before, was showing greater unity and sterness than APRA, although it had an equally vague ideology without clear principles other than anti-communism (which proved to be the common denominator between it and the military). All of the means of mass communication under the control of the state were turned in favor of the AP candidate. The fear of APRA that existed among the people did the rest, and Belaunde Terry's party swept the election by a landslide. Naturally, the decision to switch support had not been taken exclusively by national elements. The interests of powerful economic groups from North America, Europe, and perhaps even Japan (which had come to play an important role in international finance) were not absent from such a decision. But the interests of foreign groups were not entirely unified. For example, after the death of its leader, APRA took refuge in the shadow of the social democratic ideology first of Venezuela and, eventually, West Germany. In turn, the Bonn government helped finance the Aprista electoral campaign (which spent more than any other party and used modern public relations techniques and consultants). The government of the United States did not view this incursion by a major industrial competitor into its own sphere of influence with very much welcome.

Acción Popular, in contrast, had been mortgaged for some time to the United States, and Manual Ulloa (who was a minister in the first Belaúnde government) was a close associate of the Rockefeller group (Marka, Oct. 9, 1980: 28-29). Ulloa, who became Prime Minister in Belaúnde's new government, had always given considerable effort to keeping the party's channels of communication with the United States in good order. Beyond the commercial and financial factors that recommended Belaúnde and his top aides to the United States, there was also an aura of "representative democracy" surrounding Acción Popular without any of the overtones of neofascism or shades of socialism that applied to APRA. Apristas were social democrats by necessity, fascists by predilection and veritable nazis in their hearts. There was still one further element that caused the United States to favor AP over APRA. After the death of Haya de la Torre the political strength of the marxist-leninist forces began to increase. The left had already gained a respectable showing in the election for the Constituent Assembly before Haya's death, and this glimmering of its potential future strength led APRA's new leadership to take notice of what it decided to term the "responsible left." In short, a powerful faction within the APRA hierarchy began to consider the prospects for courting leftist voters. One of APRA's party secretaries, Hugo Otero, even visited the Soviet Union for several months for unspecified reasons. This mild flirtation with marxist-leninist propaganda (while not changing the true nature of APRA) made the party considerably less attractive to US interests.

The Protection of Military Interests

The military had decided to return to the barracks because there was little other choice, but the generals were still concerned with insuring that the twelve years of "sacrifice" would not pass for nothing. They were willing to surrender the exercise of _formal_ power which had cost them their institutional prestige, but they still had to do something positive to begin rebuilding their prestige, although it was understood that this would be a slow and difficult process. They were afraid of abandoning all the efforts effected to discipline an anarchical society, begin to build an industrial infrastructure, and acquire the arms necessary to defend the country in a conflict which the generals believed would not be long in coming. It was deemed essential to insure that all the work of the previous twelve years was not pushed aside by a new civilian government, whether it was progressive or conservative. Such was the outlook of the military at the beginning of 1980. The generals feared that once they dismounted the state apparatus constructed so painstakingly, their ideology of respect for the armed forces, would be displaced by another directed against the military. And they feared, finally, that military expenditures, including pay, might be cut to provide more resources for other sectors accorded greater priority by civilian politicians.

By 1980 perhaps as much as eighty percent of Peruvian military strength was based on Soviet equipment (see ACDA, 1979: 158), a fact which particularly unsettled Washington. Over the course of the Peruvian revolution the United States had watched almost helplessly as one of its former clients broke a military dependency that had lasted more than thirty years. But the Soviet arms produced a new dependency since they were so different from the weapons of other countries that replacement parts and munitions were only available from the USSR. This reality made Peru's new military dependency on the Soviet Union especially strict. The same applied to related technology for these weapons. To remain under this dependency was the only alternative for the Peruvian army and air force. The United States government attempted to convince the Peruvian government of the necessity for changing arms suppliers and returning to Peru's previous sources. But the problem was much more grave than it appeared. Aside from the cost that would be encountered in replacing an arsenal that was among the largest on the continent, it was also necessary to take into consideration the time needed to effect such a replacement program. Given the cultural level of the Peruvian population, the learning capacities of recruits would make the mastering of different techniques associated with new weapons systems protracted. The time needed to complete the retraining process would place in doubt the confidence levels of Peruvian soldiers in the use of military hardware. Tactical procedures would also have to be changed at every military level, which would require still more time and effort. In short, a transition from Soviet to Western armaments would cause chaos within the armed forces and weaken the country's defenses. And if this were not enough, the military knew that the United States would still not sell Peru the type or quantity of arms which the military desired and considered necessary.

All of these considerations brought the military to the conclusions that it could not afford to give the new government a free hand in military questions. The surrender of the Presidential Palace would have to be purely formal, and nothing more. The army would have to remain present in the councils of political decisionmaking as counselors, advisors or whatever they wanted to call themselves, but with the ability to oversee laws and programs which touched however remotely on national defense. Furthermore, the armed forces wanted to secure explicit and exclusive authority over all strictly military questions. A particular preoccupation of the military was that if the Peruvian armed forces were forced to return to their earlier dependecncy on United States' arms, they would be limited to the same levels and quality as other Latin American countries, especially Chile. Thus, the armed forces would be deprived of any material advantage, which is to say they would be left without any possibility of fulfilling the ancient desire of revenge. These and other diverse considerations caused the military to look for a way to avoid being effectively removed from power. It was essential to remain part of, or close to, the centers of decisionmaking, but in a legal manner that would not provoke suspicion, press attacks, or denunciations from anti-military factions. After much deliberation, the armed forces finally arrived at an apparent solution shortly before the actual transfer of power took place. In the following section, we will examine the legal device through which the military attempted to preserve most of its power in tact after the surrender of government.

THE MOBILIZATION LAW

Most countries of the world that need, or believe they need, armed forces for their national defense create legislation to strengthen the military in the event of war. Such laws govern the conversion of private citizens into soldiers, the mobilization of troops, the requisitioning of public communication services by the armed forces, and practically any other measures that may be needed to prevail in armed conflict. Such legislation is generally called a mobilization law, or something similar, and is usually supposed to enter into force sometime prior to the legal declaration of a state of war.

Peru also had legislation on the books appropriate for such occasions, intended to mobilize human, industrial, and agricultural resources for national defense. Nevertheless, the law was never activated, not even when hostilities occurred with Colombia in 1932 and Ecuador in 1941. There was additional recruitment of troops and stockpiling of resorces during both of those confrontations, but these were accomplished by less drastic means than those authorized by the mobilization statute of the period. Of course, there was never a declaration of war in either conflict, only a de facto state of belligerency. Thus, the provisions of the law calling for a change in authority favoring the military were not invoked since they were intended only for a time of declared war. But the military leaders in power at the close of the docenio were not satisfied with the existing legislation, and imposed a new law of mobilization with far reaching political implications.

The generals believed they had found the answer to their problems in the new Mobilization Law, which would be their means for preserving sufficient authority in time of peace to remain at the forefront of the management of the state. This "solution" consisted completely in giving legal or juridical formulation to the reality of continued military involvement in politics in order not to scare the "pisanos," and allow them to cling to the illusion that they, the citizens, actually ruled. The military put together a committee of social scientists and legal experts to draft an appropriate decree. These individuals burned the midnight oil for weeks to come up with a law which they thought accomplished the purposes of the generals; a device that would win the battle againt true and independent civilian rule. And indeed it appeared by early 1981 that they would win if the political opposition did not begin to fight with every means at its disposal to overturn, or at least modify, the law. There was little indication that the government of Belaunde Terry was willing or prepared to lead the people in this undertaking. Belaúnde's Acción Popular party, which together with its Popular Christian party (PPC) ally dominated the parliament, had already entered into an agreement with the armed forces before the elections. APRA had also promised to refrain from challenges to the military's authority. Thus, the leading parties were obligated not to deal with the theme of the Mobilization Law, as if it were not a matter of national importance but only of concern to the military. Indeed, Belaunde and his ministers consistently shyed away from any conflict whatsoever with the military during the first year in power.

The Mobilization Law has an obscure and symptomatically conspiratorial origin. The Mobilization Law, after what was probably a long period of study, was not decreed until July 9th, just nineteen days before the surrender of power to Belaúnde. It was not published in El Peruano (which has a limited circulation within legal/administrative circles) until several days later. In other words, the law was publicized only after it was too late for any effective citizen reaction. When the new government assumed power without rejecting this law, or even discussing it, the complicity of the parliament dominated by AP and the PPC seemed to have been confirmed.

This unique law did not limit itself to mobilization only in cases of war, but also in cases of "internal subversion" and "disasters," with the clarification that under the latter heading were included certain acts of men such as industrial sabotage, arson, or manifestations which might have a political end. Here lies, it would seem, the true motivation behind the law, which points to the real purpose for its existence. We will not concern ourselves with the law in all its finer details since it is far too complex to be fully analyzed here.

Turning to just a few of the particulars of the law, we will attempt to briefly outline its most important provisions. Once declared in force by the president, the law provides that mobilization becomes the responsibility of a National Defense Council composed of the Ministers of the Interior, Foreign Relations, and Economy, the Director General of Planning, and the General Staff. This means there would be four civilians and four military officers (the chairman of the general staff and the commanders of the three services) on the committee, who would be presided over by the president. By this arrangement, neither the civilians nor the military could make up a majority, and the president would be responsible for breaking tie votes. The National Defense Council's primary responsibility would entail approving plans and actions formulated by the military to deal with the particular crisis at hand. To the extent that the president of the republic would be to some extent involved in reviewing those plans before they were brought to the National Defense Council, he could be expected to vote with the military to insure their passage. Once the mobilization were decreed, and the corresponding plans elaborated by the military were approved by the Defense Council, all Pruvians and foreigners living in the country (with the exception of certain groups such as diplomatic personnel), and all property (again with some minor restrictions) would come under the provisions of the law even before the oubreak of any hostilities.

To promote mobilization, the law would also authorize the military to expropriate, intervene in, or requisition companies and services, labor and materials, and anything else necessary for securing the national defense. And requisitions could be made in time of peace by the Joint Command, by other lesser officers and, in necessary cases, by the ranking military authority present. The latter could be an officer with little or no education and without the consequent competence to adopt such measures. If, for example, a transportation strike were called in a city, a captain in charge of military conscription for that district could decree the requisitioning of all transpotation services and the workers necessary to man them. The effects of the strike would be nullified, the rights of the workers ignored, and the status of the union reduced. And the gravest aspect of the law is that all the authority for directing such measures would be placed in the hands of the military which could act against the civilian community in times of peace.

The law makes it possible for certain groups who might possibly favor military intervention to provide justifications for the implementation of the mobilization statute by provoking "disasters." The military could then place all or part of the country under its rule. The military would then have all the power needed to carry out requisitions, labor mobilizations, the calling up of reserves, etc. And the entire civilian population would come under the jurisdiction of military law which provides penalties as harsh as twenty years in prison for cases of "unfaithfulness" (infedencia); an offense that is not even legally defined.

One of the particulars of the law is that the military would be present in all the various councils that would have authority to execute and supervise the Mobilization Law. These include 1) the National Defense Council, 2) the Secretariate of National Defense, 3) the Joint Command of the Armed Forces, 4) the National Intelligence Service, 5) the Interministerial Committee, and 6) the Public Ministry and Organism. Only the first and the last councils would contain some civilian members. The others would remain exclusively in military hands.

As if this decree law were not enough to ease the surrender of power, the armed forces dictated another law that required that officials who belonged to the former military government, even if they no longer worked for the state, could only be accused of offenses before the

Supreme Court.   This protection previously   applied only
to ministers of state.

CONCLUSIONS

The   failures   of   the   Peruvian   revolution were   at
least partly the result of the   nature of the military as
an   institution.   The generals   enjoyed   absolute   power
after   1968 yet   could not   successfully implement   their
developmental   model   or   corporatist   objectives.   The
military in power   proved to be less   rationalistic, less
cohesive,   less   moral,   and   less   efficient   than
anticipated.   The   strains   of   governing   led   to
factionalism,   most   major   policies   suffered   from
inconsistencies and contradictions, and the opportunities
for personal gain in   high offices encouraged wide-spread
corruption.   As political and   economic problems began to
mount after 1975, the military rulers relied increasingly
on authoritarian measures to manage   crises.   In the end,
the military proved to have been no less political in its
appraoch   to   problem   solving   and   decisionmaking   than
civilian   governments   before   it.   And   its   former
self-confidence   and   political   progressivism   have   been
replaced by public stigma and political conservatism.   In
the   immediate post-revolutionary   setting,   the   military
has   concentrated   mostly   on   maintaining   the   new   and
expensive weapons systems it acquired during the docenio,
and establishing   procedures to   guarantee its   virtually
unlimited   authority   to   maintain domestic   order   in   the
event   of   "emergencies" or   "disasters."   The   Belaúnde
government   has   granted   the   military   nearly   complete
autonomy in its   own affairs and has   effectively blocked
efforts   by leftists   in the   legislature to   investigate
past   or   present   military   actions.   The   armed   forces
appear content for the time being   to focus on their more
strictly   military   functions,   while   exercising what   is
probably decisive influence   behind   the   scenes on   all
matters   of   national   security   and   domestic   order.
Nevertheless,   strong   interventionist   tendencies   among
officers remain present just below the surface.

7
Challenges to Peruvian Foreign Policy

Stephen M. Gorman
Ronald Bruce St John

Fernando Belaúnde Terry was ousted as president of Peru in 1968 in part because of his administration's weak foreign policies, which did not satisfy nationalistic expectations. He was returned to the presidency on July 28, 1980, the 159th anniversary of Peruvian independence. Events during the intervening twelve years of military rule had an important bearing on the foreign policy options available to the new civilian government after July 1980. During its first year, the second Belaúnde administration proved unable to escape the consequences of the foreign policies pursued during the docenio, although the new president did seek policy redirection and reemphasis in important areas. Moreover, like the revolutionary regimes which his administrations bracketed, President Belaúnde found that the success of much of his domestic policy depended in large measure on the shape and direction of his foreign policy.

This chapter focuses on three critical areas of foreign policy that confronted the second Belaúnde administration upon taking office: Peruvian dependency, regional geopolitical conflict, and the Andean Pact. Before reviewing developments in each of these areas since 1975, it is useful to briefly discuss the significant shifts in Peruvian foreign policy that resulted from the 1968 military take over. The new external initiatives of the revolutionary government experienced checkered success and contributed to the severity of the problems that beset the nation after 1975 and curtailed the options available to President Belaúnde after 1980.

NEW POLICY DIRECTIONS, 1968-1975

The foreign policy of the Juan Velasco Alvarado government (1968-1975) was designed both to generate domestic political support for the regime by playing on the themes of nationalism and anti-imperialism, and to

improve Peru's economic relationships with other
countries. In his July 1969 Independence Day address,
Velasco (1973: 25) explained that:

> . . . the Revolutionary Government has placed a
> distinctive seal on its foreign policy . . . .
> The Peruvian doctrine on problems of Economic
> Cooperation is founded in the need to destroy
> forever all types of pressures and imposed
> conditions in the field of international
> relations.

As the revolutionary government's first foreign minister
later explained, the military attempted to strengthen
Peruvian independence by seeking international solidarity
on three levels: the subregional, regional, and global
(Mercado Jarrín, 1980: 6). However, as Anibal Quijano
(1971: 47) observed, the military government was actually
pursuing the more modest goal redefining ". . . the
relations of imperialist domination in Latin America".

Under the leadership first of General Mercado Jarrín
(1968-1971) and later General Miguel Angel de la Flor
Valle (1972-1976), the Peruvian foreign ministry
endeavored to modify the terms of Peruvian dependency
through a broad range of policies. For purposes of
review, these policies can be grouped into four
interrelated categories.

First, a number of specific measures were enacted to
assert heightened Peruvian sovereignty, including the
uncompensated expropriation of the US-owned International
Petroleum Company;[1] stronger enforcement of the 200
mile thesis on the law of the sea which Peru had advanced
since 1947, involving an escalation of the seizure of
United States fishing vessels; creation of state
monopolies for the commercialization of minerals and
hydrocarbons as well as foreign exchange; and the
formulation of guidelines to insure Peruvian
participation in the profits and management of foreign
firms operating in the country (Pease García and Verme
Insúa, 1974: xxviii-xxxiii; and Quijano, 1971: 30-40).
Other important economic policies included the exclusion
of foreign investment from areas such as agriculture,
future mineral refining and fishing, and the stipulation
that foreign mining companies begin development of
mineral concessions or lose them (Malpica, 1980: 18; and
Hunt, 1975: 313, 328). In conjunction with these
domestic policies, the revolutionary government promoted
subregional economic integration to stimulate
industrialization, increase exports, and strengthen the
corporate bargaining position of the Andean nations
vis-a-vis the developed market economies and
multinational corporations. Aside from the IPC case,

these measures did not seriously disrupt US-Peruvian relations. But the seemingly erratic fashion in which rules for foreign investment were formulated tended to discourage the foreign and domestic private investment which the government still counted on to play a major role in economic development.

The Velasco administration also sought to expand Peru's diplomatic and commerical relations. The starting point for initiatives in this area was Velasco's 1969 pledge that Peru would disregard East-West rivalries and establish "contacts with countries . . . whose markets can open to our products and whose technical and economic cooperation can be very useful in the undertaking of national development" (See Gorman, 1978c: 31). Accordingly, Peru established diplomatic and commercial relations with the Soviet Union, the Peoples Republic of China, and numerous other socialist countries including Cuba. These initiatives produced some tangible benefits as Peru found new markets for non-traditional exports (Sheahan, 1979: 17), and "the socialist bloc began to provide important new loans for various development projects" (Palmer, 1980: 115). Related to Peru's search for new trading partners was the military's desire to diversify further sources of arms transfers (the military had already purchased French Mirage aircraft during the first Belaúnde administration). This policy resulted from Washington's reluctance to sell the types of sophisticated weapons systems demanded by Peru, as well as an interest in reducing overall United States influence in this area (Rouqui, 1973).

Under President Velasco, Peru also took the lead in demanding a radical reorganiztion of the inter-American political and economic systems. Peru began with a call for an end to the Organization of American States' (OAS) blockade of Cuba and later pushed for the formation of a Latin American Frente Economico directed against the United States (Pease García and Verme Insúa, 1974: 386). Peru subsequently co-sponsored resolutions in the OAS to relocate the seat of that organization from Washington to Latin America and to include within its charter a recognition of the right to "ideological pluralism" in the Western Hemisphere (the OAS subsequently approved a modified concept calling for a "plurality of ideologies") (Pease García and Verme Insúa, 1974: 496). Finally, the Velasco Government called for a reorganization of the Inter-American Development Bank to eradicate paternalism (i.e., United States control) and publically endorsed Panama's demands for the nationalization of the Panama Canal (Swansbrough, 1975: 119-120). Washington bitterly resisted these initiatives which gained some support among other Latin American countries.

Finally, the Velasco regime sought closer association with the organization of nonaligned countries

and the Group of 77. Peru quickly became one of the
leaders in the North-South confrontation, joining in the
call for a new international economic order, a
restructuring of the international monetary system, the
formation of a Third World primary producers' cartel, and
an end to the "systematic economic aggressions" of
developed countries against developing countries (Dodd,
1975: 372-377; and Pease García and Verme Insúa, 1974:
665-666). Strong verbal support was even given to
liberation movements like those in Vietnam and Angola.
Policies in this area provided the military regime with
its most powerful symbols of Peruvian independence and
were therefore instrumental in reinforcing political
support for the Velasco government.

As dynamic as some of the above initiatives
appeared, the economic policies underlaying them were, as
John Sheahan (1979: 1) has noted, "fatal". The key to
the military's strategy for breaking dependency was an
export-led development model which, in itself, was not at
all novel (Thorp and Bertram, 1978: 302-304). What was
new was the military's belief that by reducing the power
of the oligarchy and containing the role of foreign
investment, new social forces would be released to take
advantage of capital importations financed by primary
exports. In order to finance the necessary expansion of
exports to set this process in motion, the military
borrowed extensively from foreign commercial banks
(Philip, 1978: 148-149). As Carl Herbold (1979: 5)
noted, this strategy contained both high costs and high
risks, and suffered in its implementation from both "bad
luck" and gross mismanagement. The result was that by
the mid-1970s Peru was faced with an externally related
economic crisis.

By 1975 the external debt stood at $3.99 billion,
representing 29.4 percent of the GNP (in contrast to an
average 18.3 percent for Latin America as a whole) (IDB,
1979: 95-97). While the foreign debt had been expanding,
the volume of key exports had declined by about 33
percent--the effects of which were partially muted by
increasing unit prices (Gorman, 1978b: 294). Thus,
between 1971-1975 Peru required an average of 22.8
percent of its annual export earnings to service the
foreign debt, as opposed to an average of 12.8 percent
for all of Latin America (IDB, 1979: 101)). The entire
situation was further aggrevated by the military's
failure to sufficiently diversify its foreign markets to
escape the consequences of the recession in the developed
market economies beginning in 1974. In 1966 over 82
percent of Peruvian exports had gone to the developed
market economies (42 percent to the US alone). This was
reduced to 75 percent (29 percent for the US) in 1971,
and 70 percent (36 percent for the US) in 1974 (Gorman,
1980: 15). Although encouraging, this shift in trade was

still inadequate. The most important new markets were Eastern Europe and the Peoples Republic of China, but they proved insufficient to counterbalance the reduced demand in the West. All of these conditions combined to create an economic crisis in Peru that contributed to the replacement of Velasco by General Francisco Morales Bermúdez in 1975, and a gradual reorientation of Peruvian foreign policy thereafter.

HEIGHTENED PERUVIAN DEPENDENCY

Peru's economic crisis continued to deepen throughout 1975-1976 as exports weakened while the demand for imports increased. The Morales Bermúdez government attempted to correct the imbalance with a mild austerity program in late 1975, but the country's financial condition failed to improve. In mid-1976, the government resorted to more severe measures, including currency devaluations, restrictions on imports, elimination of subsidies for consumer items, wage and price regulations, and massive budget cuts for social services and developmental projects (Werlich, 1981; Gorman, 1977: 381-392; Citibank, 1976: 63-64; and Philip, 1978: 154-155). Through these measures, the government sought to stimulate exports while holding imports down, regain the confidence of Peru's foreign creditors, and stimulate private sector investment to compensate for the drop-off in public sector investment. Although these policies in themselves were extremely unpopular, reports in the Lima press that the austerity measures had been demanded by New York bankers created something of a political crisis within the military in August 1976 (Ortize de Zavallos, 1980: 24; and Pease García and Filomeno, 1977b: 2142-2145).

The specter of neo-imperialism raised by these reports of external pressure set off a debate within the military between September 1976 and May 1978 over whether or not to default on the external debt (Ortize de Zavallos, 1980). The situation was made even more critical when Peru's foreign creditors (mostly New York commerical banks) refused in 1977 to negotiate additional aid without IMF involvement (Dietz, 1980b: 3). Some encouragement was derived from an improvement in the performance of the two leading exports on which the military had depended to finance the foreign debt: copper and oil. Both of these export industries recovered in 1976-1977 from their decline during the previous two years, but by this point the recovery of exports proved to be too little too late. In 1978 the external debt reached $7.2 billion, 61 percent of which fell due within five years (IDB, 1979: 95, 99).

The 1978 external debt represented 44.4 percent of the Peruvian GNP (in comparison to an average 27.7

percent for all of Latin America) and required 31.3 percent of export earnings to service (IDB, 1979: 97, 101). Moreover, while Peru's per capita indebtedness ($426) was only the eighth highest in Latin America, all but two of the other countries with higher per capita indebtedness also had significantly higher per capita GNPs (World Bank, 1980: 134). In view of these realities, the Morales Bermúdez government had concluded by mid-1978 that it had no alternative but to meet the demands of the IMF in order to refinance the foreign debt. The conditions of the IMF stand-by agreement reached in August 1978 were harsh. It called for the elimination of subsidies to public enterprises, increases in the costs of fuels, the devaluation of the national currency, wage and price controls, and reductions in government spending (see the chapter by Dietz). Needless to say, these measures had a devastating impact on the lower classes in Peru. As damaging as the IMF agreement was to both the popularity of the Morales Bermúdez regime (which was scant to begin with) and the institutional prestige of the armed forces as a bulwark against dependency, the military leaders apparently concluded that it was the lesser of two evils. The government still believed that the export sector would eventually be able to finance development, especially given its resurgence between 1976-1977. Indeed, many of the major public sector investments in export industries were only beginning to produce returns in the late 1970s. If Peru failed to honor its international financial obligations, markets for what was still expected to be a "bonanza" in mineral exports might become difficult to find.

Peru's increasing need after 1975 to appease its creditors and attract more foreign investment had a moderating influence on many aspects of Peruvian foreign policy. General de la Flor was replaced as foreign minister by José de la Puente Radbill in July 1976 when all remaining liberal officers were purged from the cabinet. Thereafter, Peruvian foreign policy increasingly concentrated on subregional concerns, progressively disassociating itself from the political positions of the nonaligned nations movement. An illustration of Peru's new conservatism was provided after the August 1976 Conference of Nonaligned Countries when Peru announced its reservations to resolutions passed at that meeting. Specifically, Peru objected to the endorsement of Cuban support for the Angolan government, the labeling of United States control of Puerto Rico as colonialism, and the criticism of other governments with which Peru maintained normal diplomatic ties (Pease García and Filomeno, 1977b: 2141-2142). Parallel with this moderation in external policy, Morales Bermúdez publically exorcised the word "socialism" from the revolution's vocabulary, explaining that it had a negative connotation which merely served to confuse and discourage private investors (Pease García and Filomeno, 1977b: 2139-2140).

The IMF conditions agreed to by the military government remained in force after the inauguration of Belaúnde Terry in July 1980, and the foreign debt (by then more than $9 billion) continued to require an expansion of exports. This weakened state of government finances encouraged the Belaúnde government to expand the participation of private domestic and foreign capital in certain economic sectors which the revolutionary government had previously reserved for the state. In the mining and oil industries in particular, the decision to expand private foreign investment led to severe criticism by the left against the Belaúnde government (Malpica, 1980). Although restricted, foreign investment had been permitted in the mining and petroleum sectors throughout the revolution (Hunt, 1975), and in 1977 actually represented the largest area of both state and foreign investment (Juscamaita Aranguena, 1980b: 21). What made the mining and petroleum policies of the second Belaúnde administration so objectionable to some Peruvians was the decision to permit private capital to participate in the exploitation of deposits whose profitability had already been proven at considerable expense to the state. Regardless of the economic merits of these policies, the simple fact that mining and petroleum exports were expected to account for 65 percent of Peru's foreign earnings in 1980 would seem to have militated against expanded foreign involvement on political grounds. To aggravate matters further, the Belaúnde government pushed for an end to the state's monopoly over mineral exports, a policy which threatened to turn over the politically sensitive business of negotiating export prices to foreign interests (Malpica, 1980: 20-21). Although some argued that the state monopoly over mineral exports had been inefficient (see for example Sheahan, 1979: 13-14), it nevertheless satisfied nationalist demands for the state to exercise closer supervision of the marketing of Peruvian natural resources to guard against foreign price manipulations.

As of mid-1981, the long-term outlook for Peru's external economic relations did not promise any reduction in the country's dependency, even though the external sector of the economy was expected to continue to strengthen through 1981-1982. As one Peruvian economist argued:

> During 1978-1979 the bases were created for a new recuperation, thanks to the extraordinary expansion of our exportations and because of a highly recessionary economic policy. Towards the end of 1979, in consequence, . . . the

conditions were present for the initiation of a
new process of economic recovery (Schuldt,
1980: 43).

Nevertheless, this same observer predicted another
economic crisis by 1983-84 if the new govenment continued
to follow the policies of the Morales Bermúdez government
(as he expected it to do). Thus, it was projected that
inflation might top 75 percent and exports could begin to
slacken again while imports continue to rise as a
percentage of the Peruvian GNP (Schuldt, 1980: 33-51,
76-77). Accordingly, the prognosis for the Belaúnde
government in 1981 appeared to be increasing dependence
on the IMF and private foreign capital.

OLD AND NEW GEOPOLITICAL CONCERNS

Soon after assuming power in 1975, President Morales
Bermúdez put the foreign policy emphasis of his
administration on improving regional diplomatic ties and
subregional economic integration. These twin objectives
soon encountered serious obstacles, however, as conflicts
within the Andean Pact delayed implementation of
agreements for economic cooperation, and territorial
disputes complicated Peru's bilateral relations with
Chile and Ecuador. The difficulties which arose for
subregional economic integration will be discussed in the
following section, but it should be kept in mind that
they were related to the geopolitical tensions examined
below. The three primary issues that interfered with
Peruvian efforts after 1975 to strengthen relations with
neighboring countries were the conflict with Chile over
the solution to Bolivian demands for an outlet to the
sea, strained relations with Ecuador over disputed Amazon
territory, and an accelerated build-up of Soviet military
arms in Peru which was viewed with considerable alarm by
Chile and Ecuador. These problems, in turn, interacted
with broader geopolitical tensions in the Southern Cone
to increase polarization in the region.
    The dispute with Chile over control of the northern
Atacama Desert dates back to the War of the Pacific
(1879-1883) when Peru and Bolivia were forced to cede
substantial amounts of territory (including Bolivia's
littoral) to Chile. Permanent sovereignty over two
occupied Peruvian provinces (Tacna and Arica) was
originally to be decided by plebicite, but the eventual
breakdown of the process in the 1920s finally led to an
agreement to divide the two provinces between Chile and
Peru (St John, 1976: 332-335). Although Bolivia was
granted transit and port privileges in northern Chile, it
refused to accept the loss of its littoral and,
consequently, Bolivian access to the Pacific Ocean became
a permanent objective of Bolivian diplomacy in the

twentieth century (St John, 1977b).

In 1962, a frustrated Bolivia broke diplomatic relations with Chile over the general issue of access to the Pacific and the specific question of Chilean diversion of water from the Rio Lauca in the disputed area. It was not until February 1975 that the military government of Hugo Banzer Suarez re-established diplomatic ties with Chile in an attempt to negotiate a settlement. Chile responded in December of the same year with a proposal to exchange a narrow strip of land north of Arica along the Peruvian border for equivalent territorial compensation in the Bolivian altiplano. The Bolivian government, taking pains to emphasize that a firm basis for future negotiation had been established, rejected this offer on the grounds that Boliva should not have to agree to territorial compensation for land seized in an agressive war. The Bolivian military also bristled at a Chilean provision calling for demilitarization of the area in question, arguing that meaningful sovereignty necessitated the right to exercise military control (Gordon, 1979: 325; and Werlich, 1978: 366).

The Peruvian government, alarmed that the Chilean proposal entailed Bolivian acquisition of territory originally Peruvian, then sought to insert itself into the negotiations to protect what it considered to be vital national interests.[2] On November 9, 1976 Peru proposed a third round of negotiations in Lima to discuss the situation, but Chile requested a delay due to the illness of its chief delegate in the talks. In response, the Peruvian foreign ministry publically released an entirely new formula for resolving the issue on November 19, 1976; a proposal which completely undercut the earlier Chilean initiative. The heart of the Peruvian proposal called for the creation of a zone of joint Peruvian-Bolivian-Chilean sovereignty between the Peruvian border and the city of Arica, with Boliva being granted a corridor and port in the same area (Pease García and Filomeno, 1977b: 2274-2276; Werlich, 1978: 369-370). The Peruvian proposal offered Bolivia as much as the Chileans had and, at the same time, reintroduced the question of Peruvian rights in the disputed area. Moreover, since it called for trilateral economic development of the zone, it was also consistent with the Peruvian government's emphasis on Andean integration and mutual cooperation (Gordon, 1979: 325-326). Negotiations then stalemated when Chile refused even to discuss the Peruvian proposal, charging that it involved modifications to the Peru-Chile Treaty of 1929 and also introduced issues totally unrelated to the question of Bolivian access to the Pacific. At first, Bolivia expressed interest in the Peruvian proposal, but recognized that the plan had little chance of being considered by Chile. The Bolivian government later took

official notice of the impasse by rejecting both Chile's
demand for territorial compensation and Peru's plan for
tripartite sovereignty.

The dispute in the Atacama Desert coincided with a
deterioration in Peruvian relations with Ecuador over a
boundary dispute which had originated at the time of
independence. The issue resurfaced in October 1976 when
the Ecuadorean ambassador to the UN stated that a major
obstacle to Peru's goal of regional economic cooperation
was Ecuador's territorial claims in the Amazon region.
In particular, Ecuador demanded a renegotiation of the
1942 Protocol of Rio de Janeiro which had awarded
sovereignty over the bulk of the area in dispute
(situated along the Amazon frontier between Peru and
Ecuador) to Peru (St John, 1977a). Ecuador argued that
Peruvian possession of the so-called Oriente region
blocked Ecuadorean access to the Amazon river network and
thus reduced that country's participation in any future
multilateral development of the region. Relations
between Peru and Ecuador were strained further the
following month when a leading Ecuadorean daily accused
the Soviet Union of arming Peru for an invasion of
northern Chile (Pease García and Filomeno, 1977b: 2249).
Peru responded in early 1977 with a minor peace
offensive, but news of Ecuador's intention to acquire a
squadron of sophisticated jet fighters caused a certain
degree of concern in Lima, as did reports of the
mistreatment of Peruvian nationals in Ecuador later that
year.

The situation remained stable until early 1978 when
the conflicts between Peru and its two neighbors
converged with a multiplicity of factors to produce a
potential for armed conflict. The most immediate
developments involved minor armed clashes between
Peruvian and Ecuadorean forces along their Amazon
frontier in January, and the rupture of diplomatic
relations between Bolivia and Chile in March when
President Banzer, citing Chilean insincerity and
inflexibility, opted for a more confrontationist
strategy. Three broader factors also impended on
disputes in the area. The Chilean record on human rights
and Pinochet's failure to cooperate with the United
States in the Letelier case[3] contributed to a growing
international isolation of the Chilean government, which
made the country somewhat more vulnerable than might
otherwise have been the case (Gorman, 1979). In
addition, the intensification of the territorial dispute
between Chile and Argentina over the Beagle Channel
Islands in Tierra del Fuego (involving significant
military maneuvers and threats of force) provided Peru
and Bolivia with a powerful potential ally in any
confrontation against Chile. Finally, the Brazilian
government was actively promoting governments with a

compatible ideological outlook in the Andean region.
Brazilian diplomacy in this regard was presaging the
creation of a conservative, anti-Peruvian axis linking
Brazil, Bolivia, and Chile (Gorman, 1978a: 52-53; Pike,
1977: 373-374). Although the situation remained critical
throughout 1978, conflict was avoided and both Chile and
Peru actively sought a reduction in tensions (insisting
that relations between them were cordial and that rumors
of war were the fabrication of the foreign press). But
at the end of the year the discovery of an extensive
Chilean espionage network directed at the most sensitive
Peruvian military installations and coordinated through
the Chilean Embassy produced an open split between the
two countries. By early 1979, however, the configuration
of regional forces that had appeared to favor conflict
during the previous year had altered significantly.
Specifically, Papal mediation had achieved a reduction in
tensions between Chile and Argentina, Bolivia found
itself effectively preoccupied with internal political
problems, and Chile had partially overcome its
international isolation.

This protracted period of geopolitical tension
served to aggravate a growing military build-up in the
region. However, the turn toward militarism in Peru
actually preceded the deterioration in relations with
Ecuador and Chile and, therefore, cannot be attributed
entirely to the Atacama and Amazon disputes. The size of
the Peruvian armed forces remained relatively stable
until after 1973, when a greater amount of resources were
allocated to the military. While per capita GNP rose by
only 40 percent in Peru between 1968-1977, for example,
per capita military expenditures increased by over 82
percent, with most of the expansion occuring between
1974-1977 (ACDA, 1979: 100). The fact that the
escalation began even before the fall of Velasco suggests
that the new emphasis on armaments was independent of the
political divisions that began to appear within the
military leading to the Morales Bermúdez coup of August
1975.

The preponderant role of Soviet arms transfers in
Peru's military build-up caused considerable alarm in
neighboring countries. The question of Soviet motives in
supplying Peru with advanced military hardware first
surfaced in March 1974 and began to receive extensive
coverage in the Chilean press in August of the same year
(Pease Garcia et al., 1975: 807, 905). Finally, after
UPI picked up a story from Aviation and Technology in
December 1974 attributing the build-up of Soviet arms in
Peru to a plan to attack the copper deposits in northern
Chile, the Peruvian foreign ministry called for a
regional conference on arms limitation. A conference of
Andean Pact countries eventually convened in Lima in
September 1975 but failed to produce any workable formula

for ending what by that point had evolved into an arms race between Peru on one side, and Chile and Ecuador on the other. In the meantime, Peru's interest in Soviet military equipment had increased after the United States suspended military assistance to Peru in February 1975 to counterbalance the cutoff in aid to Chile (for human rights violations). Although the US decision to cutoff Peruvian arms shipments was reversed a few days later, the political damage had already been done. Progressively after 1973, the Soviet Union had become Peru's chief arms suppler, and Peru completely outdistanced its two regional rivals in arms acquisitions. Although accurate data for the period after 1977 is difficult to obtain, all indications are that Peru continued to increase its purchases of Soviet weaponry and achieved something approaching a temporary regional military superiority by the end of the decade (Smith, 1977; and Gorman, 1978a: 51-53).

As Víctor Villanueva suggests in Chapter 6, the military had at least two institutional motivations for engaging in an arms build-up. First, there was a desire to achieve a complete modernization of the armed forces in the shortest period of time possble. Second, there existed a deeply felt need within the military to avenge the country's loss to Chile in the War of the Pacific (1879-1883). Unfortunately, the military intensified its expensive modernization program at the same time that the economy plunged deeper into an economic crisis induced in large measure by a foreign currency shortage. The massive importation of military equipment, therefore, contributed significantly to a worsening external debt situation.

Both the Bolivian-Chilean and Ecuadorean territorial disputes receded after early 1979, but they remained as potential points of conflict between Peru and its neighbors. This potential manifested itself again in January 1981, the 39th anniversary of the 1942 Rio Protocol intended to resolve the dispute in the Oriente, when fighting again erupted between Peru and Equador. This was the first outbreak of fighting since 1978 and involved relatively small skirmishes in and around Paquisha in the Cordillera del Condor. Peru's southern frontier was quiet during the first year of the second Belaúnde administration, but the potential for conflict also still remained there as the three participants in the War of the Pacific continued to search for a solution amenable to all of them.

SUBREGIONAL COOPERATION AND INTEGRATION

One of the key objectives of Peru's revolutionary foreign policy was the promotion of subregional economic integration as a means for stimulating industrialization, increasing non-traditional exports, and strengthening the bargaining position of Andean countries vis-á-vis the developed market economies and the multinational corporations. Movement toward greater subregional cooperation actually began during Belaúnde's first administration with the 1966 Declaration of Bogotá. This declaration committed Chile, Colombia, Ecuador, Venezuela and Peru to begin negotiating an arrangement for economic integration (Avery and Cochrane, 1973: 87). The formal document establishing the Andean Pact, the 1969 Cartagena Agreement (signed by Chile, Bolivia, Ecuador, Colombia and Peru the same year, and Venezuela in 1973), received the enthusiastic support of the Velasco government (Gushiken, 1977: 51-56). The signatories of the Cartagena Agreement subsequently developed a number of collective policies consistent with the objectives of the Peruvian revolution, including a code for the common treatment of foreign capital, industrial programing among member countries, and the projected establishment of a common external tariff.

Although there were several areas of progress within the Andean Pact, and some specific advantages for Peru in particular, the process of subregional economic integration began to encounter major obstacles after 1975. By far the most serious difficulties arose in connection with the provisions for the treatment of foreign investments. "Decision 24" creating a common regime for the treatment of foreign capital was approved in December 1970 and came into force in June 1971. Among other things, Decision 24 set a limit of 14 percent on the profit remittances of new foreign firms, and required the transformation of foreign firms to "mixed" or "national" companies before they could participate in the common market (Ferris, 1979: 51-52). Problems were encountered almost immediately in achieving a uniform implementation of the code within all member countries. Peru went beyond the provisions of Decision 24 while Bolivia virtually ignored them, and a lengthy legal battle was necessary in Colombia before the government there succeeded in making the code binding in that country (Gushiken, 1977: 40-56). The real challenge came after the September 1973 military coup in Chile. Originally, the military junta in Chile promised to observe all of the country's international obligations, but in July 1974, the Pinochet regime issued a new investment code that effectively nullified Decision 24 in Chile. After pressure from the other Andean Pact members, the new code was repealed in November 1974. Nevertheless, by December of the following year Chile was insisting on significant revisions in the rules for the common treatment of foreign capital.

The three areas in which Chile demanded revisions involved an increase in the profit remittance limits for foreign firms, repeal of the restrictions on the sale of state enterprises to foreign interests, and changes in the definition of a "mixed" company allowed to participate in the common market. The Morales Bermúdez government expressed some sympathy for the call to permit foreign investors to repatriate a higher percentage of investments, since the cost of capital had risen considerably since 1970 when the code was originally written. As a consequence, both Peru and Chile had found themselves hard pressed to attract much needed foreign investors given the profit restrictions imposed by Decision 24 (Grosse, 1980: 85-90). Nevertheless, when the Chilean proposals for revising important aspects of Decision 24 were largely rejected by a meeting of Andean Pact ministers in Lima in August 1976[4] Peru opted to abide by the decision of the majority. Chile, for its part, refused. There followed a period of intensive negotiations between Chile and the other Andean Pact members which culminated in October 1976 with Chile's withdrawal from the Cartagena Agreement. Because of Chile's geographical location and level of economic development, its departure from the Andean Pact represented a major setback for Peru's ambition for subregional economic integration. Not only had the Chilean controversy limited progress in other areas by occupying so much of the group's attention over a prolonged period, but Chile's eventual decision to withdraw also set an unfortunate precedent for the reconciliation of Andean Pact objectives with the national development goals of member states (Ferris, 1979: 54).

Concomitant with Chile's growing disaffection, the Andean Pact experienced strains on two other issues. The first concerned slow progress in industrial programing. In addition to the overall complexity of the issues involved, production allocations were interrupted first by Venezuela's tardy agreement to the pact and then by Chile's withdrawal. By 1980 only three agreements had been reached, all of which suffered from problems of implementation.

> The Metalworking agreement, originally passed in 1972, was amended in 1979, following arduous negotiations, to incorporate Venezuela. The Petrochemical agreement--passed in August 1975--has become almost obsolete as a result of expansion in petrochemical capacity around the world. [And] the 1977 agreement of the automotive sector was the most difficult to achieve and disagreements over assignments continue to plague the Andean Pact members (Ferris, 1980: 2).

Industrial programing was intended to take advantage of the economies of scale provided by the Andean Common Market to promote heavy industrialization (Fontain, 1977: 17). But the allocation of industrial activities between countries proved extremely complicated, partly as a result of the higher levels of economic development in Colombia and Chile which favored these two Andean Pact members as the centers of heaviest industrialization (Mytelka, 1979: 44). As a result, Peru pressed for a delay in agreements on certain industrial programing schemes until it could develop its own national industries sufficiently enough to secure adequate participation in the allocation of industrial activities.

The other major issue to confront the Andean Pact was the timetable for trade liberalization within the common market and the adoption of a common external tariff. Mytelka (1979: 44-45) attributed lack of progress in intraregional trade liberalization during the seventies to 1) the failure of the Andean Pact to meet the 1975 deadline for the adoption of certain industrial programs, 2) the inability of Ecuador and Bolivia to industrialize as quickly as anticipated (which meant that they required a longer period of trade protection), and 3) continuing disagreement over the structure of the common external tariff to be adopted. After the withdrawal of Chile from the Andean Pact, the remaining members agreed to postpone by several years the deadlines for the complete liberalization of intraregional trade and the adoption of a common external tariff.

Despite these setbacks, Peru reaped important trade advantages from its participation in the Andean Pact. As Jan Ter Wengel (1980: 2-3) has explained, the real gains from integrationist movements like the Andean Pact are expected to derive from import substitution, industrialization and, by extension, an expansion of non-traditional exports. By the late 1970s fully 66 percent of Peru's intraregional exports were manufactures, compared to only 8 percent of its global trade. Moreover, "Peru had also begun to participate in intraindustry specialization and trade. . ." (Mytelka, 1979: 56). Thus, any breakdown in regional economic integration in the 1980s could be expected to have serious consequences for Peruvian industrialization which has become at least partially dependent on regional markets to maintain economies of scale.

As difficulties were encountered in achieving the Andean Pact's economic goals, political divisions between the member governments also increased. The most important of these was the opposition which developed to the Bolivian military golpe of mid-1980. This rift caused real problems for the Andean Group since the refusal of the Andean countries to recognize the new military regime in La Paz resulted in the latter's

absence from Andean Pact meetings. To emphasize their
position, the Andean presidents, meeting in Ecuador in
September 1980, issued an Andean Code of Conduct which
stated that respect for human, political, and social--as
well as economic--rights was a cornerstone of the Andean
Group and that defense of those rights was an
international obligation. Bolivia's new military
president responded two months later with a statement
that his government would not recognize any Andean
Commission decisions not approved by all five member
countries.[5]

The quarrel between the Bolivian government and the
other members of the Andean Pact forced the group to
reschedule several pending decisions, including adoption
of a common external tariff and further revisions to the
industrial programing scheme. The failure to sanction
these programs, in turn, adversely affected investment as
firms remained reluctant to invest without first knowing
the level of tariff protection available and the
countries which would be granted preferential access to
the Andean market.

The on-going dispute also left open the possibility
that Bolivia might eventually follow Chile's example and
withdraw from the Cartagena Agreement. The Andean Pact
governments, especially Peru, were reluctant to oppose
the Bolivian military government to a degree that might
result in its withdrawal. Peru's military leaders, in
particular, feared such a policy might result in a new
alliance between Bolivia and Chile, motivated in part by
the Atacama Desert dispute. Similarly, the new outbreak
of fighting between Peru and Ecuador during Belaúnde's
first year not only strained the bilateral relations of
these two countries, but also weakened the struggling
Andean Pact.

The re-election of Fernando Belaúnde Terry to the
presidency of Peru presaged a re-orientation of
post-Velasco Peruvian economic policy which has had a
major impact on the scope and direction of the Andean
Group. As Elizabeth Ferris (1980: 6) predicted,
Belaúnde's choice of a developmental model dependent on
the goodwill of the US and the international financial
community has had definite effects on the future of the
Pact in promoting the economic development of its
members. While the second Belaúnde administration
repeatedly emphasized its support of the Andean Pact in
general, and Decision 24 in particular, it also sought
during its first year in power to ease the Pact's
restrictive foreign investment regulations as well as
negotiate a more liberal, less nationalistic external
tariff schedule.

CONCLUSIONS

Peruvian foreign policy over the last two decades (and for a much longer period) has been characterized by considerable continuity in terms of the dominant external concerns if not the policies articulated to address those issues. It has also been distinguished by a strong linkage between foreign and domestic policy with domestic objectives (and domestic political considerations) strongly influencing, if not actually dictating, many aspects of the nation's foreign policy. Both of these characteristics are largely the result of the strong dependent relationship Peru has found itself in for much of the nineteenth and twentieth centuries; a situation unlikely to change in the foreseeable future.

Our analysis of Peruvian foreign policy since 1969 has demonstrated how difficult it is for a developing country to break dependent relationships. While Peru was able to take advantage of reduced global bipolarity in the late sixties and early seventies to expand its political and economic ties, and participated actively in a novel effort at regional integration, it was still unable to escape the consequences of its subordinate position within the international market. When the developed market economies experienced recession in the mid-1970s, the export-led development model adopted by the military government insured that Peru would suffer serious economic consequences. In turn, this contributed to a softening of the country's international political positions and closer ties with the United States. Similar to his first term, President Belaúnde made internal economic development the central objective of his second administration. Moreover, he elected to pursue this goal through a development model largely dependent on the support, bordering on the largess, of the United States and the international financial community. Consequently, in contrast to Velasco's policy of confrontation, Belaúnde has pursued a policy of accommodation, if not active cooperation, with the developed world in general and the United States in particular.

At the same time, Belaúnde did not seek to reverse all of the policies of the docenio. While he sought additional foreign investment in the petroleum sector, he made it clear that refining, especially the former IPC facility at Talara, would remain in government hands. Moreover, he has continued to advance Peru's 200 mile thesis on the law of the sea. On the question of arms diversification, Belaúnde continued to support a policy that had really originated during his first administration with the purchase of French Mirage jets. The related question of the appropriate level of defense expenditures for a country in Peru's strained financial condition was a more difficult one that necessitated ongoing negotiations between the civilian government and the armed forces.

In other areas of revolutionary policy, Belaúnde has sought to divest himself of initiatives which were both aberrations in terms of the nation's traditional concerns and had produced minimal tangible benefits to the nation. Two obvious policies in this regard were the Velasco administration's attempts at Third World solidarity and leadership, and modification of the inter-American system. Belaúnde continued Bermúdez's de-emphasis of these two issues because they were not of great interest to his administration and, more importantly, any revival of such polices could jeopardize the development model he sought to effect.

Notes

1. The Velasco government argued that the IPC was an exceptional case, and its seizure did not reflect a general predisposition by the military to expropriate other foreign holdings without compensation. On this subject, see Piñelo (1968).

2. Article I of the Additional Protocol of the 1929 Tacna and Arica Treaty provided that neither Peru nor Chile could cede to a third state any or all of the territories over which they were given sovereignty by the treaty without first attaining the agreement of the other signatory (St John, 1970: 202).

3. Letelier was a member of the Salvador Allende government who was later assassinated in Washington, D.C. on the apparent orders of members of Chile's military government. The refusal of the Chilean government to cooperate in the extradition of certain individuals involved in the murder led to a deterioration in relations.

4. The Andean Pact ministers did make several important changes, but they did not go far enough for Chile.

5. The statement of the Bolivian president contradicted the group's charter, the Cartagena Agreement, which provided for approval of most decisions by a two-thirds majority vote (four of the five members).

8
The Intellectual Foundations of Revolution in Peru: The Anti-Oligarchic Tradition

Stephen M. Gorman

The military-led revolution in 1968 was strongly influenced by a well developed tradition of anti-oligarchic thought in Peru stretching back nearly one hundred years. At least since the War of the Pacific, Peruvian intellectuals have sought for the causes of the nation's political and economic problems in the elite-mass relations that have evolved since colonial times. We cannot say exactly what the legacy of the docenio will be for this tradition. But it is instructive to review the evolution of social criticism in Peru to learn what the expectations of the intelligentsia were for the revolution, and speculate on what changes have been effected in elite-mass relations as a consequence of twelve years of military rule.

EARLY CRITICISM

The radical critique of the Peruvian oligarchy began primarily with the works of Manuel Gonzalez Prada (1848-1918). Born to an aristocratic family of the first order, Gonzalez Prada turned against his own class after Peru's humiliating defeat in the War of the Pacific convinced him of the need for radical reform to forge a strong and unified nation. He argued that the existing elite was incapable of either integrating the nation or developing the economy, and eventually came to the conclusion that lower-class violence would be required to remove the oligarchic obstacle to national modernization (Chang-Rodríguez, 1957: 96-98). The revolutionary theme in Prada's political thought was later adopted and expanded by a group of young militants known as the Generation of 1919, which included José Carlos Mariátegui and Víctor Raúl Haya de la Torre (Bains, 1972: 3-18). Prada described the elite as an "upper class" consisting of landowners, merchants, high military officers, leading politicians, and the Church hierarchy. Its wealth derived from land and state sponsored

197

commerce, like guano and nitrate export. This upper class represented a "ruling class" that in times of civilian government controlled the state apparatus through a restricted electoral system in which political parties functioned exclusively as economic interest groups organized on the basis of personalistic followings (Gonzalez Prada, 1964: 9-10; and 1969: 10-12). During times of military rule, however, there was still no substantial difference other than that caudillos robbed the public treasury in broad daylight while civilistas normally waited until the cover of night. The entire system of elite domination rested at bottom, he insisted, on police repression and the hierarchical structures of authority within which officials showed absolute servility to superiors and unsheathed brutality and contempt for subordinates (Gonzalez Prada, 1940: 46-47; Chang-Rodríguez, 1957: 89-94; García Salvattecci, 1972: 245-254).

The influence of the elite on Peruvian society was depicted as singularly negative. Because the elite borrowed its culture from Europe, its values were alien to the wider society. Because it held absolutely no interest in the material well-being of the masses, and because it held direct interest in the continuation of feudalistic property, it was unwilling to carry out the agrarian reform without which Peru could never develop. Prada's most bitter criticism, however, was reserved for the Catholic Church, which worked in the interest of the oligarchy to legitimize the prevailing inequalities of society and placate the masses (Bains, 1972: 12-15; Chang-Rodríguez, 1957: 87-98, 96-100; García Salvatecci, 1972: 256-257). In Prada's view, the leadership pretensions of the elite rested on pseudo-science and intellectual depravity, and the institutionalized inequalities of the society were protected by the joining of the tyranny of the oligarchic state with the fanaticism of the Catholic Church (Gonzalez Prada, 1966: 49-50, 101-102).

Prada's disappointment with the Peruvian upper class, if not his radicalism, was shared by many of his contemporaries. Even the ultramontane intellectual José de la Riva Agüero (1885-1944), grandson of Peru's first persident and a leading conservative spokesman, conceded the "Levantine egotism" and intellectual destitution of his own class (Riva Agüero, 1955: 110-120). But unlike Prada, Riva Agüero desired the regeneration of the elite, and not its liquidation. This could be accomplished, he advocated, by establishing a fascist regime in Peru which would resurrect the European roots of upper-class Peruvian culture as a means of national salvation (Pike, 1967: 321). Those who followed in the tradition of Prada, conversely, have argued for indigenismo, which advocates the superiority of pre-conquest Indian cultures as the basis of national integration and unity.

Prada's diagnosis of the superficiality of upper-class Peruvian culture also received corroboration in the early writings of the moderate conservative Víctor Andrés Belaunde (1888-1966), a distinguished diplomatist and uncle of Peru's current constitutional president. In a series of articles first published in 1912, Belaunde identified six harmful qualities of the "dominant culture" which perverted public life. Belaunde (1963: Part I) argued that the dominant culture was characterized by incoherent conduct because of 1) its lack of central ideas capable of orienting behavior; 2) sterile animosity and combativeness; 3) a pompus incapacity to perceive the gap between ideals and actions; 4) a natural disposition toward ignorance as reflected in the poverty of Peruvian philosophy; 5) a disproportionate concern with decoration over substance; and 6) a complete absence of normative values suitable for creating national cohesion and legitimizing authority.

Although many of his contemporaries shared Prada's concern for the cultural deprevity of the ruling elite, they normally thought in terms of the incomplete internalization of European values rather than, as Prada, in terms of the preferability of an indigenously derived cultural framework. Nor were they inclined to embrace the radical political solutions that Prada advanced. These gained wider acceptability only during and after the First World War, when the resulting economic expansion mobilized formerly marginal groups who began to demand greater participation in urban wealth. Along side the nascent workers' movement that grew out of these conditions arose a university reform movement. Student and worker demands came together briefly in 1918-1919 to nearly topple the oligarchic state, but the elite succeeded in consolidating power in the Leguia dictatorship (1919-1930), and the challenge from below was defeated (Villanueva, 1973a: 149-160). From this experience emerged the Generation of 1919 whose two leading figures were José Carlos Mariátegui (1895-1930) and Víctor Raúl Haya de la Torre (1895-1979). Both men took their first inspirations from the works of Prada and made significant contributions to the understanding of elites in Peru. Haya de la Torre and the political party which he formed, however, generally functioned as supports for the oligarchic system after the mid-1950s in the estimation of several observers (Chaplin, 1976: 5-7; Bourque, 1970: 33-38; and Villanueva, 1977).

THE GENERATION OF 1919

It was Mariátegui who adapted marxist analysis to the essentially literary criticisms developed by Prada, and provided a more precise historical framework for understanding the economic foundations of elite power (Bains, 1972: 3-5). As a lower-class mestizo, Mariátegui was deprived of a university education and evolved his ideas during a truncated career in journalism. His political thought began to acquire some theoretical unity late in his short life, as reflected in his major work Siete ensayos de interpretación de la realidad peruana. His work provided the foundation for the majority of subsequent leftist critiques of the oligarchic state.

In his analysis, Mariátegui (1968: 57-58) explained that the struggle for independence in Peru brought together the landowning aristocracy and bourgeois merchants into a political alliance in which the liberal principles of the latter group served to legitimize the break with Spain. In the republic that followed, however, the absence of a strong bourgeoisie whose economic interests would have compelled it to enforce the liberal legislation that was encacted allowed the state to be used exclusively to promote the feudalistic interests of the "aristocracy." The first decades of the republic, accordingly, were dominated by military strongmen (caudillos) who pretented to institute liberal reforms, but who in one way or another served only the interests of the feudalistic landowners (Mariátegui, 1968: 57-69). The native and foreign urban merchant classes therefore alligned themselves with the aristocracy in a subordinate fashion.

These political-economic circumstances meant that when guano and nitrate export began in the 1840s the aristocracy was the primary beneficiary and was thus "forced by its economic role to assume the function of a bourgeoisie in Peru, although without loosing its colonial and aristocratic prejudices and habits" (Mariátegui, 1968: 61). The wealth from guano and nitrate export allowed members of the aristocracy to transform themselves between 1860-1872 into a plutocracy that consolidated its ties with international capital and followed a policy of development that emphasized state favoratism rather than market competition as the means of accumulation and investment (Mariátegui, 1968: 29). The only solution to this state of affairs that locked Peru into a position of underdevelopment and dependency was a socialist revolution based on nationalism and indigenismo.

Mariátegui died a young man while working to establish a political party which would be able to mobilize the masses to overthrow the oligarchic state. Subsequently, a minority within the nucleus of Mariátegui's movement transformed it into an avowedly communist party (Communist Party of Peru) which today, along with many other movements of the left, claims to represent the ideals of Mariátegui.

The career of Víctor Raúl Haya de la Torre presents
a marked contrast to that of Mariátegui, although for a
brief period the two men shared a common political
approach between 1919-1926. Haya de la Torre was born to
an aristocratic family in the northern coastal city of
Trujillo, where he enjoyed all the advantages of his
class. The major force that seems to have pushed him
into a posture of political opposition to the established
order was the penetration of foreign capital into the
aristocratic estate agriculture of his native province
(Bourricaud, 1970: 57). Indeed, Peter F. Klaren (1973)
sees the unsettling effects of agricultural consolidation
under foreign economic impetus as one of the principle
moving forces behind the formation of Haya de la Torre's
Aprista movement. Haya de la Torre became involved in
the university movement and subsequently took up his
studies in Lima. There he played an important role in
coordinating student-worker cooperation during the
disturbances of 1918-1919, which launched him on his
political career (Chang-Rodríguez, 1957: 213-226; Cox,
1940: 41-50; and Stein, 1980, Ch. 6). During his first
period of exile in the 1920s, he formed the Alianza
Popular Revolucionario Americana (APRA) as a pan-Latin
American political movement drawing upon other
expatriates for the original membership. On his return
to Peru in 1931 he assumed control of the recently
founded Peruvian Aprista Party over which he maintained a
firm grasp for the remainder of his life (see Kantor,
1966: 12-13). Peru turned out to be the only country to
establish a viable Aprista party, which in its earlier
phase (1931-1941) was an anti-imperialist, anti-
oligarchic populist movement.

Haya de la Torre described the elite as a "governing
class" or, alternatively, a "dominant class," consisting
of landowners and merchants holding power by virtue of
their concessionary association with North American
imperialism (which had replaced British imperialism
during the 1920s as the primary economic force in Peru).
He distinguished between the elite and masses of the
criterion of who benefited and who suffered from
imperialism. The first to suffer were considered to be
the nascent middle class capitalists who were destroyed
by the superior techniques of advanced capitalist modes
of production that penetrated the native economy. The
proletariat suffered as well from the incomplete
development of the consumer economy and the limited
opportunities and remuneration of many forms of labor.
The peasantry suffered, finally, through the imposition
of a dualistic society that marginalized the rural poor
that the foreign dominated urban economy could not
accomodate. Those who benefited from this situation were
the provincial hacendados, the agro-industrial sugar and
cotton producers, and their many retainers who formed the

national component of the oligarchical-imperial network (Kantor, 1966: 37-42; Alexander, 1973: 98).

Haya de la Torre suggested that the rigidification of the exisiting socioeconomic conditions derived in large measure from the traumatic clash of civilizations of widely separated "historical Space-Times" brought together through imperialism (Alexander, 1973: 64-85, 149-158). Indirectly, this implied that the continuity of anachronistic elite-mass relations within Peru (and "indo-america" generally) was the result of external interference. Such interference could exist in one or both of two fashions: imperialist support for the continuation of the oligarchy in power, and/or the adoption of foreign sociopolitical formulas for the solution of Peruvian problems that are inappropriate for an organic evolution of the society (Alexander, 1973: 94-96).

This conceptualization of the nexus between the oligarchy and imperialism, while not entirely novel, represented an important contribution to the understanding of Peruvian elite structures (especially as it was developed by later Peruvian intellectuals). But its later refinement by Haya also facilitated a fateful flaw to appear in Aprista reasoning. During the Second World War (largely because of Haya's antifacism and admiration for the role of the United States in the war), a distinction emerged between the presumed political and economic effects of imperialism. External political influence was negative, it was argued, but the economic diffusion that came with foreign capital was now considered positive (Interview, 1976). On the heels of this revision, APRA quickly accomodated itself to at least those elements of the prevailing order which reflected the "positive" influences of imperialism. Another, perhaps more important, consideration in the increasing conservatism of APRA, according to David Chaplin (1976: 5-11), was the integration into the existing socioeconomic framework that had been achieved by APRA's more politically articulate members (its clientele).

POST-SECOND WORLD WAR CRITIQUES

The political thought of Mariátegui and Haya de la Torre permeated, and to some extent dominated, the analysis of elite-mass relations up to the 1960s, when significant new ideas entered the scene. To be sure, the newer formulations built extensively upon the earlier work of Mariátegui and Haya de la Torre; but they also introduced new perspectives or rigorously re-examined older ones. Two individuals in particular stand out: one a respected Peruvian philosopher, Augusto Salazar Bondy, the other a French sociologist, Francois

Bourricaud.

In a collection of essays written during the 1960s and published together as Entre escila y caribdis in 1969, Salazar Bondy reflected on the psycho-social qualities of Peruvian life which contributed to the injustice and decadence of his nation. Two important conclusions concerned the ubiquity of what he termed the "hauchafo spirit" and the absence of an organic and unifying national culture. In the Peruvian lexicon, a huachafo is an individual who pretends to be what he is not in order to achieve acceptance (especially referring to a parvenu). In the broader sense in which Salazar Bondy employed the term, it refers to a pervasive attitude that infests virtually all facets of Peruvian life with an "inauthentic" character. This, he argued, explains in large measure the universal superficiality of Peruvian institutions and civic virtues which corrupts both public and private life. This observation seems clearly within the tradition of González Prada, Víctor Andrés Belaunde, and even Mariátegui (Salazar Bondy, 1969: 36). The absence of an organic and unifying culture, on the other hand, derived both from the heterogeneity of Peruvian society in which each individual is alienated from himself, the state, and the society in general, and the nation's dependent position within the global capitalist system (Salazar Bondy, 1969: 47-53). The only shared national culture, insisted Salazar Bondy (1969: 56), is the "Culture of Domination." The only viable solution, he concluded, is the path of revolution (Salazar Bondy, 1969: 55). Salazar Bondy died in 1974 while serving as an advisor to the Ministry of Education of the Velasco government.

Francois Bourricaud is noted foremost for his 1967 work Pouvoir et societe dans le Perou contemporain, and his subsequent contribution to La oligarquia published in Peru in 1969 under the editorship of Jose Matos Mar. In these works, Bourricaud advanced a thesis which has quickly become an integral part of the body of Peruvian literature on elites, which is not to suggest, however, that his arguments are uniformly accepted in all quarters. Bourricaud's analysis draws extensively on two important Peruvian novelists, José María Argüedas and Ciro Alegria, to present a composite portrait of elite-mass relationships in the highland provinces, and on sociological and historical materials to depict the form and nature of the national elie grounded in the dominant urban-coastal economy. Focusing on the latter, Bourricaud (1970: 39-40) designated the elite an "oligarchy" because it enjoys absolute power and is extremely restricted in its membership. Its members dominated agro-export, rural and urban landowning, mining, industry, and banking. Finance, however, was by far the most important activity of the oligarchy because

it formed the hub of outward expanding economic empires
based on clan ties (Bourricaud, 1970: 40-43). He is in
essential agreement with Mariátegui on the origin of the
oligarchy's control of national credit: guano wealth
between 1850-1869 served to capitalize newly established
national banks under the direct control of the plutocracy
of that era. The most outstanding attributes of the
oligarchy, however, are its behavioral propensities for
export, speculation and quick profits, and its
inclination to rule through others rather than directly
on its own.

The influence of González Prada is evident when
Bourricaud (1969: 45) explains that the oligarchy's
domination of the country has been "simultaneously aided
in its realization by two conditions: the marginalization
of the illiterate masses and the neutralization of the
middle class." And he is in fundamental agreement with
Mariátegui and the early Haya de la Torre when he
observes that therefore the oligarchy's "greatest danger
lies in a coalition of the underpriviledged and the most
intensely radicalized sector of the middle class"
(Bourricaud, 1969: 45). But Bourricaud's emphasis on the
internal conditions of the oligarchy's existence led him
to attribute to it a greater degree of autonomy and
decisionmaking independence than many contemporary
Peruvian dependista intellectuals are willing to accept.

CONTEMPORARY CRITICISM

There are many contemporary intellectuals in Peru
who have developed positions on the nature of elite
domination and the direction that reforms should take.
In this section we will focus on three in particular who
stand out either because of their political activism or
their insight into the existing social relationships of
Peru. It is fair to say that all three have been both
highly visible social comentators and fall generally
within the tradition of anti-oligarchic thought in the
country. Yet, as what follows demonstrates, each
observer began from somewhat different premises, and
reached substantially different conclusions about the
conduct of the military's revolution.

Ismael Frías

Ismael Frias began his political career as one of
the leaders of the Trotskyist Revolutionary Workers Party
which attempted to form a proletarian party as the only
viable means for achieving a revolutionary restructuring
of Peruvian society. After 1952, as Hugo Blanco (1972:
19) recalls, "Frias began to retreat from this concept"
because he came to doubt the ability of the workers to
succeed in their goals without some form of alliance with

the progressive middle classes. Consequently, he led his
own faction awary from POR and toward a quasi-association
with APRA. At the time of the 1968 revolution, Frías was
director of Inkarri, the review of the Revolutionary
Socialist League. He supported the goals of the
revolution from the outset, and became a leading
journalist with the Lima daily La Crónica when it was
nationalized in 1971. Frías later participated in the
state's decision to expropriate all remaining independent
Lima dailies in mid-1974 (Gorman, 1978b: 302-303), and
became director of Ultima Hora after its "socialization."
When the government shifted to the right after the
Francisco Morales Bermúdez coup of mid-1975, Frías was
forced into a posture of mild opposition and established
the openly pro-APRA weekly Equis X. He continued to hold
an increasingly hostile attitude toward the labor left
which he had acquired during his tenure with the
state-controlled press because of what he viewed as
labor's counterproductive policy of pressing for economic
concessions during a period of national economic
dislocation.

Although Frías tended to equivocate in his political
views over time, his conceptualization of elite-mass
relationships and the nature of elite domination were
cogently presented in his 1970 work La revolución
peruana y la via socialista. In this work, Frias
identified five hierarchically organized classes. At the
bottom of the society are the peasants and urban workers
who represent the largest class with 65 percent of the
population. The combination of peasants and workers into
a single class reflects the continued influence of
Trotskyist formulations in Frías' thought. The next
lowest class is composed of the petty agricultural,
cattle, and commercial bourgeoisies (which we must assume
includes "rich" peasants), and contains 31.4 percent of
the population. The third class is the petty and middle
industrial and service bourgeoisie which is said to
represent only 1.8 percent of the population. Well above
this industrial and service bourgeoisie are the high
public and private bureaucrats and independent
professionals representing about 1 percent of the
population. Finally, at the apex of the socioecnomic
pyramid is the bourgeoisie and oligarchy with 0.3 percent
of the population and 20 percent of the national wealth
(Frías, 1970: 54). To simplify this scheme, Frías saw a
mass of peasants and proletarians dominated by a
minuscule class of bourgeois oligarchs controlling the
political-economic life of the nation through a small
subsidiary class of high public and private bureaucrates
and professionals. Clearly, the "swing" classes were
considered to be the petty and middle bourgeoisies of the
countryside and city who needed to be weaned away from
their attachment to the existing order and into an

alliance with the peasants and proletarians.

The highest two classes--the bourgeoisie and oligarchy, and the high public and private bureaucrates and professionals--together formed the "Dominant Class." This elite was considered by Frias to be both bourgeois and oligarchic because of the manner in which it held power and the nature of its economic interests. Its primary and traditional techniques for retaining exclusive power included 1) the marginalization of the rural population, 2) the neutralization of the urban population, 3) the active recruitment of those in control of lower-class organizations to enlist their assistance in the continued marginalization of the rural population and neutralization of the urban workers, and 4) the exclusive use of state power to promote private interests. The basis of this Dominant Class's wealth is historically capitalistic and has come to depend on its association with the global capitalist system for its continued survival (Frías, 1970: 54-55). Although Frías alternatively refered to this upper stratum as an elite and a Dominant Class, the best label for it he concluded is "Intermediary Bourgeois Oligarchy" (Frías, 1970: 55). As a class, it was and is highly differentiated, and includes those elements variously defined as the "national," "native," "middle," "industrial," and "progressive" bourgeoisies. Not only is this class variegated, according to Frías (1970: 56), it is also capable of permutations over time. Its most recent "metamorphosis" before the revolution was brought on by a shift in its power base away from agro-export (especially sugar and cotton) in favor of its expanding role as agent for international monopoly capital. But although the Dominant Class might change periodically in form or appearance, for Frías it remains the same in substance.

Frías (1970: 60-64) maintained in 1970 that the chances for breaking elite domination were improving as a consequence of several converging patterns of social change. The most important factors working to weaken elite domination were: 1) the increase in rural-urban migration since World War II; 2) the penetration of the countryside by modern forms of economic organization and production; 3) the cholification or social mobilization of dynamic elements of the peasantry along with the breakup of the large haciendas and the unionization of the rural poor; and 4) the intensification of class struggle and political conflict in reaction to the increasing pauperization of the peasantry (caused by the more efficient methods of capitalist exploitation that had been recently introduced into the countryside). Frias seems to have believed that for these and other forces to bring about the destruction of the Dominant Class it was necessary to install a revolutionary government that could deprive the elite of external assistance from the forces of global capitalism. He mistakenly assumed the Revolutionary Government of the Armed Forces that came to power in 1968 was such a regime. But the failure of the revolution to either destroy all the forms of elite domination or extricate Peru from its dependent international position suggests that Frías was mistaken in some fundamental aspect of his thought.

Carlos Delgado

Carlos Delgado Olivara was at one time personal secretary to Haya de la Torre and, at least during that early period, a confirmed supporter of APRA. Delgado's formal training in sociology and the seemingly more academic than political orientation of his early work provided him with a technocratic image appealing to the military. In 1969 he became then-president Velasco's leading speech writer and, together with the radical colonels who had originally conspired with General Velasco to execute the coup of 1968, exercised exceptional influence in the government (Lowenthal, 1975: 34-35, 39). In July 1971, Delgado was appointed director of the newly formed SINAMOS. At that time, it was alleged in Ultima Hora (July 21, 1971) that Delgado had been the predominant voice in the formulation of the ideology of the revolution, and not the radical colonels who were normally credited with the doctrinal direction of the revolution. Whether true or not, the allegation reveals to what extent Delgado belonged to the inner-most circle of the revolutionary leadership. Delgado survived the fall of Velasco in mid-1975, although his position and influence within the regime declined drastically. As late as May 1976 Delgado was defending the military government in the state-controlled press (La Prensa, May 26, 1976) against demands by leading political parties for the election of a new government. Delgado opposed the call for elections between 1974-1977 on the grounds that the parties that would participate were the instruments of the oligarchy and imperialism. The government could not condone elections that would subvert the goals of the revolution, he argued.

Delgado's most direct treatment of elite-mass relation is presented in his 1974 work Problemas sociales en el Perú contemporaneo (which contains some essays published previously). Delgado (1974: 39) set out in this work to elaborate a "new scheme of social composition in Peru" which would break with the repetitive and imitative patterns of earlier works. His standing premis was that the conclusions of social science in the developed countries had no reliable applications in developing societies where social conditions were so radically different. Only the methodology of science and the rigors of theory building enjoy a universal application, according to Delgado, and not the conclusions they yield in particular settings. It is worth noting that this perspective echoed Mariátegui's position on the utility of marxian analysis in understanding Peruvian reality independently from the conclusions that that analytical mode had yielded for other societies. Specifically, Delgado argued against the usability of the "traditional tri-class scheme" (upper-middle-lower) which through imitation of Western scholarship has become rooted in Peruvian social science. This cognative inclination to understand societies in terms of stratification leading to a concentration on hierarchically organized classes is, claimed Delgado (1974: 43), "too simple to reflect the social reality of Peru and facilitate interpretation, and too rigid to capture the natural change" within Peruvian society.

As an alternative to this "class stratification" model, Delgado (1974: 43-45) proposed his own which he felt would better depict the "complexity, fluidity and dynamism of the Peruvian social order." The position of groups within Peruvian society, and their relationships to each other, argued Delgado (1974: 48-49), could best be determined in relation to their relative "domination." The extent and nature of the domination experienced by social groups was considered to be a function, primarily, of their access to the "mechanisms of power." Access, in turn, was determined, among other things, by the following factors:

Race and Ethnicity. Peruvian society discriminates against individuals and groups on the basis of the presumed racial superiority of blancos (those of European extraction). Indians are excluded from formal channels of influence, as are orientals, negros, and mestizos to lesser degrees, because of their "race." But since race and ethnicity are increasingly determined by cultural, linguistic, and economic criteria (because of the nearly universal miscegenation throughout the population), upward mobility (for example from the status of Indian to mestizo) can be achieved fairly quickly through acculturation.

Geographical Location. The Peruvian political and economic system discriminates in favor of the coast over the sierra, and in favor of cities over countryside. Consequently, those residing on the coast generally wield more influence in the "mechanisms of power" than those in the sierra, and urban dwellers enjoy greater influence than do rural inhabitants. The greater the geographical disadvantage in access to power, the more marginalized a group is.

Organization for Collective Defense. Access to power, or the ability to moderate the degree of domination imposed by those in power, is achieved by collective organization (cooperatives, collectives, unions, etc.). Those groups with the strongest organization and the largest memberships succeed, all other things being equal, better than others in exercising influence or defending their members against the influence of their adversaries.

By focusing on the above considerations, Delgado sought to offer a structural interpretation of Peruvian society based not on stratification, but domination. The most dominated members of society are those whose race or ethnicity, geographical location, and relative lack of organization prevent them from either gaining access to, or mitigating the adverse effects of, the mechanisms of power. Using this perspective (which looks not at who is on top and who is on the bottom, but who is inside and who is outside), Delgado arrived at a schematic picture of Peruvian society that distinguishes between fourty-two socioeconomic groups, classified into nine categories of relative domination, and divided between four "sectors" or classes (Delgado, 1974: 51-52). The most disadvantaged sector is the Social World of Total Marginalization which contains those completely insulated from national life (primarily jungle tribes). Their very marginalization, however, reduces the degree to which they are dominated by the center of the system. Next in order of relative disadvantage is the Sector of the Predominantly Rural and Indian Social World, containing three subcategories of relative domination. (Completely Dominated, Partially Dominated, and Transitional Dependent) between which are divided some sixteen socioeconomic groups of shared identities. Within this variegated class, there are wide variations in status and domination: the most diadvantaged socioeconomic groups being the unsalaried workers on sierra latifundia, while the most advantaged group would be the urban artesians and skilled workers in the provincial towns. The third sector or class is the Predominantly Urban and Mestizo Social World. This is an intermediary sector, in contrast to the previously noted sector which is considered completely dominated. This sector contains four subcategories of relative domination (Stationary Subordinate, Emergent Subordinate, Emergent Transitional, and Dynamic Upwardly Mobile) into which are grouped nineteen socieoeconomic groups. Once again, there are wide variations of status and opportunity between the socioeconomic groups aggregated into this heterogeneous class: the least advantaged being those in static positions of subordination like army recruits, petty civil servants, and unskilled workers; the most advantaged being successful entrepreneurs, high military officers, and high professionals and public administrators. Members of these latter groups are considered viable candidates for recruitment into the fouth sector: the Dominant Class.

The Dominant Class, Delgado (1974: 53) argued, lies in an insular world that is predominantly white and metropolitan. Its six constituent socioeconomic groups are labeled "Power Groups," and consist of the large commercial interest, the highest military chiefs, the leaders of the major political parties, the big industrialists, the big mineral, rural and urban property owners and, finally, the bankers and financiers. One notices immediately that these are the same constituent members of the elite identified by Gonzalez Prada, Mariátegui and, most recently, Bourricaud.

Julio Cotler

Julio Cotler was educated in sociology at the University of Burdoes (Ph.D. 1960) and has published widely in both English and Spanish. Unlike Frías and Delgado, Cotler was not an unqualified supporter of the military regime that came to power in 1968, although he did selectively endorse certain policies of the new government. Together with Anibal Quijano Obregón, Cotler participated in the publication of the review Sociedad y Política which served as an important forum of criticism of the military government. Through this publication, Cotler questioned the intent and likely impacts of many revolutionary programs, especially those directed toward labor. This provoked public responses from Delgado, who defended the government's policies in the Lima press. A particular issue of dispute concerned whether the government's policies could actually achieve a reconciliation between labor and private capital by providing the former with partial ownership in the means of production. Delgado, arguing for the government, insisted that the policy would succeed. Cotler, for his part, suggested that the policy could not successfully end all forms of class conflict. The opposition of Sociedad y Política to the Velasco government finally brought about its closing and the exile of Cotler and Quijano (Pease García and Verme Insúa, 1974: 618, 633). Cotler was subsequently allowed to return to Peru and became associated with the prestigeous Institute of Peruvian Studies.

One of Cotler's areas of focus has been the techniques of domination in Peruvian society. In an article describing conditins before the 1968 revolution, Cotler (1970) depicted Peru as a society of structural dualism. But by dualism he did not mean that Peru contained two isolated subsystems, but rather that one part of the society dominated the other. In a manner similar to Delgado, he explained that the coast exercises a type of internal colonial control over the sierra, whose masses are marginalized and deprived of access to the opportunities and resources of the wider society. Cotler attempted to illustrate how the system of domination functioned by focusing on the most destitute region of the sierra: Mancha India (an area in south-central Peru containing the departments of Ancash, Apurimac, Ayacucho, Cuzco, Huancavelica and Puno). Within this region, a distinction formerly existed between Indians and mestizos based on language, place of residence, consumption patterns, occupation, and prestige. The bulk of the population of Mancha India was marginalized from the mainstream society by provincial oligarchs exploiting the cast-like distinctions between Indians and mestizos. Mestizos were recruited into the system of domination by the provincial oligarchs as the direct overseers of the Indian masses. Indians seeking upward mobility were limited to the path of taking on the appearance and habits of mestizos and participating in the system of domination. (This observation bears striking resemblence to Prada's argument that the stratification of Peruvian society depended on the servility of intermediary groups to their superiors and absolute distain for their inferiors.) The sum result was that only a few members of the Indian caste entered the larger political-economic system, and then only on conditions of serving the oligarchy in marginalizing the remaining bulk of the rural population (Cotler, 1970: 423-427).

The system of marginalization in the sierra was paralleled by an alternative mechanism for neutralizing the urban masses. In the major cities and along the coast, political parties served as devices for the segmental incorporation of the proletariat into the prevailing order. Political parties employed their access to state resources to forge clientelistic relationships with their members. Three important consequences of this process were: the subordination of the individual to the party that served as his patron; occupational immobility since benefits were normally tied to a person's specific economic activity (such as party-sponsored wage increases for certain industries in which the party had a strong position); and the maintenance of the distance between segmentally incorporated urban groups and the marginalized Indian masses of the sierra. This last characteristic derived from the reality that segmentally incorporated groups often received benefits which the system could not afford on a nation-wide level (like higher wages, social security benefits, or job security). Hence, many members of the urban lower classes were provided with at least an implicit interest in the continued marginalization of the rural population (Cotler, 1970: 428-430).

Returning to the rural situation, the entire system of domination before 1968 was grounded, according to

Cotler (1970: 423), on the political-legal authority of
the oligarchic land owners. Elites monopolized political
offices in their respective provinces so that the
hacienda remained the real seat of power, and not the
municiple, provincial or even departmental governments.
At the local and national levels the system produced
excessive bureaucratic clientelism and privatization of
state power. Within this context, few if any
opportunities for self advancement existed for the Indian
masses other than those that re-enforced the system of
domination. But Cotler detected a fracture in the
edifice of elite domination with the appearance of a new
social type: the Cholo. The Cholo provided a new role
model for Indians which weakened the prestige of
mestizos and provided alternative paths of upward
mobility that did not strengthen elite domination. More
specifically, Cholos were (and are) individuals who
independently integrate themselves into the wider
political economy by taking advantage of the increasing
opportunities appearing in the countryside as a
consequence of "cholification" (a process involving rural
urbanization and urban ruralization).

Obviously, the appearance of new opportunities
reflected the simultaneous collapse of the oligarchical
forms of control from within, and the penetration of
external forces (especially market forces). The dynamics
of cholification led Cotler (1970: 432-440) to identify
"a change in the patterns of social stratification of
Mancha India, with an emphasis upon the elimination of
caste lines." This, in turn, contributed to a breakdown
of the system of elite domination as it became
increasingly difficult to effectively marginalize the
bulk of the rural population.

The revolution of 1968 interrupted, to some extent,
the axis of the struggle between elites and masses both
in the countryside and the city. This required a
corresponding adjustment in Cotler's analysis. In two
articles first published in Peru in 1972 and 1973, and
later revised and published together in English, Cotler
(1975) examined the "new mode of political domination"
which he felt the military regime was working to
institutionalize. For Cotler (1975: 47-50), the 1968
revolution had resulted from the "oligarchic crisis of
the 1960s" which involved a breakdown of the traditional
elite structure. That structure had rested on
cooperation between two distinct sets of elites--those
involved in export and those owning semi-colonial
haciendas--joined together in a political alliance. The
overall economy, therefore, was a mix of semi-colonial
feudalism and capitalist coastal activity which permitted
a high degree of concentration of economic, social, and
political power within an institutionalized structure
dominated by foreign (and especially North American)

capital. The provincial elites marginalized campesinos while the native bourgeoisie restricted itself to those economic activities neglected by foreign capital. The scant opportunities within this setting for native accumulation and distribution of wealth locked the society into a state of underdevelopment. To the extent that the dominant class was visably responsible for the continuation of this state of affairs, it was unable to legitimize its authority and was forced to rely on the military to preserve the existing order during times of political crisis (Cotler, 1975: 47-48).

The weakening of this system began after the Second World War when the more complete integration of the Peruvian economy into the world market stimulated a development of the urban economy along more fully capitalistic lines. This was paralleled by expanding migration to the cities and a certain degree of participation by the middle and lower classes in the wealth generated by a diversification of national exports and increasing domestic production. But the shift in the economy was not complemented by a shift in the political system, which remained essentially as before. The impact of the new economic activities stimulated social mobilization aimed at forcing basic political-economic reforms. The unresponsiveness of the oligarchic and dependent state sparked an abortive guerrilla movement in the early 1960s that contributed to the alienation of the military and the Church from the existing political system. The military, fearing that the intransigence of the elite would lead to a revolution from below, intervened in 1968 to authoritatively restructure the polity from the top down, while simultaneously suppressing the social mobilization that necessitate the reforms. The military's approach was to impose corporatist structures which, to a certain extent, continued to rely on segmental incorporation of lower-class sectors as a means of neutralizing them politically (Cotler, 1975: 63-75). The military, therefore, eschewed political participation, and its revolution endeavored to create new techniques of centralized control over a population that would still remain essentially neutralized and segmentally tied to the state in clientelistic ways. The objective, nevertheless, had not been achieved with any great success. Thus, Cotler (1975: 78) optimistically looked forward to the prospect that the increasing social mobilization stimulated by the military reforms would pave the way to a mass-based, popular revolution at some near point in time.

The importance of social mobilization and popular organization have been stressed by Cotler in Clases, estado y nación en el Perú (1978). In this work, Cotler traced the influence of Peru's colonial heritage on the early republican era, the role of commerce and guano in the formation of an urban elite, and the critical alliances made by the nascent bourgeoisie at the turn of the century with international capital, on one side, and the provincial feudalistic interests, on the other. A recurrent theme in the study is the frustration of popular aspirations to achieve an integration of the nation capable of facilitating its social, economic, and political development free of external, imperialistic forces. In this work, Cotler revealed clearly the role of independent, anti-oligarchic, anti-imperialistic and essentially socialistic popular movements in toppling the old system of domination in the 1960s. In short, Cotler argued the indispensability of class conflict in resolving Peruvian problems in the tradition of Gonzalez Prada and Mariátegui. Frías and Delgado, although in essential agreement with earlier works of the anti-oligarchic tradition in Peru, looked more to the military as the solution of elite domination in Peru than open class conflict. Their optimism that an alternative existed to popular revolution from below is less credible now than in the early 1970s, and the post-revolutionary critique of the upper classes will likely follow the more radical line advanced by Cotler.

CONCLUSIONS

With the return of civilian government in Peru, a new chapter is being written in the history of elite-mass relations. The military government did not obliterate the oligarchy even if it did significantly alter its composition and force it to restructure its social, political, and economic relations. Wealth remains concentrated, the state remains in the hands of what Delgado called the traditional oligarchic parties, and the military has reverted to its previous preoccupation with order and security. The ties between Peru's entrepreneurial class and foreign economic interests have been reforged, and the national economy has begun to slide back into its earlier status of dependent integration in the global capitalist system. Salazar Bondy argued that only a socialist revolution could break the bonds of dependent capitalist development and the malais of national political life. The docenio was not a socialist revolution, and its outcome appears to have been the rationalization of elite domination rather than any meaningful distribution of power among the popular classes. The oligarchy has passed through one of its "metamorphoses" of which Frías wrote, disregarding its provincial component and adopting more indirect means of promoting its interests.

Elite-mass relations in the post-revolutionary period will likely be conditioned by four primary considerations: the role adopted by the state, the organizational solidarity of organized labor, the accentuation or lessening of rural marginalization, and the performance of centrist parties like Acción Popular. The docenio increased the size and scope of the state apparatus, and the Belaúnde administration attempted to employ the expertise and resources of government during its first year to mediate between workers and owners. Labor, for its part, is well organized as Scurrah and Esteves illustrated in Chapter 4. But a tripartite mechanism for resolving labor disputes (involving unions, management, and government) set up after Belaúnde took office threatened to divide the working-class movement. A process similar to the segmentary incorporation described by Cotler appeared to be taking shape as some unions were enticed into competition for clientelistic concessions. At the same time, the gulf between the rural poor and the struggling urban working class was reinforced by the new constitution which effectively guaranteed that provincial concerns would not be placed on the national agenda. For example, the method of electing senators (at large) insured that Lima, with perhaps one third of the national population, will largely determine the membership of the upper chamber. Thus, the enfranchisement of rural marginals, mostly illiterate and economically insignificant, amounted to very little. Compounding the situation is the reality that, as McClintock pointed out in Chapter 5, sufficient resources simply do not exist to meet the needs and demands of most of the rural poor. Finally, even the broadest labor organization, the CGTP, did not adequately bring together rural marginals with urban workers. Thus, although Cotler may be correct in suggesting that new avenues of upward mobility have come into existence in the countryside, the conditions of geographical isolation and insufficient organization discussed by Delgado will continue to contribute to the subordination and marginalization of the rural poor.

By far the most important determinant of elite-mass relations in the future will be the performance of centrist parties like Accion Popular or APRA. More than ever before, the state apparatus is the pivotal institution of domination in Peru and, if civilian democracy survives, elections will be the crucial test of who gets what, when, and how. The chapters by both Woy-Hazleton and Villanueva demonstrated that in the 1980 general elections the military was willing to tolerate the victory of either of the two leading parties (neither of which could be considered hostile to the upper class). In future elections, should the leftist parties become unified and present a realistic challenge, the situation might not be the same. The performance of the leftist coalition IU in the November elections suggests that perhaps one third of the electorate could be expected to vote for the left in future elections, meaning that the centrist parties would need to become more institutionalized and cohesive. The political traditions of Peru do not suggest that this is likely.

Little seems to have changed from the time when Gonzalez Prada and Víctor Andrés Belaunde examined the political propensities of the upper class. At the end of its first year in office, Acción Popular was at war with itself, its legislative leaders openly attacking their executive counterparts. APRA, in turn, was divided between one faction drifting to the right, and another flirting with the left. Although many of these disputes seemed to center around important policy questions, closer examination indicated that they were essentially clashes between personalistic factions. The oligarchy has always understood that the protection of its interests rests with control of the state apparatus. Yet hitorically it has never been successful for any extended period in competing in the electoral arena (in spite of its vast resources). In the past, it has overcome this handicap by either the appearance of a more or less charismatic politician or military intervention. There do not appear to be any charismatic figures on the horizon of Peruvian politics, and the stage is set for a repetition of the crisis in oligarchic domination of the sixties described by Cotler and Frías.

9
The Post-Revolutionary
Political Economy in Peru

David Scott Palmer

On July 28, 1980 Peru returned to civilian rule
after almost twelve years of military government. In a
moment of high drama, Fernando Belaúnde Terry, architect
by training and politician by experience, took over as
Peru's 102nd president from the very military
establishment which had wrested power from him in the
dead of night on October 3, 1968. In his inaugural
address, he pledged his administration to the resolution
of the country's continuing economic, social, and
political problems in a spirit of national unity. During
his first months in office the preliminary outlines of
the directions he would take during his term of office
began to take shape: real wage and salary improvements,
local self-help in both the burgeoning urban squatter
settlements and the countryside, partial devolution of
the responsibilities of some state enterprises to the
private sector, return of newspapers to their former
owners, large-scale welfare projects in marginal urban
and rural areas, substantial international financial
community assistance, export promotion, municipal
elections, and appeals for increased foreign investment.

THE LEGACY OF THE REVOLUTION

In order to appreciate the new civilian government's
initiatives and to assess the prospects for success, one
must examine briefly the legacy of the military regime it
replaced.[1] The political economy parallels between
1967-1968 and 1978-1980 are remarkable. In both periods,
the government in power had lost legitimacy over time for
similar reasons: growing inflation, a rapidly rising
foreign debt, mismanaged nationalizations, currency
devaluation, worker unrest, and corruption scandals.
Large segments of the population actively supported an
alternative during both periods. In 1968, however, the
military proclaimed its commitment to righting the wrongs
of its civilian predecessor; in 1980, the reverse was the

case. As similar as the political economy contexts were
for the changes of government in 1968 and 1980, the
reforms of the intervening period produced a much more
complex situation both quantitatively and qualitatively
for the new civilian administration to deal with. The
military inherited a foreign debt of less than $1 billion
in 1968; the civilians, about $9 billion in 1980.
Inflation for 1968 was about 19 percent; in 1979, 67
percent. The percentage of GDP and employment within the
public sector increased from 11 percent and 7 percent,
respectively, in 1968 to 21 percent and 13 percent by
1975. The Peruvian sol was valued at about 44 per US
dollar in 1968 and about 260 per US dollar in mid-1980.
In 1968 there were 364 major strikes affecting 108,00
workers; in 1975, 779 affecting 617,000.[2]

Between 1968 and 1975 the military, with the
enthusiastic support of key civilian advisors, dedicted
itself with unprecedented vigor to carrying out the
social, political, and economic reforms it felt the
situation required. These reforms were to have
far-reaching consequences--including, ultimately, the
military's own demise. The main goal of the program was
national security, redefined to include economic
independence, political incorporation, and social
leveling. Rarely in Latin America had a military
establishment espoused reformist goals upon taking power;
even less frequently had one followed through with a wide
variety of concrete actions.

The military leaders initially mistook popular
acquiescence for support and eventually squandered the
very genuine political space they inherited in 1968 by
trying to do too much too quickly with too few resources.
Process often came to substitute for results; sectoral
plans often overlooked contradictions across sectors;
impressive new ministry buildings conveyed an illusion of
significance largely lacking in the gritty day-to-day
labor of making a policy work at the grass roots. The
willingness of Occidental and Southern Peru Copper to
make major investments may have deceived government
leaders into believing others would soon be forthcoming
in spite of the impressive array of foreign investment
disincentives.[3] Increases in sugar production after the
cooperatization of the plantations, dramatic increases in
the fish catch and production, rising prices for copper
and the discovery of apparently substantial oil deposits
shortly before the OPEC embargo, and the easy
availability of large foreign loans combined to lull
military leaders into believing that they had finally
broken for Peru the bonds of dependence and resulting
underdevelopment which many believed had been their
country's historic fate.

The eventual results are now history. The
government used up existing political space faster than

it could create the new order to give new and different kinds of space.[4] The military, furthermore, turned into weakness its greatest strength--a hierarchical command structure--because it was largely sealed off from the various feedback mechanisms by which more open political systems usually adjust policy over time. The illness of President Juan Velasco Alvarado reduced the effectiveness of the individual most able to keep the various parts of the growing government complex in reasonable synchronization at the very moment when inspired implementation was most required. Fish disappeared, copper and sugar prices fell, oil remained elusive, loans began to come due, inflation and popular dissatisfaction rose in tandem, corruption tainted individuals within the military, and the national police finally refused to continue to be the government's enforcer without adequate pay or prestige. In summary, a combination of bad luck and policy errors undermined many of the military's reform goals.

The Morales Bermúdez administration, which took over from Velasco through a bloodless coup in August 1975, tried to consolidate the reforms without abandoning them altogether. It largely succeeded, but at an economic and social cost that the new civilian government will have to bear for most of its term in office. Inflation rose to rates not seen in a generation and wages plummeted, along with health and nutrition standards.[5] Even though government bankruptcy was narrowly averted in 1978 and international accounts improved substantially thereafter with a series of strict economic measures and improved foreign market prices for primary products, the legacy of unemployment and human suffering remained. So too, however, did many of the important institutional reforms which gave thousands of citizens new opportunities in their workplaces and government; new powers to carry out their will.

In a somewhat perverse way, then, the new civilian government took over at an auspicious moment. The situation was bad enough domestically and the previous military regime had been sufficiently "desprestigiado" (deprived of prestige) that the civilian successor represented a hopeful alternative for millions of Peruvians. At the same time, the new government had the opportunity to build on many of the reforms of its predecessor. As long as it did not promise more than it could deliver and moved cautiously but responsibly in a political arena in which routinized citizen-system feedback mechanisms had been reintroduced (e.g., parties and interest groups, congress, and elected local governments), and got cooperation from the weather, world market prices, and oil exploration efforts, the civilian government appeared during its first year to have a good chance of finishing its term without yet another coup.

One basis for this sanguine appraisal can be set forth by
a summary description and analysis of the major actors in
the system.

KEY POLITICAL AND ECONOMIC ACTORS

The array of sectors, organizations, and groups with
a particular stake in Peru's political and economic
systems is quite complex due to both remote and recent
history. As previous chapters have demonstrated, the
twelve years of military rule brought into existence a
number of new actors. These included new unions and
union confederations, neighborhood and community
organizations, and new forms of economic organizations
controlled by workers.

In spite of such organizational proliferation under
the 1968-1980 military regimes, however, the traditional
pre-established parties and unions were neither abolished
nor pushed completely aside. These included the
political party AP (Acción Popular) of Belaúnde; APRA and
its union confederation, the CTP (Confederación de
Trabajadores del Perú); the political party PCP (Partido
Comunista) and its union confederation, the CGTP
(Confederación General de Trabajadores del Perú); as well
as a variety of smaller parties and unions or
federations. The eventual result, therefore, was
organizational proliferation both across the system and
down into it. This meant that one of the most important
legacies of the docenio of military rule was a sharp
increase in the number and variety of actors in the
political economy of Peru.

Such a diversity of organized groups in a relatively
open civilian-controlled political system carries with it
a number of important implications. One is the
relatively greater access to the peak actors in the
system by interested individuals and groups through the
utilization of one or another of the multiple channels
available. Another is the greater likelihood of
conflicting demands being placed on the system by its
very accessibility, and the impossibility of satisfying
the concerns of all the actors. The multiplicity of
organizations and groups within specific sectors
increases competition for support, and heightens the
possibility of substantial crosspressuring or even
conflict on the basis of differences in ideology,
strategy, or specific patron-client relationships. The
possibility of promoting system instability rises to the
degree that some groups can accomplish their objectives
in one issue area only to find that the negative effects
on another high priority area for other groups prod them
into counterreactive behavior. In short, while a more
open system favors demand aggregation and articulation by
the various actors, Peru's present complex and

overlapping pluralistic system is likely to make outcomes
uncertain, tentative, and even unpredictable. A short
discussion of each of the major actors will illustrate
the complexity of the new political process in Peru.

The Military

The armed forces of Peru, which today total some
60,000 (80,000 if the national police, the Guardia Civil,
are included), have historically been a key political
actor (Wilkie, 1980). The first elected civilian
president to spend more than a few months in office did
not take his post until 1872, forty-eight years after
independence! More recently, the military has occupied
the presidency for thirty of the past fifty years,
including the past twelve years. Even though officers
turned formal authority back over to civilians in
mid-1980, the interests and concerns of the armed forces
still need to be carefully taken into account.

The traditional role of the military as governor in
Peru was to restore order and protect the interests of
the so-called oligarchy. Between 1931 and 1975 a further
concern of the military was to keep APRA from occupying
the presidency: first, because of APRA's radical
tendencies, but later more in response to Aprista efforts
to subvert and undermine elements of the military.
However, developments within Peru and within the
military, beginning in the CAEM (Centro de Altos Estudios
Militares) in the 1950s, gradually gave the bulk of the
officer corps a very different perspective on what its
role in Peru should be. Much greater stress was placed
on the national development components of national
security, which included a heightened perception of, and
rationale for, what the military could do in this regard
(Villanueva, 1973b). When the civilian government of
President Belaúnde stumbled along its own growth and
development path in the late 1960s, the military had the
opportunity to put its own evolving theories identifying
national security with national development to work. As
these theories interacted with practical realities over
the following twelve years they placed the Peruvian
military squarely behind agrarian and industrial reform,
large scale expropriation of foreign investment, and the
expansion of government (even though intra-military
differences required careful attention and often delayed
or altered some policies).

The years of military rule also gave the military
establishment the opportunity to update its equipment on
its own terms, which it largely accomplished. While the
debt repayment effects of such re-equipping will be felt
for some years after 1981, new material requirements
during those years have been substantially reduced. When
combined with the military's loss of prestige and respect

from the populace, military demands on the civilian government after 1980 were less onerous than would otherwise have been the case. One can probably also speculate that the toll on the Peruvian military institution through the long period of governing was sufficiently great to discourage any impulse toward taking over power again anytime soon after 1980. This seemed likely to remain the case even if the civilian government did not give a particularly good accounting of itself.

Political Parties

With the 1978 Constituent Assembly elections and the 1980 presidential, congressional, and municipal elections, the Peruvian political party system has returned to prominence after a long hiatus of military rule. As in the 1963 election following a very short period of military rule, the parties cover the political spectrum, only more so. From five parties running in 1963, the number jumped to 15 in 1980.

Most of the expansion in numbers is explained by the proliferation of parties of the left. Their combined percentage of the vote in the presidential elections dropped in comparison to the Constituent Assembly election two years earlier, but leftist parties substantially increased their percentage of the vote in the November municiple elections (to 34 percent). The significance of the leftist parties as a force in Peruvian politics should not be underestimated. While they continue to have considerable difficulty agreeing among themselves on common strategy or candidates, virtually all of them are willing to play by the rules of the civilian political game. Furthermore, they occupy a segment of the political spectrum which the major estalished parties have virtually abandoned.

Another important change has been the expansion of the franchise in 1980 to the approximately 30 percent of the adult population which is illiterate. The vast majority of these illiterates were rural residents. This meant that, for the first time in Peru's history, national party organizations had a real stake in the problems of the country's hinterlands, and the hitherto marginal populations. Competition for votes is bound to increase, and with it greater efforts to solve such traditional problems as low prices for agricultural products, poor roads, and inadequate education and health facilities.

Except for APRA, the parties are not well institutionalized. Both Belaúnde's centrist AP and Luis Bedoya Reyes's center-right PPC are to a significant degree personalist vehicles for their leaders. This indicates that some erosion of the majority the AP-PPC coalition enjoyed in both houses of congress seemed almost inevitable over time. Therefore, while the majority itself represented a significant and positive departure from Belaúnde's last term as president, his administration needed to move quickly to get its programs passed. APRA, though undergoing the worst internal party crisis in its fifty-six year history, was still a formidable opponent. If it continues to make common cause with the left on particular issues which come before congress (which seems likely as long as Armando Villanueva remains in charge of the party apparatus) APRA could easily play the same obstructionist opposition role which has characterized it in the past.

What united most parties at the most general level during the first year of this civilian government, however, was a common perception of the desirability of avoiding another military intervention. It is very possible, then, that in the future they will avoid those confrontations which could undermine popular confidence in the civilian system once more. Even so, AP and PPC remained linked to business and middle-class interests, and committed to reducing government's role, at least in the modern sector; while APRA and the left were tied to organized labor and were bent on enlarging still further the scope of the public domain. Wherever possible each was likely to work for its own conception of the criteria for a modern and developed Peru. But during the initial phase of the Belaúnde administration, the government forces of AP and PPC held the advantage.

Labor Unions and Federations

As with the political party system, the labor movement expanded markedly in numbers and complexity over the past 15 years. Part of this was conscious government strategy by the Velasco administration (1968-1975) to weaken the hitherto APRA-dominated union movement under the CTP by recognizing new unions and federations. The CGTP (pro-Moscow, Communist Party-controlled), the CNT (Christian Democratic), and the CTRP (Government-Velasquista) were all officially legitimized during this period. The CGTP was the greatest beneficiary of these years; its favored position with the government enabled it to attract many of the locals which APRA's out-of-favor CTP had difficulty supporting (Sulmont, 1977). The mining and metallurgical unions, typically among the most militant in Peru, split off to form their own independent association (FNTMMP-Federación Nacional de Trabajadores Mineros y Metalurgicos Peruanos). The equally radical teachers union, SUTEP (Sociedad Unica de Trabajadores Educacionales Peruanos) waged long strikes over salary issues and the right to recognition. As previous chapters have indicated, real wages began to decline after Velasco, and strikes increased. The Morales Bermúdez government's relations with the unions became extremely hostile.

For all the criticisms which might be directed against the Velasco administration, wages improved substantially in real terms for both white- and blue-collar workers between 1969 and 1974. Furthermore, wages improved more quickly for blue-collar workers than white-collar and declined more slowly, at least through 1977. There remained in the early 1980s, therefore, a legacy of support for the goals and policies of the military-reformist government among organized blue-collar groups found in few other sectors of Peruvian society. Nevertheless, the sharp decline in real wages for both groups between 1977 and 1979 made continuing labor turbulence likely.

The government parties, AP and PPC, were in the most vulnerable position in this area because they controlled few unions and no federations at the outset of the civilian administration. The capacity of APRA and the left to wreak havoc with the AP and PPC plan of government was, therefore, greatest within organized labor. In response, the parties of the administration had little choice but to use the considerable powers of government itself to portray themselves as labor's friend and ally. Whipsaw strategies by opposition forces became increasingly likely by which they would use their organizational strength to threaten or wage strikes and then claim the concessions wrung as proof of their power to control the situation.

Peasant Leagues and Federations

Traditional agriculture still retains more workers than the modern sectors combined and has been perceived for some time as a potentially fruitful area for organizing.[6] Initiatives by the military government tended to concentrate on organizing peasants through local cooperative organizations set up after 1969 and, for a time, a peak entity at the provincial, departmental, and national levels, the CNA (Confederacion Nacional Agraria). In practice, these efforts tended to concentrate on the relatively more mobilized and more integrated parts of this sector, as in the central highlands. The strategy, as in the organized labor area, seemed to be to wean peasants from party-connected unions or federations so as to eventually create a completely new organizational framework. While the strategy was not ultimately successful due to the tendency of the government-created or sponsored entities to become quite independent of officialdom, many of the organizations remained in place. The CNA was one of these, even though it lost its legal standing before the close of the revolution. Its more radical marxist counterpart was the CCP (Confederacion de Campesinos Peruanos), at one time very active in the more marginal sierra departments of Ayacucho, Apurimac, and Cuzco, and still a potentially significant base of rural support for the leftist parties in the early 1980s.

Much of the peasantry generally backed AP and the Belaunde candidacy in the May 1980 presidential and congressional elections. The new administration's emphasis on self-help and "popular cooperation" specifically directed at more marginal rural areas suggested that these people might be priority targets for organization and integration by AP. While the government was likely to have plenty of competition from other parties, given the new universal suffrage laws, this segment of the population represented the government party's best chance for creating a mass movement capable of providing the electoral support necessary to retain national political power.

Urban Migrant Organizations and Federations

The popular base for urban organizations rests on the spectacular increase of migrant populations in the urban centers of Peru. In sheer numbers, however, Lima experienced the greatest expansion; from a population of 450,000 in 1945, the city was estimated in 1980 to have a total population approximating 6,000,000. At least since the Manuel Odría administration (1948-1956), governments have perceived ripe opportunities for garnering popular support among the recent urban migrants to the capital. They are closer to the national center of power and are, therefore, more visible and they tend to include the more dynamic elements of lower-class society. Historically they have not represented a radical force, largely because most are in the process of getting a stake in society; they seemingly want stability and predictability rather than turmoil and uncertainty (Dietz, 1980a).

The cooperative or collective ownership strategy which the military government pursued in the countryside generally between 1969 and 1980 was not followed among the squatter settlements. An opposite strategy prevailed, one which cleared and gave out property titles in large numbers to individual owners (Collier, 1976). While the pre-existing networks of local community squatter organizations were downplayed by the government, they could not be ignored. For the so-called "young towns" (pueblos jovenes), the approach taken was that of cooptation rather than attempting to build parallel organizations. Even though the electoral incentive for organizing was lacking during most of the docenio, many existing local bodies continued to serve as conduits for local contact points of the government bureaucratic structure.

Both Dietz and Woy-Hazleton have already discussed the voting behavior of new urban groups. Although the urban poor moved toward the political center in the 1980 general elections, the unification of the left or the failure of the Belaúnde government to fulfill expectations could produce a shift back to the left in future elections (as suggested by the November municiple elections). The formation of new urban organizations will facilitate the increased political influence of this sector of the population.

In 1980 a new sqatter settlement-barriada dwellers federation was established, the CGPP (Confederación General de Pobladores del Perú), which may become an effective aggregator of local squatter settlement interests. To the degree they do become well organized as a collectivity rather than by separate and fragmented settlement groups, they will very likely challenge the government on such key issues as food and basic necessity prices. Recent urban migrants now come very close to equaling their rural countrymen in numbers, and in some areas their interests have become incompatible. At the very least, they will be competing for scarce resources during the early 1980s; there is probably no way short of the discovery of massive new resources that the government can satisfy the legitimate needs of both sectors of the population (the urban and rural needy).

The Bureaucracy

The central government has expanded markedly over the past fifteen years, both in terms of the number of government employees (from 165,000 in 1964 to 480,000 in 1977) and the state's share of the GNP (from 11 percent in 1968 to 21 percent in 1975) (Fitzgerald, 1976). Such expansion will be difficult to reverse in the future. Government employees organized in 1978 to protect their interests, specifically against the threat of being laid-off, by forming the CITE (Central Interministerial de Trabajadores Estatales). The government's interest in achieving development goals, many in areas where private investment remained unlikely or unfeasible, also militated against lowered levels of public employment, investment, or provision of services. Further inhibiting considertions were the issues of nationalism and national patrimony, both of concern to the public, which were used in the past to generate support for government and the expansion of public control over the means of production. In addition, the civilian government needed to be more sensitive to popular pressures than its predecessor, and there was little indication that most of the important groups favored smaller government.

Agricultural, Industrial, and Mining Societies

The historic "wheelers and dealers" of the Peruvian economy may be divided into three major groups. One has been the "old" line oligarchy, whose bases of power were established during the economic regeneration of Peru following the devastation of the War of the Pacific (1879-1883). These bases came to be centered on agricultural production for export, with some interests in mining, the banks, and newspapers. A second has been the nouveau riche, mostly immigrants of the late 19th and early 20th centuries, whose interests were concentrated in industry and services. A third group has included foreign business interests, mostly English in the 19th century, primarily American since the Second World War. While their interests were based in mining, important investments were also made in export agriculture, services, and manufacturing. The peak associations of these groups included the SNA (Sociedad Nacional Agraria), primarily representing old line export and commercial agriculture; the SNM (Sociedad Nacional de Minería), including domestic and foreign mining interests, and the SNI (Sociedad Nacional de Industrias), which counted among its membership most of the larger investors in modern manufacturing.

The military government changed considerably the ground rules and bases of operation of these groups after 1969-1970. In the process, both the SNA and the SNM were abolished.

The miliiary's reforms forced the oligarchy to look for alternative opportunities and set a framework of incentives within which domestic mining and industrial interests could be both beneficiaries and motor forces for economic growth. One source of tension, nevertheless, is the "new" SI (Sociedad de Industrias) itself, which continues to want import tariff protection. Although some members welcomed fair and measured tariff reductions by the new administration, the Belaúnde government had a difficult time persuading other SI associates that competition could be good for them. Private agricultural interests were markedly reduced between 1969 and 1980 and were not very well organized in 1981, in contrast to small and medium sized mining concerns, who established a rather effective new peak organization, the SM (Sociedad de Minería). With the generation of new incentives for the private sector by the civilian government, these organizations and their members gained both access and influence.

POLICY PREFERENCES OF KEY ACTORS

The issues and interests of the major groups noted above have been incorporated into a preliminary matrix to

TABLE 9.1
Selected Key Actors in the Political-Economy of Peru

1. The Armed Forces (MILITARY)
2. Political Parties
   A. Acción Popular (AP)
   B. Alianza Popular Revolucionaria Americana (APRA)
   C. Partido Popular Cristiano (PPC)
   D. Parties of the Left (LEFT)
3. Labor Federations
   A. Confederación General de Trabajadores Peruanos (CGTP)
   B. Confederación de Trabajadores del Perú (CTP)
   C. Frente Nacional de Trabajadores Mineros y Metalurgicos del
      Perú (FNTMMP)
4. The Peasantry
   A. Confederación Campesina Peruana (CCP)
   B. Confederación Nacional Agraria (CNA)
5. Urban Migrants
   A. Confederación General de Pobladores del Perú (CGPP)
   B. Local squatter settlement organizations (LOCALS)
6. The State Bureaucracy (GOVERNMENT)
7. Industrial, Agricultural, and Mining Interests
   A. Agricultural cooperatives (COOPS)
   B. Industrial Communities (INDCOM)
   C. Sociedad Minera (SM)
   D. Sociedad de Industrias (SI)
8. Indians (INDIANS)

TABLE 9.2
Key Issues Related to the Political Economy of Peru

1. Encourage foreign investment (FINV)
2. Reduce size and scope of government (SGOV)
3. Reduce inflation (RINF)
4. Increase real wages (IWGS)
5. Increase total external indebtedness (IDBT)
6. Reduce import tariffs (RITR)
7. Promote exports, particularly "non-traditional" exports (PEXP)
8. Promote national defense (PDEF)
9. Raise prices on essentials (food, gas, electricity) to real market
   levels (IPRC)
10. Maintain civilian government (MCIV)
11. Increase production of agricultural and other primary products (IPRD)
12. Promote self-help and local infrastructural development projects
    (PHLP)
13. Maintain vigorous support for the Andean Pact (PACT)

TABLE 9.3
Preliminary Matrix of Policy Orientations of Key Groups

+ = favors   N = Neutral   - = opposes   * = high priority issue   ( ) = considerable power to affect

Stakeholders	FINV	SGOV	RINF	IWGS	IDBT	RITR	PEXP	PDEF	IPRC	MCIV	IPRD	PHLP	PACT
						Key Issues							
MILITARY	N-	-	+*	+*	-	-	+	(+)*	-	(+)	+	+	+
PARTIES													
AP	(+)*	(+)*	(+)*	(+)*	(+)*	(+)*	(+)*	+	(+)	(+)*	(+)*	(+)*	(-)
APRA	N	-	+*	+*	+*	-	-	+	-	(+)*	+	+	+
PPC	(+)*	(+)*	(+)*	(+)*	(+)*	(+)*	(+)*	+	(+)*	(+)*	(+)*	N	(+)*
LEFT	-*	-*	+*	+*	-	-	+	(-)	-*	(+)*	+	+	+
LABOR													
CGTP	-*	-*	(+)*	(+)*	-	-	+	+	-*	(-)	+	N	N
CTP	+*	-	(+)*	(+)*	-	-	+	+	-*	(+)*	+	N	+
FNTMMP	-*	(-)*	+*	(+)*	-	-	+	(-)	-*	(-)	(+)*	N	N
PEASANTRY													
CCP	-	-	+*	+*	N	N	N	-	+	+	+*	+*	N
CNA	N	-	+*	+*	N	N	N	N	+	+	+*	+*	N
URBAN MIGRANTS													
CFPP	N	-	+*	+*	+	N	N	+	(-)*	+	+	(+)*	N
LOCALS	N	-	+*	+*	+	N	N	+	(-)*	+	+	(+)*	N
GOVERNMENT	(N-)*	(-)*	(+)*	(+)*	(+)	N	+	+	-	+	+	+	+
ECONOMIC GROUPS													
COOPS	N-	N+	+*	+*	N	+	N	+	+	+	(+)*	+	+
INDCOM	N-	N+	+*	+*	N	-	+	+	-	N	+	N	+
SM	N+	+	+*	N	N	+	+	+	-	+	(+)*	N	N
SI	N+	+	+*	N	+	-	(+)*	+	-	+	+	N	+
INDIANS	N	-	+*	+	+	N	N	+	+*	+	+*	(+)*	N

suggest more graphically the range of concerns, the
intensity with which these power contenders view the
issues, and their relative capacity to affect particular
outcomes. Table 9.1 identifies some of the key political
actors in the immediate post-revolutionary period, while
Table 9.2 lists the principle issues relating to the
political economy of Peru in the early 1980s. In Table
9.3 we present the basic policy preferences of the key
political actors on each of the principle issues.

With civilian government, AP and PPC became the most
significant actors, although the capacity of "outsiders,"
such as organized labor, the bureaucracy itself, or the
military should not be overlooked. The capacity of the
current administration to operate will be determined to
an important degree by the particular arrangements or
alliances between stakeholders and, ultimately, by the
willingness of the "heaviest" actor of all, the military,
to allow the civilian political "game" to continue. The
matrix does not take into account the international
environment, including markets and prices, or possible
conflicts with neighboring countries, including
intra-Andean Pact issues. It also does not consider the
possible influence of such international actors as
foreign governments or corporations. But as an
indication of the internal dynamics of domestic actors
and issues, the matrix purports to reflect current and
projected conditions within Peru. In the following
sections we will examine the political and economic
environments within which key groups will have to pursue
their policy objectives in the forseeable future.

THE CONTEMPORARY POLITICAL SETTING

As other chapters have already made clear, Belaúnde
Terry and his Acción Popular party won a surprising and
stunning victory in the 1980 general elections. This
surprising popular mandate simultaneously accomplished
several important objectives. It dispelled any lingering
doubts that might have existed among elements of the
military over the wisdom of transferring power back to
the civilians. It also gave the incoming administration
a high level of legitimacy as it began to deal with the
severe domestic economic and social problems the country
faced. Furthermore, with significant help from the small
PPC (6 Senate seats, 10 Chamber of Deputies seats), AP
gained a working majority in the legislative branch.
Finally, the large mandate enabled Belaúnde to assemble
his own team, by and large, and also encouraged a number
of the best available people to accept.

Such an auspicious beginning seemed to augur well
for the new civilian government. Some of the outlines of
the major policies the administration would pursue were
beginning to come into focus by early 1981. Economic

policies, under Prime Minister and Minister of Economy, Finance, and Commerce Manuel Ulloa, were oriented toward export promotion, domestic business incentives, a more market-oriented economy, and substantial international participation through loans and investments in such large scale projects as hydroelectric power, oil exploration and production, and copper mining. Agricultural production for domestic consumption was stimulated through loans, credits, irrigation projects, technical assistance, and higher prices. Real wages were permitted to increase through collective bargaining and government deuce. Massive short-term relief was sought for imminent electrical power shortages and widespread nutritional deficiences. A large job creation program attempted to alleviate the 40 percent un- and underemployment, much of the responsibility for which was to rest with the private sector. Local public works programs, promoted largely through self-help projects with government assistance, were expected to improve living conditions among the marginal populations of both rural and urban Peru. New lands were in the process of being opened up through completion of irrigation projects and expansion of the marginal highway through the more fertile lands of the upper jungle. The existing cooperative and community structures were to remain, but with greater emphasis on small scale private ownership in future projects. Government bureaucracy was targeted to be whittled down, but only through natural attrition over time.

This was an impressive agenda, although there were a number of obstacles to overcome between inauguration and the 1985 elections to insure that this administration would be remembered as a successful one. Some of the major difficulties facing the country by early 1981 follow.

1) Peru will probably cease to be a net oil exporter within three years at present rates of production if no new reserves are found and brought into production by that time.

2) Electric power is scarce in several parts of the country, particularly in the Lima area, making likely brown-outs and black-outs and the postponement of energy intensive industrial projects until new capacity is constructed.

3) The president's party is a personalist one and it is not likely to hold all its members when the problems begin to mount.

4) The leadership style of Belaúnde is somewhat aloof and distant; there may be difficulties in getting him to focus on particular issue areas.

5) Higher food prices may make peasants and farmers happy, but will have precisely the opposite effect on urban migrants and marginals.

6) There is no clear candidate in the wings for 1985

who would be likely to fashion a working majority,
leading to a near certain rise in pre-electoral tension
in the latter part of the Belaúnde administration.

7) Important entrepreneur elements within the SI oppose
substantial lowering of import tariffs due to their fear
of the adverse effects on their companies of more open
competition for domestic markets.

8) A large number of wage, salary, and working-
condition demands by organized labor and employees remain
to be resolved.

9) Even if circumstances are exceptionally favorable,
it will be difficult to meet campaign promises of one
million new jobs in two years.

10) In spite of the success of the agrarian reform in
distributing land, more landless or subsistence farmers
still lack land than received it, and a scarcity of
arable land makes it very difficult to respond to the
needs of the large numbers of marginal persons remaining
in rural areas.

11) The large state apparatus needs to be substantially
redirected and trained to meet the development
requirements of the new administration.

12) While the military hierarchy is both politically
exhausted and deprived of prestige, there is a younger
generation of officers coming up through the ranks who
did not participate in the benefits of military rule and
may press to do so.

13) A Mobilization Law published by the outgoing regime,
gives the military wide ranging special powers when a
state of emergency due to war, internal subversion, or
natural disaster is declared. Should conditions
deteriorate markedly, the military could press for a
declaration of a state of emergency and use the resulting
power to reassert indirect political control.

CURRENT ECONOMIC SITUATION

The economic picture for Peru is mixed. The change
in Peru's international economic relationships between
1977 and 1980 was very positive. A combination of
governmental financial policies, IMF structures,
production increases, and improved world prices turned a
near financial disaster into a substantial foreign
exchange surplus (although at considerable human costs,
as Dietz points out in Chapter 3). Several hundred
million dollars of debts were rolled over, making a more
reasonable export/debt repayment ratio. Oil, silver, and
copper sales surged in 1979. Peru's historic diversity
of exports once again proved to be a stabilizing
force--no single export accounted for more than 20
percent of export earnings. Non-traditional, mostly
manufactured, products were the largest single export
earner for the first time (19.5 percent or $677 million

of $3,474 million total exports) (<u>LAER</u>, May 16, 1980).
On international accounts, then, the assessment was
moderately sanguine by 1980, at least for the following
two or three years, in spite of continuing high levels of
foreign debt. Just two and one-half years before, when
Peru seemed on the verge of bankruptcy, such a position
appeared virtually impossible to achieve.

The domestic economic scene was much less bright in
1980. Open unemployment was 6.5 percent and
underemployment was estimated at 33 percent. Inflation
appeared headed for a 50 to 60 percent increase in 1981
when allowances were made for the "dam effect" of
allowing price increases scheduled but postponed by the
outgoing military government to take effect.
Devaluations increased to over 4 percent per month; by
mid-May 1981 the exchange rate was over 40 percent below
May 1980 levels at 405 soles to the dollar). A severe
drought in most of northwest Peru and a good deal of the
central sierra in 1980 also sharply reduced food and
agricultural production, thereby contributing to sharp
falloffs in such traditional export crops as sugar and
cotton, and forcing increased imports of such staples as
rice. Daily caloric intake had fallen, and malnutrition,
disease, and infant death rates all increased. The real
wages of most Peruvians continued to be well below 1973
levels and hardship and suffering were to be found even
among the middle classes. In fact, by some surveys,
white-collar wages had tended to fall relatively even
more than blue-collar. Although real wage levels had
once again begun to increase and the new government was
committed to further improvements, Peruvian wage levels
remained among the lowest of the countries at middle
levels of development. The domestic economic shocks of
the previous several years had been felt at most levels
of Peruvian society, but had brought greater hardship on
the lower and middle classes.

However, signs were pointing to modest turnarounds
in many economic indicators. Also working in the new
civilian administration's favor was a climate of
considerable international good will. Sister Andean Pact
countries, international financial institutions, foreign
banks and the foreign investment community, and the
United States government were all supportive of the
government and its efforts to build on the work of the
preceding military regime of Morales Bermúdez to restore
economic growth and economic and political development to
Peru. Many key members of the international financial
community were acquainted personally with members of the
new political-economic team in the government of Peru,
since most spent the military years in exile, often among
these same organizations and institutions. One could
expect the Peruvian government to take utmost advantage
of this good will and personal relationships, improving

still further the rather promising short-run economic prospects.

With respect to economic policies, the Belaúnde administration began to pursue the following development strategies during its first year.

1) Traditional and non-traditional export promotion policies through direct (tax rebates) and indirect (exchange rates) measures.

2) Some reduction of government agency domination or monopoly status in certain production and marketing areas.

3) Greater autonomy for government agencies such as PETROPERU, MINEROPERU, and ELECTROPERU by converting them to limited liability public companies.

4) Incentives for direct- and mixed-venture investment by domestic entrepreneurs.

5) Incentives for foreign investment in high technology or special skill requirement areas, with some possibilities for joint ventures, such as oil exploration or the expansion of copper mining.

6) International financial institution borrowing for high capital investment areas, such as irrigation or hydroelectric projects. These would involve considerable foreign corporate participation in bringing the projects on line, but low involvement once operating.

CONCLUSION

Belaúnde's ability to accomplish these goals seemed dependent in large measure on his administration's capacity to deal with a wide range of problems. Considerable erosion in his administration's legitimacy over time is almost inevitable for several reasons. Governing is always more difficult and complicated than running for office. A number of the hard decisions which should be made will be unpopular with some sectors. The AP is not a well disciplined party and elements are bound to disagree with the president on some issues and vote accordingly. International market forces, natural disaster, failure to discover and extract more oil, and other forces largely beyond the government's control could undermine the best laid plans and programs. Finally, some political and economic groups in the new expanded and open political environment will likely perceive that it is to their advantage to try to challenge the administration through strikes, disruptive tactics, or the witholding of financial commitments for priority projects. The probable political result of these adverse considerations will be an increase over time in tension, confusion, and the perception of an administration reducd to "muddling through." On balance, however, even with the problems and challenges, this civilian government in 1981 appeared to have the best chance of any in recent memory to hand power over in 1985 to its elected successor.

The reopening of the political system and the prospects for continued economic recovery had given most of the system's stakeholders opportunities and alternatives for linking up to various kinds of benefits that the national system will probably be in a position to provide, at least in part. Despite many pressing problems, the political and economic propsects for most key actors in 1981 were more promising than they had been for a number of years.

Notes

1. The reformist phase of the Peruvian revolution has been discussed in a number of works published in English including Lowenthal (1975), Chaplin (1976), Middlebrook and Palmer (1975), and Stepan (1978) to name a few.

2. Figures for the foreign debt and exchange rates are from the Inter-American Development Bank's annual reports, Social and Economic Progress in Latin America (Washington, D.C.). Employment in the public sector is duscussed extensively by Fitzgerald (1976), and strike statistics are from a study by Sulmont (1977).

3. The disincentives to foreign investment stemmed in large measure from the military's nationalization of the US-owned International Petroleum Company's facilities during the first week of the revolution; the expropriation of coastal agro-export operations belonging to the Grace interests, and government moves to establish state monopolies in leading extractive industries. The 1970 legislation establishing worker participation in the management and earnings of manufacturing companies, and measures enacted to control international commerce also discouraged foreign investment.

4. The term "political space" refers to the room available to a government to carry out policies. It is mainly a contextual or environmental factor, and is determined by such considerations as the objective resource base of the state, public perceptions of the existing regime in comparison to the previous regime, the level and rate of social mobilization, the capacity of social and political institutions for channeling and responding to

demands, and the perceived performance of the government. Leadership style, prevailing ideological currents, and the behavior of leading organizations within the political arena all contribute to determining the amount of political space enjoyed by a particular regime, as do other environmental developments such as the performance of trade or the discovery of new exportable resources.

5. World Bank estimates indicate that wages in 1979-1980 were close to one-third below their 1974 levels, and that the average daily caloric intake fell while infant mortality rose. See World Bank Annual Report, 1980 (Washington, D.C., 1980).

6. During the agrarian reform the Velasco administration produced an internal study in 1971 indicating that about 750,000 farm families existed in the traditional agricultural sector for which the reform was intended. This compared with 250,000 families in the modern agricultural sector (commercial and export), and an additional 150,000 farm workers entirely excluded from any reform benefits (Dirección General de Reforma Agraria, Ministerio de Agricultura, 1971).

Bibliography

Abugattas, Luis (1979) La economía peruana en 1978: analysis de
conyuntura económica. Lima: Universidad del Pacifico, Centro
de Investigación.

ACDA (1979) World Military Expenditures and Arms Transfers, 1968-
1977. Washington, D.C.: Arms Control and Disarmament Agency,
United States Printing Office.

Adrianzen, Blanca and George Grahm (1974) "The High Cost of Being
Poor." Archives of Environmental Health 28 (June): 312-315.

Agut, James R. (1975) The "Peruvian Revolution" and Catholic
Corporatism: Armed Forces Rule Since 1968. Ph.D. dissertation.
Miami: University of Miami.

Alexander, R. Alberto (1922) Estudio sobre la crisis de habitación
en Lima. Lima: Imprenta Torres Aguirre.

Alexander, Robert (1973a) Aprismo: The Ideas and Doctrines of Víctor
Raúl Haya de la Torre. Kent, Ohio: Kent State University Press.

_____ (1973b) Trotskyism in Latin America. Stanford: Hoover
Institute Press.

Angell, Alan (1980) "Peruvian Labour and the Military Government
Since 1968." Working Paper Number 3. London: London Institute
of Latin American Studies, University of London.

Asheshov, Nicholas (1977) "Peru's Flirtation with Disaster."
Institutional Investor (October): 181-190.

Astiz, Carlos A. (1969) Pressure Groups and Power Elites in Peruvian
Politics. Ethica: Cornell University Press.

Avery, William P. and James D. Cochrane (1973) "Innovation in Latin
American Regionalism: The Andean Common Market." International
Organization 27 (Spring): 181-223.

Bains, John M. (1972) Revolution in Peru: Mariátegui and the Myth.
University: University of Alabama.

Barrenchea Lecari, Carlos (1979) El Decreto Ley 17716 y la estruc-
tura agraria peruana. Lima: Centro de Investigaciones Socio-
Economicos.

Bejar, Hector (1976) La revolución en la trampa. Lima: Perugraf
Editores.

Belaunde, Víctor Andrés (1963) Meditaciones peruanos. Lima: unspecified publisher.

Bell, William S. (1977) "Unequal Redistribution: Post Agrarian

Reform Differentiation in Coastal Peru." Discussion paper, Peasants Seminar. London: Centre of International and Area Studies, University of London.

Belleveau, Nancy (1976) "What the Peruvian Experiment Means." Institutional Investor (October): 145-148.

Berenbach, Sara (1979) "Empresas autogestionarias industriales en el Perú: una perspectiva." Lima: memeo.

Bernales, Enrique (1980) Crisis política: solución electoral? Lima: DESCO, Centro de Estudios y Promoción del Desarrollo.

Blanco, Hugo (1972) Land or Death: The Peasant Struggle in Peru. New York: Pathfinder Press.

Bollinger, Willaim (1980) "Peru Today: The Roots of Labor Militancy." NACLA Report on the Americas 14 (November-December): 31.

_____ (1977) "The Bourgeois Revolution in Peru: A Conception of Peruvian History." Latin American Perspectives 4 (Summer): 18-56.

Bomat, Thomas (1979) "The Middle Classes and the Military Regimes in Peru Since 1968." Paper presented at the Latin American Studies Association National Meeting, Pittsburgh.

Bourque, Susan C. (1970) Cholification and the Campesino: A Study of Three Peruvian Peasant Organizations in the Process of Social Change. Ithica: Cornell University Dissertation Series.

_____ and David Scott Palmer (1975) "Transforming the Rural Sector: Government Policy and Peasant Response," pp. 179-219 in Abraham F. Lowenthal [ed.] The Peruvian Experiment: Continuity and Change Under Military Rule. Princeton: Princeton University Press.

Bourricaud, Francois (1970) Power and Society in Peru. New York: Praeger.

_____ et al. (1969) La oligarchía en el Perú. Lima: Moncloa Campodonico.

Caballero, José María (1980) Agricultura, reforma agraria y pobreza campesina. Lima: Instituto de Estudios Peruanos.

_____ (1977) "Sobre el caracter de la reforma agraria peruana." Latin American Perspectives 4 (Summer): 146-159.

_____ (1976) "Reforma y reestructuración agraria en el Perú." Working paper, Department of Economics, Catholic University of Peru.

Cabieses, Hugo and Carlos Otero (1978) Economía peruana: un ensayo de interpretación. Lima: DESCO, Centro de Estudios y Promoción del Desarrollo.

Cabrera, Cesar Humberto (1978) Perú: la crisis y la política de estabilización. Lima: Fundacion Friedrich Ebert Ildis, Serie Materiales de Trabajo Numero 17.

Castells, Manuel (1972) Los campamentos de Santiago: movilización urbana. Santiago.

Caycho, Hernan (1977) Las SAIS de la sierra central. Lima: Dirección de Investigación.

CEDES (1980) El agro en el Perú. Lima: Centro de Documentación y Estudios Sociales.

CENCIRA (1975) Los cometes de educación de las empresas campesinas del Valle de Canete. Lima.

Chang-Rodríguez, Eugenio (1957) La literatura política de Gonzalez Prada, Mariátegui y Haya de la Torre. Mexico City: Ediciones Andrea.

Chaplin, David (1976) "Revolutionary Change and Peruvian Militarism," pp. 1-29 in David Chaplin [ed.] Peruvian Nationalism: A Corporatist Revolution. New Bruswick, N.J.: Transaction Books.

Cleaves, Peter S. (1980) Agriculture, Bureaucracy and Military Government in Peru. Ithica: Cornell University Press.

_____ and Martin J. Scurrah (1976) "State-Society Relations and Bureaucratic Behavior in Peru." CICA series paper number 6. Hayward: Department of Public Administration, California State University.

Cline, William (1979) "Economic Stabilization in Peru, 1975-1978." Washington, D.C.: Brookings Institute unpublished manuscript.

Collier, David (1976) Squatters and Oligarchs. Baltimore: Johns Hopkins University Press.

_____ (1975) "Squatter Settlements and Policy Innovations in Peru," pp. 128-178 in Abraham F. Lowenthal [ed.] The Peruvian Experiment: Continuity and Change Under Military Rule. Princeton: Princeton University Press.

Cotler, Julio (1978) Clases, estado y nación en el Perú. Lima: Instituto de Estudios Peruanos.

_____ (1975) "The New Mode of Political Domination in Peru," pp. 44-78 in Abraham F. Lowenthal [ed.] The Peruvian Experiment: Continuity and Change Under Military Rule. Princeton: Princeton University Press.

_____ (1970) "The Mechanics of Internal Domination and Social Change in Peru," pp. 407-444. Masses in Latin America. New York: Oxford University Press.

_____ and Felipe Portocarrero (1969) "Peru: Peasant Organizations," pp. 297-322 in Henry A. Landsberger [ed.] Latin American Peasant Movements. Ithica: Cornell University Press.

Cox, Carlos Manuel (1940) Cartas de Haya de la Torre a los prisoneros Apristas. Lima: Editorial Nuevo Día.

Craig, Wesley W. (1969) "Peru: The Peasant Movement of La Convención," pp. 274-296 in Henry A. Landsberger [ed.] Latin American Peasant Movements. Ithica: Cornell University Press.

_____ (1968 " El movimiento campesino en La Convención, Perú." Memeo. Lima: Instituto de Estudios Peruanos.

Delgado, Carlos (1974) Problemas sociales en el Perú contemporaneo. Lima: Instituto de Estudios Peruanos.

DESCO (1977) Estado y política agraria. Lima: DESCO, Centro de Estudio y Promoción del Desarrollo.

_____ (1975) Propiedad social: polémica. Lima: DESCO, Centro de Estudio y Promoción del Desarrollo.

Dew, Edward (1969) Politics in the Altiplano: The Dynamics of Change in Rural Peru. Austin: University of Texas Press.

Dietz, Henry A. (1980a) Poverty and Problem-Solving Under Military Rule: The Urban Poor in Lima, Peru. Austin: University of Texas Press.

_____ (1980b) "The IMF From the Bottom Up: Social Impacts of Stabilization Policies in Lima, Peru." Paper presented at the Latin American Studies Association National Meeting, Bloomington,

Indiana.

_____ (1978) "Metropolitan Lima: Urban Problem-Solving Under Military Rule," in Wayne Cornelius and Robert van Kemper [eds.] Metropolitan Latin America: The Challenge and the Response. Latin American Urban Research, Vol. 6. Beverly Hills: Sage Publications.

Dodd, Thomas J. (1975) "Peru," pp. 360-380 in Harold Davis and Larman Wilson [eds.] Latin American Foreign Policies: An Analysis. Baltimore: Johns Hopkins University Press.

Drysdale, Robert S. and Robert G. Myers (1975) "Continuity and Change: Peruvian Education," pp. 254-301 in Abraham F. Lowenthal [ed.] The Peruvian Experiment. Princeton: Princeton University Press.

Eguren, Fernando (1980) "Política agraria vs. producción de alimentos?" Quehacer 3 (March): 34-41.

_____ (1975) Reforma agraria, cooperativización y lucha campesina: El Valle de Chancay-Huaral. Lima: DESCO, Centro de Estudio y Promoción del Desarrollo.

Einaudi, Luigi, and Alfred Stepan (1971) Latin American Institutional Development: Changing Military Perspectives in Peru and Brazil. Santa Monica: The Rand Corporation.

Fagen, Richard [ed.] (1979) Capitalism and the State in US-Latin American Relations. Stanford: Stanford University Press.

Fano, Rodriguez, Jorge and Maximo Valencia (1980) Analisis de consumo y nutrición en Lima metropolitana. Tarma, Perú: Seminario taller sobre probelmática alimentária y nutricional.

Feder, Ernest (1971) The Rape of the Peasantry. New York: Doubleday.

Ferris, Elizabeth G. (1980) "Peru and the Andean Pact." Paper presented at the State Department briefing for the US ambassador to Peru, Washington, D.C. (October).

_____ (1979) "Foreign Investment as an Influence on Foreign Policy Behavior: The Andean Pact." Inter-American Economic Affairs 33 (Autumn): 45-69.

Fitzgerald, E.V.K. (1979) The Political Economy of Peru, 1956-1978. London: Cambridge University Press.

_____ (1976) The State and Economic Development: Peru Since 1968. London: Cambridge University Press.

Fontaine, Roder (1971) The Andean Pact: A Political Analysis. Beverly Hills: Sage Publications.

Franco, Carlos (1979) Peru: participación popular. Lima: Ediciones CEDEP

_____ (1975) La revolución participatoria. Lima: Mosca Azul.

Frenkel, Roberto and Guillermo O'Donnell (1979) "The Stabilization Programs of the IMF and their Internal Impacts," in Richard Fagan [ed.] Capitalism and the State in US-Latin American Relations. Stanford: Stanford University Press.

Frías, Ismael (1970) La revolución peruana y la vía socialista. Lima: Editorial Horrizante.

Germana, Cesar (1980) "Las elecciones del mayo y sus implicancias políticas." Sociedad y Política lll (July): 7-16.

Gilbert, Dennis (1979) "Society, Politics and the Press: An Interpretation of the Peruvian Press Reform of 1974." Journal of Inter-American Studies and World Affairs 21 (August): 369-393.

_____ (1977) The Oligarchy and the Old Regime in Peru. Ithica: Cornell University Dissertation Series.

Gonzalez Prada, Manuel (1969) Figuras y figurones. Lima: Libreria y Distribuidora Bendez.

_____ (1966) Pagines libres. Lima: Editorial Thesis.

_____ (1940) Anarquia. Santiago de Chile: Ercilla.

Gordon, Dennis R. (1979) "The Question of the Pacific: Current Perspectives on a Long-Standing Dispute." World Affairs 141
(Spring): 321-335.

Gorman, Stephen M. (1980) "Peruvian Foreign Policy, 1968-1980: An
Overview." Paper presented at the State Department briefing for
US ambassador to Peru, Washington, D.C. (October).

_____ (1979) "Present Threats to Peace in South America: The
Territorial Dimensions of Conflict." Inter-American Economic
Affairs 33 (Summer): 51-71.

_____ (1979a) "The High Stakes of Geopolitics in Tierra del Fuego."
Parameters: Journal of the US Army War College 8 (June): 45-56.

_____ (1978b) "Peru Before the Elections for the Constituent
Assembly: Ten Years of Military Rule and the Quest for Social
Justice." Government and Opposition 13 (Summer): 288-306.

_____ (1978c) "Corporatism with a Human Face? The Revolutionary
Ideology of Juan Velasco Alvarado." Inter-American Economic
Affairs 32 (Autumn): 25-37.

_____ (1977) "Creole Liberalism and Revolutionary Corporatism in
Peru: A Socio-historical Analysis of the Revolution of 1968."
Unpublished Ph.D. dissertation. Riverside: University of
California.

Greaves, Thomas C. (1968) The Dying Chalan: Case Studies in Change
in Four Haciendas of the Peruvian Coast. Unpublished Ph.D.
dissertation. Ithica: Cornell University.

Grosse, Robert (1980) "Foreign Investment Regulations in the Andean
Pact: The First Ten Years." Inter-American Economic Affairs 33
(Spring): 77-94.

Guillet, David (1979) Agrarian Reform and Peasant Economy in
Southern Peru. Columbia: University of Missouri Press.

Gushiken, Anita M. (1977) "Political Factors in the Creation and
Implementation of the Andean Foreign Investment Code."
Unpublished Masters thesis. Denton: North Texas State University.

Handelman, Howard (1975) Peasants, Landlords, and Bureaucrats: The
Politics of Agrarian Reform in Peru. Unpublished manuscript.

_____ (1975a) "The Political Mobilization of Urban Squatter
Settlements." Latin American Research Review 10: 35-72.

_____ (1975b) Struggle in the Andes: Peasant Political Mobilization in Peru. Austin: University of Texas Press.

Harding, Colin (1975) "Land Reform and Social Conflict in Peru," pp.
220-253 in Abraham F. Lowenthal [ed.] The Peruvian Experiment:
Continuity and Change Under Military Rule. Princeton: Princeton
University Press.

Herbold, Carol F. (1979) "Peru: The Political Economy of a Failed
Revolution, 1968-1975." Paper presented at the Latin American
Studies National Meeting, Pittsburgh.

Hernandez Perez, Víctor Manuel (1980) "Niñez y nutrición -- la
paradoja del Perú." Tarma, Peru: Seminario taller sobre problem-
ática alimentaria y nutricional.

Hilliker, Grant (1974) The Politics of Reform in Peru: The Aprista
and Other Mass Parties of Latin America. Baltimore: Johns

Hopkins University Press.

Horton, Doublas E. (1975) "Land Reform and Group Farming in Peru."
Washington, D.C.: International Bank for Reconstruction and
Development, Department of Economics, Studies in Employment and
Rural Development Number 23.

_____ (1974) "Land Reform and Reform Enterprises in Peru. Report
submitted to the Land Tenure Center and the International Bank
for Reconstruction and Development, Washington, D.C.

Huamantinco Cisneros, Francisco (1979) Andahuaylas: reforma agraria
y campesinado. Ayacucho: Investigaciones de la Realidad Peruana.

Hunt, Shane (1975) "Direct Foreign Investment in Peru: New Rules for
an Old Game," pp. 302-349 in Abraham F. Lowenthal [ed.] The
Peruvian Experiment: Continuity and Change Under Military Rule.
Princeton: Princeton University Press.

Huntington, Samuel P. (1968) Political Order in Changing Societies.
New Haven: Yale University Press.

IDB (1979) Economic and Social Progress in Latin America. Washington,
D.C.: Inter-American Development Bank.

ILO (1976) Yearbook of Labour Statistics. Geneva: International
Labour Organization.

IMF (1978) "Peru -- Request for Stand-by Arrangement." Confidential
memo. Washington, D.C.: International Monetary Fund.

INDA (1979) "La autogestación ante una alternativa histórica." Memeo.
Lima: Instituto de Investigacion y Desarrollo de la Autogestion.

Jaquette, Jane S. (1975) "Belaúnde and Velasco: On the Limits of
Ideological Politics," pp. 402-438 in Abraham F. Lowenthal [ed.]
The Peruvian Experiment: Continuity and Change Under Military
Rule. Princeton: Princeton University Press.

_____ (1971) The Politics of Development in Peru. Ithica: Cornell
Dissertation Series.

Juscamaita Aranguena, Enrique (1980a) "Nuestra económica es una ven-
tana al imperialism." Marka 161 (June): 22-24.

_____ (1980b) "El oxigeno del régimen actual." Marka
168 (August): 20-21.

Kantor, Harry (1953) The Ideology and Program of the Peruvian Aprista
Movement. Berkeley: University of California Press.

Klaren, Peter F. (1973) Mobilization, Dislocation, and Aprismo:
Origins of the Peruvian Aprista Party. Austin: University of
Texas Press.

Knight, Peter F. (1975) "New Forms of Economic Organization in Peru:
Toward Workers' Self-Management," pp. 350-401 in Abraham F.
Lowenthal [ed.] The Peruvian Experiment: Continuity and Change
Under Military Rule. Princeton: Princeton University Press.

Landsberger, Henry A. (1969) "The Role of Peasant Movements and
Revolts in Development," pp. 1-61 in Henry A. Landsberger [ed.]
Latin American Peasant Movements. Ithica: Cornell University Press.

Larson, Magali S. and Arlene G Bergman (1969) Social Stratification
in Peru. Berkeley: Institute of International Studies,
University of California.

Lecaros, Fernando (1975) Propiedad social: teoría y realidad. Lima:
Ediciones Rikchay Peru.

Lehman, David (1978) "The Death of Land Reform: A Polemic." World
Development 6 (March): 339-345.

Long, Norman and Bryan R. Roberts [eds.] (1978) Peasant Cooperation
and Capitalist Expansion in Central Peru. Austin: Institute of
Latin American Studies, University of Texas.

Lowenthal, Abraham F. (1975) "Peru's Ambiguous Revolution," pp. 1-43
in Abraham F. Lowenthal [ed.] The Peruvian Experiment: Continuity
and Change Under Military Rule. Princeton: Princeton University
Press.

Maletta, Hector (1978) "El subempleo en el Perú: una visión crítica."
Apuntes 4: 2-48.

Malpica, Carlos (1980) "Transnacionales: el Perú como una mina."
Marka 177 (Octubre): 19-22.

Mariátegui, José Carlos (1968) Siete ensayos de interpretación de la
realidad peruana. Lima: Amauta.

Martz, John and Enrique Baloyna (1976) Electoral Mobilization and
Public Opinion: The Venezuelan Campaign of 1973. Chapel Hill:
University of North Carolina Press.

Matos Mar, José (1976) Yanaconaje y reforma agraria en el Perú: el
caso del Valle de Chancay. Lima: Instituto de Estudios Peruanos.

_____ and José Manuel Mejia (1980) Reforma agraria: logros y
contradicciones, 1969-1979. Lima: Instituto de Estudios Peruanos.

McClintock, Cythia (1981) Peasant Cooperatives and Political Change
in Peru. Princeton: Princeton University Press.

_____ (1980a) "After Peru's Agrarian Reform: Are the Peasants
More Conservative, or More Radical?" Paper presented at the Latin
American Studies Association National Meeting, Bloomington,
Indiana.

_____ (1980b) "Velasco, Officers, and Citizens: The Politics of
Stealth." Unpublished manuscript.

_____ (1977) Self-Management and Political Participation in
Peru, 1969-1975: The Corporatist Illusion. Beverly Hills: Sage
Publications.

Medina, Oswaldo (1980) Perú 1978-1980: Analesis de un momento político.
Lima: C'est Editorial.

Mejia, José and Rosa Dias Suarez (1975) Sindicalism y reforma agraria
en el Valle de Chancay. Lima: Instituto de Estudios Peruanos.

Mercado Jarrín, Edgardo (1980) "Planteamentos sobre política exterior."
El Comercio (Peru) (September 21): 6.

Michl, Sara (1973) "Urban Squatter Organization as a National Govern-
ment Tool: The Case of Lima, Peru," in Francine Rabinovitz and
Felicity Trueblook [eds.] Latin American Urban Research. Vol. 3.
Beverly Hills: Sage Publications.

Ministerio de Agricultura (1978) Información basica sectoral. Lima:
Memeo.

_____ (1974) Reforma agraria en cifras. Documento
de trabajo No. 11-74 (November).

Ministerio de Trabajo (1979) Situación occupacional del Perú. Lima:
Ministerio de Trabajo, Dirección General del Empleo.

Ministerio de Vivienda (1978) Plan diagnóstico del sector vivienda y
construcción, 1978-1980. Lima: Ministerio de Vivienda.

Monteforte Toledo, Mario (1973) La solución militar a la peruana,
1968-1970. Mexico City: Instituto de Investigaciones Sociales.

Moore, Barrington (1966) Social Origins of Dictatorship and Democracy:
Lord and Peasant in the Making of the Modern World. Boston: Beacon

244

Press.

Mytelka, Lynn Krieger (1979) Regional Development in a Global Economy: The Multinational Corporation, Technology, and Andean Integration. New Haven: Yale University Press.

Neira, Hugo (1973) "Peru," pp. 399-400 in Richard Bott [ed.] Political Parties of South America. Middlesex, England: Penguin Books.

OIT (1975) Estudio sobre ingresos de los trabajadores rurales en el Perú. Lima: Organización Internacional del Trabajo.

ONE (1980a) Informe estadístico: enero-deciembre 1979. Lima: Instituto Nacional de Planificación, Officína Nacional de Estadistica.

_____ (1980b) Informe estadistica: enero-marzo 1980. Lima: Instituto Nacional de Planificación, Officína Nacional de Estadística.

Ortiz de Zavallos, Felipe (1980) "Hacía la transferencia." Equis X 196 (June): 24-25.

Padrón Castillo, Mario and Henry Pease García (1974) Planificación rural, reforma agraria y organización campesina. Lima: DESCO, Centro de Estudios y Promoción del Desarrollo.

Paige, Jerry M. (1975) Agrarian Revolution, Social Movements and Export Agriculture in the Underdeveloped World. New York: The Free Press.

Palmer, David Scott (1980) Peru: The Authoritarian Tradition. New York: Praeger.

_____ (1973) Revolution from Above: Military Government and Popular Participation in Peru. Ithica: Cornell University Dissertation Series.

Pasara, Luis, Jorge Santistevan, Alberto Bustamente and Diego García-Sayan (1974) Dinámica de la comunidad industrial. Lima: DESCO, Centro de Estudios y Promoción del Desarrollo.

Pasara, Luis and Jorge Santistevan (1973) "Industrial Communities and Trade Unions in Peru: A Preliminary Analysis." International Labor Review 108: 127-142.

Pease García, Henry (1979) Los caminos del poder: tres años en la escena política. Lima: DESCO, Centro de Estudios y Promoción del Desarrollo.

_____ (1977) El Ocaso del poder oligárquico: lucha política en la escena oficial, 1968-1975. Lima: DESCO, Centro de Estudios y Promoción del Desarrollo.

_____ and Alfredo Filomeno (1980) Perú 1978: cronología política. Tomo VII. Lima: DESCO, Centro de Estudios y Promoción del Desarrollo.

_____ and Alfredo Filomeno (1979) Perú 1977: cronología política. Tomo VI. Lima: DESCO, Centro de Estudios y Promoción del Desarrollo.

_____ and Alfredo Filomeno (1977a) Perú 1975: cronología política. Tomo IV. Lima: DESCO, Centro de Estudios y Promoción del Desarrollo.

_____ and Alfredo Filomeno (1977b) Perú 1976: cronología política. Tomo V. Lima: DESCO, Centro de Estudios y Promoción del Desarrollo.

_____, Julio Calderón and Alfredo Filomeno (1975) Perú 1968-1974: cronología política. Tomo III. Lima: DESCO, Centro de Estudios y Promoción del Desarrollo.

_____ and Olga Verme Insúa (1974) Peru 1968-1973: cronología política. Tomo I y II. Lima: DESCO, Centro de Estudios y Promoción del Desarrollo.

Perlman, Janic (1975) The Myth of Marginality: Urban Poverty and Politics in Rio de Janiero. Berkeley: University of California Press.

Petras, James and Robert Laporte (1971) Perú: transformación revolucionaria o modernización? Buenos Aires.

Philip, George D.E. (1978) The Rise and Fall of the Peruvian Military Radicals, 1968-1976. London: Athlone.

Pike, Frederick B. (1977) The United States and the Andean Republics: Peru, Bolivia and Ecuador. Cambridge: Harvard University Press.

_____ (1967) The Modern History of Peru. London: Weindenfeld and Nicolson.

Pinelo, A.J. (1968) The Multinational Corporation as a Force in Latin American Politics: A Case Study of the International Petroleum Company in Peru. New York: Praeger.

Powell, John D. (1971) Political Mobilization of the Venezuelan Peasant. Cambridge: Harvard University Press.

Powell, Sandra (1969) "Political Participation in the Barriadas: A Case Study." Comparative Political Studies 2 (July): 195-215.

Quijano, Anibal Obregón (1971) Nationalism and Capitalism in Peru: A Study in Neo-Imperialism. New York: Monthly Review Press.

Riva Agüero, José de la (1955) Paisajes peruanos. Lima: Editoria Peruana.

Roncagliolo, Rafael (1980) Para las elecciones de mayo: política y estadística. Quehacer 4 (April): 28-47.

Rouqui, Alain (1973) "Military Revolution and National Independence in Latin America, 1968-1971," in Phillippe C Schmitter [ed.] Military Rule in Latin America: Function, Consequence and Perspectives. Beverly Hills: Sage Publications.

Salazar Bondy, Augusto (1969) Entre escila y caribdis: reflexiones sobre la vida peruana. Lima: Casa de la Cultura del Perú.

Salvattecci, Hugo García (1972) El pensamiento de Gonzalez Prada. Lima: Editorial Arica.

Sanchez León, Alberado and Raúl Guerrero de los Rios (1979) Tugurización en Lima metropolitana. Lima: DESCO, Centro de Estudios y Promoción del Desarrollo.

Santos, Milton (1979) The Shared Space. London: Methuen.

Sartori, Giovanni (1976) Parties and Party Systems: A Framework for Analysis. Volumn I. Cambridge: Cambridge University Press.

Schuldt, Jurgen (1980) De la promesa al fracaso: Perú 1980-1984. Lima: Centro de Investigación, Universidad del Pacífico.

Schydlowsky, David and Juan Wicht (1979) Anatomía de un fracaso económico: Perú 1968-1978. Lima: Universidad del Pacífico.

Scott, Christopher D. (1978) "Agrarian Reform and Agricultural Labor Markets." Paper presented at the Ninth World Congress of Sociology, Uppsala, Sweeden.

Seligson, Mitchell A. (1980) Peasants of Costa Rica and the Development of Agrarian Capitalism. Madison: University of Wisconsin Press.

Shapiro, Harvey (1976) "Monitoring: Are the Banks Biting off More than They Can Chew?" Institutional Investor (October): 140-142.

Sheahan, John (1980) "Peru: Economic Politics and Structural Change,

1968-1978." Journal of Economic Studies 7 (Spring): 3-27.

_____ (1979) Peru: Economic Policies and Structural Change. Research Memorandum 72. Williams College, Center for Development Economics.

Smith, Gavin A. and Pedro H. Cano (1978) "Some Factors Contributing to Peasant Land Occupations in Peru: The Example of Huasicancha, 1963-1968," pp. 163-191 in Norman Long and Bryan R. Roberts [eds.] Peasant Cooperation and Capitalist Expansion in Central Peru. Austin: University of Texas Press.

Smith, Norman M. (1977) "The Buildup of Soviet Gear in Peru's Army and Air Force." Armed Forces Journal International 114 (May): 22-24.

St John, Ronald Bruce (1977a) "The Boundary Dispute Between Peru and Ecuador." American Journal of International Law 71 (April): 322-330.

_____ (1977b) "Hacía el mar: Bolivia's Quest for a Pacific Port." Inter-American Economic Affairs 31 (Winter): 41-74.

_____ (1976) "The End of Innocence: Peruvian Foreign Policy and the United States, 1919-1942." Journal of Latin American Studies 8 (November): 325-344.

_____ (1970) Peruvian Foreign Policy, 1919-1939: The Delimitation of Frontiers. Unpublished Ph.D. dissertation. Denver: University of Denver.

Stallings, Barbara (1979) "Peru and the U.S. Banks: Privatization of Foreign Relations," pp. 217-253 in Richard Fagen [ed.] Capitalism and the State in US-Latin American Relations. Stanford: Stanford University Press.

Stein, Steve (1980) Populism in Peru: The Emergence of the Masses and the Politics of Social Control. Madison: University of Wisconsin Press.

Stepan, Alfred (1978) The State and Society: Peru in Comparative Perspective. Princeton: Princeton University Press.

Stephens, Evelyne Huber (1980) The Politics of Workers' Participation: The Peruvian Approach in Comparative Perspective. New York: Academic Press.

Sulmont, Denis (1980) El movimiento obrero peruano, 1890-1980: reseña histórica. Lima: Tarea.

_____ (1977) História del movimiento obrero peruano, 1890-1977. Lima: Tarea.

Swansbrough, Robert H. (1975) "Peru's Diplomatic Offensive: Solidarity for Latin American Independence," in Ronald G. Hellman and Jon Rosenbaum [eds.] Latin America: The Search for a New International Role. New York: John Wiley and Sons.

Tai, Hung-Chao (1974) Land Reform and Politics: A Comparative Analysis. Berkeley: University of California Press.

Taylor, Charles Lewis and Michael C. Hudson (1972) World Handbook of Political and Social Indicators. New Haven: Yale University Press.

Thorp, Rosemary and Lawrence Whitehead [eds.] (1979) Inflation and Stabilization in Latin America. London: MacMillan.

_____ and Geoffrey Bertram (1978) Peru 1890-1977: Growth and Policy in an Open Economy. London: MacMillan.

Torres, Mario (1980) "Radicalismo o izquierdismo político en el Peru." Socialismo y Participación 9 (febrero): 41-70.

Tullis, F. LaMond (1970) Lord and Peasant in Peru. Cambridge: Harvard
University Press.
United Nations (1979) Statistical Yearbook, 1978. New York: United
Nations Statistical Office.
_____ (1977) Statistical Yearbook, 1976. New York: United
Nations Statistical Office.
Van den Berghe, Pierre L. and George P. Primov (19) Inequity in the
Peruvian Andes: Class and Ethnicity in Cuzco. Columbia: University
of Missuouri Press.
Van Ginneken, P. (1977) El desarrollo del cooperativismo y la educación
cooperativa en el Perú. Lima: Ediciones del Centro.
Valdez Angulo, Enrique (1974) El Sector Agrario. Lima: Ministerio de
Agricultura.
Vela, Jaime (1980) "Hasta la mujer me van a pedir: La disolucion de la
SAIS Huancavelica." Quehacer 4. Lima: DESCO.
Velasco Alvarado, Juan (1973) La revolución peruana. Buenos Aires:
Editorial Universitaria de Buenos Aires.
Villanueva, Victor (1980) "Doce años bajo la cruz y la espada." Paper
presented at the Latin American Studies National Meeting,
Bloomington, Indiana.
_____ (1977) "The Petty-Bourgeois Ideology of the Peruvian
Aprista Party." Latin American Perspectives 4 (Summer): 57-76.
_____ (1973a) Ejército peruano: del caudillaje anárquico al
militarismo reformista. Lima: Mejia Vaca.
_____ (1973b) El CAEM y la revolución de la fuerza armada. Lima:
Instituto de Estudios Peruanos.
_____ (1969) Nueva mentalidad militar en el Perú? Lima: Mejia
Vaca.
Walton, John and Joyce Sween (1971) "Urbanization, Industrialization,
and Votin in Mexico: A Longitudinal Analysis of Official and
Opposition Party Support." Social Science Quarterly 52 (December):
721-745.
Webb, Richard Charles (1977) Government Policy and the Distribution
of Income in Peru, 1963-1973. Cambridge: Harvard University Press.
_____ (1974) Trends in Real Income in Peru, 1950-1966. Research Paper
in Economics. Princeton: Woodrow Wilson School, Princeton
University.
Wengel, Jan Ter (1980) Allocation of Industry in the Andean Common
Market. Boston: Martinus Nijhoff.
Werlich, David P. (1981) "Peru: Encore for Belaunde." Current History
80 (February): 66-68, 85.
_____ (1978) Peru: A Short History. Carbondale, Ill.: Southern
Illinois University Press.
Wilkie, James W. [ed.] (1980) Statistical Abstract of Latin America.
Los Angeles: UCLA Latin American Center Publications.
World Bank (1980) World Bank Annual Report, 1980. Washington, D.C.:
International Bank for Reconstruction and Development.
_____ (1978) Land Reform in Latin America: Bolivia, Chile,
Mexico, Peru, and Venezuela. Washington, D.C.: International Bank
for Reconstruction and Development.
Woy-Hazleton, Sandra L. (1979) "Political Participation in a Non-
Electoral System." Paper presented at the International Studies
Association Annual Meeting, Toronto, Canada.

248

_____ (1978a) Political Participation in Peru: A military Model for Mobilization. Unpublished Ph.D. dissertation. Charlottesville: University of Virginia.

_____ (1978b) "Infrastructure of Participation in Peru: SINAMOS," pp. 189-208 in Joh Booth and Mitchell Seligson [eds.] Political Participation in Latin America. Vol. I. New York: Holmes and Meir.

Zimmerman Zavala, Augusto (1975) El Plan Inca: Objectivo revolucion peruano. Barcalona, Spain: Ediciones Grefalbo.

Magazines and Journals

Actualidad Económica (Peru)
Analisis Laboral (Peru)
Andean Report
Avances de Investigación (Peru)
Caretas (Peru)
Economia y Política (Peru)
El Comercio (Peru)
Equis X (Peru)
La Crónica (and La Nueva Crónica) (Peru)
LAER -- Latin America Economic Report (London)
LAPR -- Latin America Political Report (London)
La Prensa (Peru)
LAWR -- Latin America Weekly Report (London)
Marka (Peru)
Oiga (Peru)
Peruvian Times
Realidad (Peru)
Resumen Semanal (Peru)
Revista Semanal (Peru)
Sociedad y Política (Peru)
Ultima Hora (Peru)

Index